# TRAUTMANN

## THE BIOGRAPHY

# TRAUTMANN

## THE BIOGRAPHY

Alan Rowlands

First published in Great Britain in 1990 by The Breedon Books Publishing
Company Limited, Breedon House, 3 The Parker Centre, Derby, DE21 4SZ.
Paperback edition 2005, Hardback edition 2009.

The Derby Books Publishing Company Ltd.
Paperback edition 2011

This edition published in Great Britain in 2012 by The Derby Books
Publishing Company Limited, 3 The Parker Centre, Derby, DE21 4SZ.

ISBN 978-1-78091-119-9

# CONTENTS

# DEDICATION

For Jo

# ACKNOWLEDGEMENTS

*Manchester Evening News*; The *St Helens Reporter*; Gordon Banks; Central Library Staff, Manchester; Bobby Charlton, Deutscher Fußball-Bund; Tommy Docherty, English Football Association; Tom Finney, Tony Gleave and the staff of the *St Helens Reporter*; Jimmy Hill; Jack Kelsey; Nat Lofthouse; Sir Stanley Matthews; Jackie Milburn, Manchester City FC; Trevor Porteous, Public Records Staff, Kew; Bobby Robson, St Helen's Town FC; Bob Wilson and Lev Yashin.

# SPECIAL ACKNOWLEDGEMENTS

Marlis Trautmann for her knowing understanding.
B.C. Trautmann for his inspiration and friendship.

# NORTH-WEST ENGLAND, 1949

HE WAS in a deep sleep when Jack Friar peered around the bedroom door. A sleep induced by Beecham's Powders and whisky to help sweat out his illness. Friar closed the door quietly and returned to the living room. He looked at the newspaper report again. Most of the content was speculation, but he had to face up to the fact that his goalkeeper would be leaving St Helens by the end of the week.

Friar and the team manager, George Fryer, had built a successful side in the Lancashire Combination. Attendances had increased to around 2,000, which was phenomenal for such a small club in a town that was dominated, in sport, by Rugby League.

St Helens Town, holders of the Mahon Cup, had started this new season with great anticipation of more success. Football League scouts had been present at their matches for a while now, and they had all been impressed by the labourer, who was showing such astonishing form in the St Helens goal. Friar, however, knew the reason why no one had rushed in to sign him: regardless of his ability, the accompanying problems of his background would present a great dilemma.

Burnley had made the first official approach and in a couple of days Jack would talk over a possible transfer with their officials. Having resigned himself to losing the player, he now had to consider what monetary advantage, if any, he could get for St Helens, particularly as his man was on amateur forms. Jack's immediate plan was to keep his appointment in Manchester that evening.

Meanwhile, Jock Thompson, the manager of Manchester City, had made a decision. His scout's report had so astounded him that he had gone to watch the player himself. The news of Burnley's approach had increased the urgency of moving, and that move would be made tonight.

There was an early autumn chill in the air as Thompson looked around the huge, empty Maine Road stadium. Rain clouds were building up into a grey mass as they bounced off the Pennines, that greyness unique to Manchester. It was on a day such as this that Frank Swift had told him he would be retiring.

Swift was a supreme goalkeeper. The crowds revered the man. They loved his eccentric mannerisms and his spectacular dives into territory where most mortals would have held back. They laughed at his nonchalance as he sat at the foot of a goal post while play was up field.

Thompson, as ever pragmatic, also knew that Swift's immense ability instilled so much confidence into the rest of the team. He had the knack of keeping them amused in those taut moments before a game and helped to relieve the boredom when on the road. He had been persuaded to stay on for the start of the season until the problem of a replacement had been resolved. That problem had now developed into a crisis. Alex Thurlow, who had been showing so much promise as Swift's successor, had developed a serious chest complaint – he later died from tuberculosis – and the two other goalkeepers on the playing staff were both raw and inexperienced youngsters. Thompson thought Swift had two or three years to offer yet, but felt that the goalkeeper had lost his enthusiasm for playing and wanted to concentrate on his developing business interests.

When he returned to his office Thompson looked at his files again, making notes for Walter Smith, one of the club directors, who would be joining him later. The registration papers had been prepared earlier in the day and he was checking through them when Smith arrived. Smith seemed mysteriously confident of making the signing that night, but Thompson, having spoken to Jack Friar at St Helens, thought it more likely to be in a week or so. He had prepared the papers just in case. In view of the controversy that might surround the signing, Smith said that the board would handle the Press interest, but his judgement that it would represent only a novelty value for a few days was seriously underestimated.

Smith and Thompson set off along the East Lancashire Road as Jack Friar arrived for his appointment at the Kingsway Hotel, Manchester. They arrived in Marshalls Cross Road, St Helens, just after eight o'clock. It was 6 October 1949. In the house, a recently released German prisoner of war lay in bed, suffering from influenza.

# BREMEN, GERMANY, 1918–1933

*Children of every age are adventurous and their favourite games are always*
*games of adventure, and do not change very much with the passing of the years.*
*Boys climb trees now just as they always did, and march their armies to victory*
*and sail upon voyages of exploration.*

ELIZABETH GOUDGE

WHEN THE Allied soldiers arrived home from the battlefields of France and Belgium in 1918, victory parades and celebrations were held for the returning heroes. Carl Trautmann had returned to Bremen without fuss or ceremony. No flags or people lined the streets to welcome him home that November, just a few days before his 20th birthday. He had been away for two years fighting the war, and as he returned to be reunited with his parents and brothers and sisters their faces reflected only the abject misery and humiliation of defeat.

The victorious Allied countries had signed the Treaty of Versailles and the German Government quickly ratified the terms. The war repayments that Germany would be forced to pay were enormous, and huge areas of territory were to be split among the victors, who had also occupied the Rhineland and placed great limitations on the German armed forces.

Carl, like the majority of the German people, felt cheated by inept politicians and bad military leadership. He was an introspective youth and had entered the war through conscription rather than military or political zeal. But defeat affected him deeply, the deaths of his army friends, the chaos of retreat and capitulation and now the atmosphere on his return reeked of revolution.

After a few weeks at home, Carl started to pick up the threads of his life again in the elegant old port on the River Weser. Bremen had always been a thriving place with a long and proud history and enjoyed free *Hansestadt* status, an autonomy of self-rule. It had been a market town for over 900 years and the 500,000 inhabitants had enjoyed a prosperous and comfortable lifestyle.

In the old harbour one could smell the coffee and tobacco contained in the warehouses. The port had also built up rubber, textile and, latterly, chemical trades. Merchants had established businesses in the Far and Near East, and the ships that navigated the shallow waters of the Weser carried cargoes from Africa, India and Malaysia.

Kalle Chemicals had a manufacturing plant in the docks, the main product being fertilisers. On leaving school Carl had been apprenticed as an electrician and after his discharge from the army he was taken on at the chemical plant, mainly through the influence of his father, who worked in a minor administrative role in the docks. Carl's friends and former army colleagues could not find any work so, despite the long hours and unhealthy conditions, he had some security that others did not. The prospects for these others were bleak indeed.

Carl Trautmann met Frieda Elster shortly after he joined Kalle. She was a pretty, self-confident girl from a fairly middle-class background in Bremen. Her father had run a prosperous carpentry business and had aspirations for his future and those of his seven children, but the war had changed so many plans and ambitions. His prosperity suffered and he lost most of his workers, first to the army and then to economic recession. He liked Carl as an honest and down to earth working-class lad and allowed the couple to begin a formal two-year courtship.

In the autumn of 1920 they married, renting a small house in Walle, West Bremen. Shortly after their wedding, Frieda became pregnant, but such was the mortality rate at the time that her first-born, an unnamed son, died shortly after his birth.

By the bitter winter of 1921–22, the harsh terms of the Allies had brought the German nation to its knees. Most of the population were without work, had little or no heating and were hungry and desperate. Political parties seemed to mushroom overnight, and, at Kalle, Carl was under constant pressure to join one of the mainly left-wing groups. His marriage and the relative security of his job had helped to diminish the bitterness of the war and his political allegiance was to the Social Democrats as opposed to any of the more extreme groups.

His main instinct was to keep a low profile and avoid trouble. His responsibility now lay in maintaining a home for Frieda and himself. He continued to work hard and they tried to shut out the social problems developing around them. Frieda found difficulties in buying food. Supplies were hard to find, but as a prudent woman she managed to maintain a comparatively comfortable lifestyle, which was just as well as Carl liked to visit the odd *bierstube* on the way home from work, and he was known as a generous man to others without the pfennigs for a drink.

As 1922 progressed the economic and social conditions became even worse, and on the outskirts of Bremen the unemployed and homeless set up camps of despair. Walle was mainly a middle-class area. The Trautmanns' neighbours were small businessmen, teachers and engineers, but all were struggling to maintain their standards amid the growing crisis. Christmas was greeted with little enthusiasm or joy.

One evening, in February 1923, Carl returned home later than usual. He travelled to and from work each day on his bicycle, but this particular evening his journey had been hazardous. It was a volatile night in Bremen and transport was chaotic. Trains and buses were at a standstill as marchers and demonstrators clashed with police desperately trying to separate the various political and anarchist groups. It had been another miserable beginning to a year. The value of the German mark had fallen so quickly that the economy was on the brink of total collapse.

Carl was finding it difficult to meet the constant increase in food prices and the mounting cost of the house. This particular night he arrived home to discover Frieda was pregnant once again.

During her confinement, the mark fell to 1,800 to the US dollar, by July it was 160,000, and by August it took one million marks to buy a single dollar. Carl was bringing home his wages in sacks.

On 22 October 1923, Frieda gave birth to a son. The day Bernhard Carl Trautmann was born, the German currency was virtually worthless. The purchasing power of wages had been reduced to nothingness and anyone with money in the bank had seen their savings wiped out. The economic structure of Germany was destroyed and everyone was affected, not least this young hard-working couple with a child.

When people queued for bread, the price would double or treble by the time they had made their purchase and the queues for every commodity were getting longer and longer. Also, in 1923, the French marched into the Ruhr and food riots, including all social strata of German society, were occurring each day.

Carl found it difficult to avoid politics now. A number of his workmates were members of the NSDAP, the new political party that was eventually to become known as the Nazis, and they would put forward the ideas and philosophy of its charismatic leader, whose rhetoric and vision reflected the views of so many in the stricken country. The man had spoken at the famous Ratskeller in Bremen and had adopted, at that very place, the salute that would soon become infamous throughout the world.

On her shopping trips, Frieda had seen the raucous men handing out pamphlets and hounding the hapless Jewish shopkeepers, and she was also aware of their involvement in the fights against the Communists, which were happening throughout the city. She felt apprehensive about raising her boy in such a torrid, odious society.

The support for the NSDAP in northern Germany was increasing and the general consensus among Carl's workmates and neighbours was that, despite his extravagant speech making, Adolf Hitler made a lot of sense when speaking of his vision of a strong and united Germany. Frieda thought Adolf Hitler was a funny and idiosyncratic little man. The food riots and the French occupation of the Ruhr had inspired Hitler to march against the Government, which culminated in the notorious Beer Hall *Putsch* in Munich. As a result, the Government banned the NSDAP and the funny little man with a moustache was incarcerated in Landsberg prison. Carl and Frieda thought that in all probability it would be the last anyone would hear of Hitler or his political thugs.

The imprisonment of Hitler coincided with an improvement in the economy. Germany arranged massive loans, mainly from the United States, and slowly but surely trade began to build up again. As more capital flowed into the country, Bremen once again found itself a prosperous port. Increased work at the Kalle plant meant more hours and money for the labour force and the troubled streets became quieter.

Frieda's worries for Bernhard receded and she was a fastidious mother, spoiling the boy who, in comparison to her first child, was so strong and healthy. Those splendid Germanic features of blond hair and blue eyes 'would cause much heartache with the fräulein', she was told.

In March 1926 Frieda gave birth to another son, Karl-Heinz, and as they grew the boys became unusually close. Karl-Heinz idolised Bernhard, who was both protective and caring towards his younger brother, but Bernhard was a rumbustious boy who always seemed up to some mischief. Frieda displayed a benign tolerance to his antics, even allowing for sudden flashes of his temper. Karl-Heinz, on the other hand, was already displaying that introspection so prevalent in his father's character, and he tended to brood if things did not go his own way. The first sign of sibling rivalry began when Bernhard started his education at the Walle Junior School. The catalyst was Frieda's favouritism for the older brother and this was further enhanced by his academic promise.

Bernhard's numeracy and reading abilities developed quickly, which pleased his mother, who had great ambitions for him. Her own middle-class background nurtured hopes for an eventual university place and then professional status for him. Bernhard's rate of growth was, however, causing problems. Carl would often grumble about having to pay for more clothing and Frieda said little about the clothes that she was constantly patching as a result of endless climbing and tumbles.

Frieda was in admiration of his keenness and ability for sports, but, although seeing it as a healthy sign of his development, she was convinced that he would become less interested in games as he found academic life more stimulating. Carl, on the other hand, had a 'bruised-body' philosophy – if a child did not have the bruises and cuts of a rough and tumble he argued that the child could not be enjoying life. The problem for Frieda was that Carl featured so little in the boys' upbringing. He was so rarely at home and they were being left more and more to their own devices.

Within Germany, a healthy society was developing and it was both modern and lively. Bremen Council had provided so much for the young, with sports facilities, education, health-care and the social services structure unrivalled. The Teutonic obsession with outdoor pursuits and camping was growing, and each summer tanned and healthy youngsters enjoyed their lives. Young Bernhard seemed to personify this. He had great energy and was in constant search of adventure. As a result, he became involved in scrapes at school, some because of his temper but mainly due to his developing sense of mischief. The teachers recognised, however, that he was not a malicious boy. His behaviour and standard of work in class were excellent and they were as tolerant of his escapades as Frieda.

Carl had been promoted to loadmaster at Kalle and was now supervising the loading of ships. He was involved with ships masters and officers, which allowed him to participate in the hospitality on board. Indeed, he was drinking regularly with the crews.

In common with all dock areas, the life was hard and the men who worked there were tough and uncompromising. The Kalle workers were a particularly close-knit group and the lightermen employed on a casual basis often found themselves excluded from conversation and allocated the dirtiest work and, therefore, Kalle was an unpopular place for the casual labour force.

At the end of each shift the stevedores and labourers would congregate in the dock area bars and pubs, the Kalle workers covered in fertiliser dust. They would quaff more steins of beer than most, in order to irrigate their clogged throats. The conversation was mainly of conditions and their rate of pay, a debate fuelled by the mainly Communist union leaders. Carl would listen with little interest and a certain cynicism. All he wanted was to participate in his two pleasures, drinking with his mates and music. He was an accomplished trumpeter and flautist and a member of the Kalle band. He attended practice once or twice a week and the band would play at dances or march in parades on public holidays and festival days. Unfortunately, this left him little time for Frieda and the boys, who were seeing him less and less.

Carl's wages paid for a good home, and he regarded his role in the marriage as that of provider and little more. He was not aware of any alienation between himself and his family and tended to compensate for his absence from the house with generous presents. Bernhard and Karl-Heinz always had toys and games or money for sweets. Frieda accepted her docile role in the relationship as Carl provided the security for the family, and the future for the Trautmann boys looked promising. Unfortunately, the events in the rest of world negated that promise.

On 29 October 1929 the Stock Market in New York collapsed. Germany's economic recovery had been based on loans and these loan sources disappeared overnight. Trade slumped as a world recession started. The country could not pay for the raw materials of production, or for foodstuffs, and, by Christmas, Carl and Frieda were left to contemplate what had happened. They could not understand how things could change so quickly. There was extreme poverty again, factories closed, millions were unemployed and food queues snaked along the streets. The boys saw soup kitchens appear, and Frieda would often steer them away from beggars, more of whom appeared each day. The value of the mark fell again and the stability of the last few years ended abruptly.

Dramatically, the funny little man with the moustache was back on the scene. Frieda saw the men with the pamphlets return to the streets, but now they were dressed in odd items of uniform with various insignias on their brown shirts. The fights with the Communist groups flared up as before, but now there were many killings and political assassinations. Carl saw a resurgence of the NSDAP at Kalle and in the docks. The disciples were once again distributing propaganda leaflets, but now the emphasis on racism and political violence was more pronounced.

The dock area became the focus of militancy and unrest. The inevitability of some form of revolution was omnipresent, but the fear of losing his secure and well-paid job made Carl justifiably hesitant in endorsing his workmates' views, with the NSDAP and the Communists offering radical alternatives to the vapid policies of the Government. Carl chose to stay with the Social Democrats. He did so because he still had a job, even though he had started to work double shifts, and he was always able to supplement his earnings by wheeling and dealing in various commodities. It was not unusual for Scandinavian watches to appear on the market for just a few marks, and on one infamous occasion, a whole train of food items disappeared.

Inevitably, inflation and the downturn in the economy meant the cost of houses became an overwhelming financial burden. Early in 1932 the Trautmanns moved three kilometres away, to a home in Wisch Husen Straße in Gröpelingen. The flat, at the top of the apartment block containing four other families, was rented from Bremen Council and, although having its own bathroom and toilet, Frieda had to accept it as a big reduction in their circumstances. Again, the top floor of a council home did not meet her expectations for her family due to her middle-class expectations. After a few months a larger flat in the house became vacant and they were able to move down a floor, but Frieda never came to terms with uprooting from Walle into the working-class area.

Gröpelingen, at the time, was not a particularly ugly area. Indeed, the whole city of Bremen, stretching 34 kilometres or so, was known as a city of low-rise buildings and was surrounded by a flat, agricultural countryside. Just a few streets away was the rural landscape and fresh air – for Bernhard and Karl-Heinz it was a new playground. At the same time, the children of the area were both streetwise and tough and, although Bernhard, because of his formidable size, was not undaunted, Karl-Heinz found this new environment a little intimidating.

Bernhard helped Frieda to run the home. He helped with cleaning the stairs and polishing the wood, he ran errands for his mother and for neighbours and generally did the chores that his father was unable to do.

Bernhard was attending the local Humann School now and still making good progress. It was the practice at the school for the teachers to read out the results of tests by naming the pupils with the least marks first, Bernhard's name was always one of the last to be called.

Karl-Heinz, on the other hand, was having a thoroughly miserable time. The local junior school was severely overcrowded and a few classes had to attend Hut Schule, a health or 'open-air' type school established for educationally sub-normal children. The stigma for having to attend was considerable and the local children were merciless in their teasing. Karl-Heinz became more solitary. He was a good-natured child somewhere inside, but the effect of attending this new school led to displays of wild tantrums. He would tear up his school books in a rage or throw them into puddles of water and stamp them into a pulp. Once, he broke up his school writing slate, the cost of which was borne by his mother. In the past it was always Bernhard who managed to calm him down but, as their lives were taking separate paths, it became more difficult for him to do so.

Bernhard tried to include him in games and expeditions, but Karl-Heinz would either stay at home or play with the younger boys in the street. He also liked to make balsa-wood model aeroplanes and gliders and there was always a smell of glue in the shared bedroom.

During 1932 Bernhard's academic progress began to wane as his talent and enthusiasm for sport accelerated. Even at the age of nine he was competing with, and beating, older boys at athletics. He was a good footballer and developing as a handball and völkerball player. Völkerball, a uniquely German game, was played by two teams of 10 on a small 10-metresquare pitch divided into two halves. The rules were simple: each participant would throw the ball at the opposition; each player hit was then removed from the game until only one player was left, sometimes playing against three of four opponents. With acrobatic twisting and diving, this player could manage to avoid being hit by the ball. By developing his throwing ability with power and curving, the outnumbered player could win the game. Young Trautmann often did.

Carl and Frieda had been told of the possibilities for him in higher education at the Gymnasium school if he could concentrate more on his studies, but his parents were concerned about the high cost of books and the fees they would have to pay. Frieda's ambition for his future became less hopeful, school reports were now deteriorating and, as his interest in lessons declined, his zeal for sport increased. Lack of parental guidance meant that he and Karl-Heinz were often bored and Bernhard, as the more intrepid, was always on the look out for things to do.

Events in Bremen were now also affecting their lives. The boys would start school at eight each morning and be home shortly after one. Frieda would prepare their lunch and then Bernhard would cycle over to the docks with food for his father. He would pass queues at the 'peoples' kitchen, long poverty lines waiting for one-pot meals, and he would notice their dirty and ragged clothing. Even some of his schoolmates were subsisting on bread and potatoes.

At the docks, Bernhard would hang around with his father for as long as he could, and Carl sometimes took him on board a ship, a treat he looked forward to with eager anticipation. He often came away from the ships with a gift of sweets or money.

It was an exciting time for Bernhard, his sense of adventure being fuelled by the events of politics and violence unfolding all over the city. Each day, stories of mass arrests and killings were discussed by anxious parents. Road cordons were common, particularly around the docks where an increasing number of disturbances were taking place, and police vans with heavily grilled windows were frequently seen speeding through the streets. One of the main union leaders was abducted and political executions were now an everyday occurrence, the Communists being the main targets. Anyone denounced as a Communist was arrested and taken away for questioning and detained without charge. At schools the children, with naive innocence, would pick on certain individuals by calling them 'Commies' as a form of insult. This was happening in an area that was already a violent place anyway because of drunken sailors arguing and fighting over whores or bar bills. Even at school the windows had been shattered by gunshots and Bernhard's teacher, Herr Konig, kept them all at floor level until the danger passed.

Bernhard's visits to the docks ceased because Frieda and Carl were concerned for his safety, but he had his sporting interests and boyish pursuits to follow, particularly with his closest friends, Herbert Behrens and Richard Hohnemeyer. The Humann School they attended was a large L-shaped building with 1,000 pupils, the girls being taught in a separate part. Bernhard's friendship with Herbert had started after they had a fight because Herbert had picked on Richard, who was smaller, over some trivial incident. With bizarre schoolboy reasoning, the fight brought some mutual respect and all three became firm friends, with Bernhard the undoubted, mischievous leader.

A natural target for the boys' energy was an orchard on part of a farm near the school, and they made regular assaults on the apple trees. The farmer, being naturally unimpressed by these raids, would chase the boys. After regular complaints to the school authorities and parents, his patience snapped and one day he fired his shotgun at a whole army of apple stealers. They rushed away squealing with pain, eventually meeting to remove the pellets from each other's buttocks like a family of grooming monkeys.

Football, above all else, was now the main purpose of their lives. They would take part in those ridiculous street games of up to 30 a side, chasing the ball about in huge swarms and arguing over the score after each side had scored at least 25 goals. At other times, just the three friends would play, or Bernhard would play on his own if the others were not around. One of his uncles, Hans von Salzen, lived nearby and Bernhard often had to call at his house for Hans to good-naturedly help him to patch-up shoes, battered by hours of kicking. If Hans was out, Bernhard had to return home, pink and sweaty, to face the wrath of a scolding Frieda.

In an effort to channel his energy in a more organised and constructive way, he was allowed to join the YMCA and also the Blau und Weiße Football Club. Blau und Weiße ran several football teams and he would play for the juniors on Sunday mornings and travel to watch the senior teams in the afternoon. The YMCA normally met at around five in the evenings, when the boys would all turn up adorned in their khaki uniforms. Bernhard found the activities dull, the leaders boring, and he disliked the emphasis on church and spiritual matters. By seven o'clock he would often be back at the sports field helping the groundsman.

Sunday was certainly his busiest day and also the only opportunity that he had to see Carl for any length of time. It was usual for the whole family to meet at the Elster or Trautmann grandparents' homes for Sunday lunch, and Bernhard would rush home from his football game to change into his best clothing. This made him cringe with discomfort as he put on his sailor suit and polished shoes.

Invariably, Carl would visit one of the local bars before lunch and the boys would be dispatched to bring him back for the meal. His generosity meant his *stammtisch*, the local table, was always the centre of attention. Bernhard and Karl-Heinz would sit with Carl and listen to the stories of the latest outrage in the city, but not really taking anything in. They amused each other with belching competitions after drinking their lemonade, until Carl was ready to leave.

Frieda had always shown tolerance of Carl's drinking. He worked hard and deserved time with his friends, but now her tolerance was exhausted and she had to accept that their chauvinistic marriage would never change. She retreated quietly into her shell without a fight.

The boys would bolt down their lunches and sit and fidget until they were allowed to leave the table. They played outside and were frustrated at not being able to play in any street games because they were wearing their Sunday best.

During the summer the whole family would travel into Bremen and visit the Burger Park. They would take pieces of bread to feed the swans and often met friends strolling with their parents. The boys felt conspicuous and awkward in their attire and stared into each other's gleaming shoes to avoid eye contact.

The visit to the city was always a holiday, especially the pleasure steamer trips along the Weser. Carl always tried to compensate the boys for the little time he spent with them by his generosity, with copious amounts of ice cream or lollipops. Bernhard was always relieved to get home, however. He would rush into his room, pull off the repugnant clothing and rush out in his street clothes to get a last hour of play.

His only real interest with the YMCA was the occasional excursion outside Bremen for a camping trip. He had a restless spirit, the only other journeys he had made were during summer holidays when he visited relatives in Hamelyn, but he even found the camping trips staid and unadventurous and now yearned for some other form of activity that would capture his attention.

The pamphlets and booklets first appeared at his school and a number of boys had joined this new organisation. People who read the literature learned of the qualities of Adolf Hitler. They read about the ways that boys would be moulded into men of action and steel and how they would be instilled with German Nationalism. In August 1933 Bernhard Carl Trautmann became a member of the *Jungvolk*.

# THE JUNGVOLK, THE HITLER YOUTH, SILESIA 1933–1939

*The old parties train their youth in the gift of the gab, we prefer to train them to use their bodily strength.*

*For I tell you, the young man who does not find his way to the place where in the last resort the destiny of his people is most truly represented, only studies philosophy and in time like this buries himself behind his books or sits at home by the fire, he is no German youth! I call on you. Join our storm troopers.*

ADOLF HITLER

B Y 1933 Adolf Hitler and the NSDAP had schemed and plotted their way to the very pinnacle of power. The party had captured the imaginations of industrialists, workers and farmers, the minds of intellectuals and, through fear and violence, subjugated its enemies. The structure of the party was a revelation in organisation and its tentacles had spread everywhere. To build on the fanatical allegiance to a true Aryan race, seeds of a youth movement started at the birth of the party.

The power of Nazis in northern Germany had become considerable and youth groups had been formed under various guises for several years. The Hitler Youth movement began its formal organisation in 1926 and an auxiliary for teachers had started in the same year. The appeal of the organisation was its stance on morality and order and many anxious parents, after experiencing the disorder of the last few years, actively encouraged their children to join. The curriculum of schools changed suddenly; hours of physical training were introduced and racial biology and German history and literature became compulsory. The system changed rapidly as it focused more on character building and fitness. The acceptance of NSDAP philosophy was absorbed by the authorities and the indoctrination of the young began.

Life in Bremen had certainly become orderly and red and black swastika banners swirled everywhere. For Carl, the changes at the plant and docks were remarkable. The Communist Party and Press were banned and the union leaders had gone. The unions were taken over by the Labour Front, which was run by the NSDAP and, while this brought stability of a kind, Carl now found his wage structure was altered considerably. His wages were now based on productivity and to earn extra payments or increments he had to increase that productivity – and this was a man who was already working two-thirds of his day. In addition to personal taxes, he also had to contribute to sickness plans, the Labour Front required subscriptions and he was always under pressure to make donations to Nazi charities. In some cases there were veiled threats to jobs if these donations were considered insufficient. Carl was now paying up to one third of his wages to the State.

He always maintained that he had not voted for Adolf Hitler, a claim difficult to prove considering 98 per cent of the population were reported to have done so, but he looked in awe at the momentous changes happening within the social and economic structure. The fact that these changes had happened in a corrupt and insidious way became of little consequence to a German nation experiencing full employment again.

The conditions at the plant and docks also changed. The workers were given better welfare and medical facilities, cleaner and safer work practices were introduced and more social activities organised, all linked to the NSDAP priorities. Kalle were awarded a 'Gold Flag' in recognition of their efforts for the workers and adapting their role to the National Socialist economic structure. The company fulfilled the strict criteria laid down for German workers and industrialists.

Carl accepted his loss of civil liberties with docile resignation. The Press and radio were now heavily censored and churned out huge amounts of propaganda.

Carl's activities with the band increased, although the content of the music became increasingly nationalistic. Discipline within the band was tightened and a more militaristic stance was introduced.

The *Jungvolk* was an organisation that prepared boys of 10 to 14 for the Hitler Youth movement, which had itself been formed to lure teenagers away from Communists and later church-based youth organisations like the YMCA. For Bernhard, the attraction was irresistible and he thrived on the outlets provided for his energy. The local leader of *Jungvolk* held regular meetings in a wooden hut on a large allotment near the school. The boys were taught basic marching drills using broom handles as rifles and they were organised into self-disciplined teams.

For the first time, Bernhard succumbed to a real discipline, greater than his school offered and, more significantly, a discipline that he had missed in his home life.

Since his return from the war, Carl had concerned himself solely with keeping his job and providing for the family. He had managed to keep working right through the troubles of the last two decades but, unfortunately, at a cost of great neglect to the family's emotional needs. The new problem for Carl and the other workers was that the fear of unemployment was now being replaced by fear of the state that now controlled their employment. The job and stability were his main considerations, his cynicism of politics remained, but he willingly accepted the policies of the Nazis. There was no outright condemnation of the NSDAP from workers and no leaders in the docks that foretold any form of revolt. The result became a workforce at Kalle that was timid and tamed.

Frieda accepted her passive role as wife and mother, providing the love and affection in her own way, but she found it difficult to cope on her own with two boys of differing characters. On the one hand there was Karl-Heinz and his increasing inhibitions, on the other Bernhard becoming more self-confident and gregarious. Carl and Frieda's acceptance of Bernhard's entry into the *Jungvolk* were merely perfunctory.

The literature of the *Jungvolk* was a reflection of the Nazi dramatic sensibilities and contained evocative imagery. 'The *Jungvolk* is the newly won element of eternity in inexorable truth'. In other cases it was more clearly nationalistic. 'So stand before your German father, German mother, we, the young leaders of German youth, we train and educate your son and mould him into a man of action, a man of victory. He has been taken into a hard school so that his fists may be steeled, and his courage strengthened, and he may be given a faith, a faith in Germany.'

Carl and Frieda abrogated to the *Jungvolk* the right to mould Bernhard's character. Admission to the *Jungvolk* was not automatic, Bernhard had to pass tests in athletics, camping and Germanic history. The fittest and more adaptable boys were invited to join, in Bernhard's case as a *Pimpf* – little one – until his full acceptance into the organisation on his 10th birthday.

The boys were not aware that they were being moulded into the movement's definition of a true German youth and they were also unaware, at the time, of others being excluded. No Jewish, Slavic or infirm boys were involved. On his acceptance into the *Jungvolk* proper Bernhard had to stand in front of his group, hand held high in the movement's salute, and swear the oath of allegiance before a red swastika background: 'In the presence of the blood banner, which represents our Führer, I swear to devote all my energies and my strength to the saviour of our country, Adolf Hitler. I am willing and ready to give up my life for him, so help me God.' Such was the indoctrination of the young.

He attended the *Jungvolk* meetings once or twice a week and was taught about Nordic and Viking festivals, evoking images of warrior races and invincible armies. His group spent days and weekends developing their camping skills, learning basic survival techniques and the value of comradeship. The group would sit around the camp fires and listen to stories of Varangian rovers from the ninth century, hardly comprehending the significance but absorbing the tales of battle and conquest with wide eyes of innocence.

Bernhard competed against other groups in sports events or field crafts, and he learned to march in disciplined formations. His healthy adolescent lifestyle developed his confidence and a noticeable arrogance appeared as his sporting progress became more prominent. In June 1934 he was one of two boys in Bremen to be presented with a certificate of achievement, signed by President Hindenberg, for their unsurpassed level of athletic ability. He was not yet 11 years old.

Bernhard was now enjoying his life to the full, his involvement with the *Jungvolk* and his football were fulfilling all his needs and his athletic ability was being

THE JUNGVOLK, THE HITLER YOUTH, SILESIA 1933–1939

harnessed by regular competition. He was a local champion at 60-metre races and at various throwing competitions. One particular throwing event with an overarm action involved a half-kilo piece of metal shaped uncannily like a World War One hand-grenade.

By 1936 his sporting pursuits were actively encouraged by the changing priorities of the education system. Hitler's book *Mein Kampf* had been introduced as the main focus in schools and even text books had been rewritten. Teachers were retrained or replaced by ones embracing Nazi doctrines and the Ministry of Education took over the administration of the schools from Bremen Council.

Academic standards were now falling as fitness and health became more important than intellect. Bernhard's school and after-school activities were now irretrievably linked to those of the NSDAP. Any further development of his academic progress was arrested by his sporting activities.

The State, by this time, had introduced 'work books'. Carl had been issued with one at Kalle. It documented his work record, skills and commitment to the company. Any disaffection or lack of loyalty was recorded and could affect or limit his ability to apply for promotion or change employer.

Similarly, Bernhard, as a member of the *Jungvolk* serving his apprenticeship for the Hitler Youth proper, was issued with a performance book, which would appraise his progress through his entire involvement with the youth movement.

The *Jungvolk* were involved in regular marches throughout Bremen, marches which were held at any opportunity. The local NSDAP group would meet up under banners and march to a central meeting point with exemplary precision. Stirring music was played over loudspeakers and the sound of thousands of voices, chanting slogans and tributes to the Führer, pumped up the level of excitement. One particular evening Carl was standing in the doorway of the flats watching the local Nazi group forming up a march, when he was torn off a strip by the leaders for being disrespectful to the banners and the Führer. Bernhard's father was absent-mindedly playing 'pocket billiards'.

It was in August 1936 that the Hitler Government staged the most publicised and well-organised Olympic Games of modern times, and it was an ideal opportunity for their propaganda experts to extol the virtues of German strength.

Bernhard listened avidly to the radio broadcasts, so avidly in fact that he once smashed the radio in a fit of temper as the noise in the family kitchen prevented him from hearing the results of some of the races. He could recite the names of all the winners in the track and field events, together with their times and distances. Indeed, more than 50 years later he could still remember most of the names and times. His ambition in sport increased, and he began training for athletics under the watchful eye of the school coaches and party officials. Rem Riefenstahl produced one of the most atmospheric and visually stunning sports films of the 1936 games, a film that had a lasting impression on Bernhard.

His friendship with Herbert and Richard continued. When they were not involved with the school and youth groups, the River Weser was always an adventure for them. The Trautmann gang of three would often cross the river on the rowing-boat ferries and visit the surrounding farmland, or spend sunny afternoons on the banks of the river, lying in the sun, fishing or waving to the ships' crews as they navigated up or down to the docks or out to the North Sea. During the winter the canals and the river would overflow into the fields and provide huge areas of free ice-skating as the water froze over. The boys could skate for kilometres on the ice.

Their mischievous streak remained. They trampled through the fields looking for birds' nests or would steal fruit or vegetables. Although not malicious boys, they still had streaks of mischief that always contained an element of Inspector Clouseau about them. One of their favourite games would be to grab one of the sails of a slowly revolving windmill so they were carried for a few metres before letting go. One day the trio grabbed the sail together and rose into the air. Suddenly, a crack like thunder echoed over the fields as the sail snapped and deposited a bundle of bruised bodies on to the ground. They limped and scrambled away through the cabbage and potato fields, receiving involuntary acupuncture from the thorn bushes, before an outraged farmer discovered the damage. Although he was not to know it, farms were to become a formative part of his early life.

Football at school was now a significant part of the sports programme and the Humann School had a successful team in the local schools league. Bernhard was in charge of the footballs and would talk tactics with his teammates in the classroom before a game. To emphasise a particular point, he was juggling with the ball and then lost control as he tried to pass it to a pal. They watched with heart-stopping horror as it sailed upwards and smashed into a glass art-plate that had been placed on top of a cupboard. The plate shattered into hundreds of shards. The boys tried desperately to clear up the mess before the coach arrived. When he did come into the classroom he talked calmly about the game as the team looked shiftily at each other. As they left the room after the talk, Trautmann was grabbed by the ear and asked if he had noticed a large amount of glass littering the floor. He recalled having the note from the headmaster in his pocket for days before he had the courage to hand it over to his parents. Despite several hundred marks-worth of damage, remarkably nothing was heard or said about the incident. The privileges accorded to a young and gifted member of the party had started to pay off.

Bremen, as all German cities, was now under direct control of the Government in Berlin and the mayor and the council officials were appointed by the party. The Government had instigated the *Kraft durch Freude* – Strength through Joy – programme, part of which brought sports clubs under direct National Socialist organisation. As a result, the Blau und Weiße club was taken over by the larger Tura club, creating a huge sports club, which ran athletics, football and handball teams. Most of the boys in the junior teams were also members of the *Jungvolk* or Hitler Youth.

Bernhard and his friends were making regular visits into the city. The pubescent boy was cutting adrift from his home life rapidly. The bedroom he shared with

Karl-Heinz, the interludes at mealtimes he spent with Frieda and Carl's brief appearance in his life were all the family ties that had existed. Some of the trips into Bremen were on school outings, visiting art galleries or museums. The teachers often allowed the children to make their own way home and this gave them an hour of rare freedom with no inhibitions of discipline. The shops and large stores were an immediate attraction. Bernhard showed great reluctance to take part in the petty thefts, but he did participate in the general mayhem caused by large groups of unsupervised boys let loose in a city centre. This large, gangling lad, however, was always pleased to get back to the familiarity of the suburbs, as he always had a feeling of unease in the centre.

Bernhard and his mates were now making regular visits to watch Werder Bremen during the football season. After his game for Tura in the morning, he was allowed to bolt down his lunch before travelling the 16 kilometres or so to the football ground.

The tram journey from Gröpelingen to Bremen and then to the stadium cost 10 pfennigs. Normally the boys had 20 or 30 pfennigs each, plus the cost of entrance to the match, but they rarely bothered with the tram, running all the way instead. On arriving at the ground, the first action was to buy an ice cream. The *Hedamannsisse* was especially good, costing 10 pfennigs each, then a second one, and third. Their dilemma then was that if they paid to get in to the game they would have insufficient money to get home on the tram. The alternatives to paying were either to climb the fences or walls or to sandwich between the adults, often with their encouraging conspiracy as they passed through the turnstiles.

The problem for Trautmann was summed up succinctly by one of the men: 'We can get the little buggers in, but this sod's taller than most of us.' Bernhard had to climb. His problem of entrance was further compounded by the lurking enemy, the Cross Keys. They were the stadium security men, a wicked bunch of grey-uniformed guardians who wore the insignia of two crossed keys on their arms. The battle of wits began with Bernhard teaming up with other boys trying to sneak in. Some of the lads would call insults, which resulted in the Cross Keys chasing after them. The remaining boys would then rush to the fence and climb into the ground. Others would tell the guards they had been separated from their fathers and ask if they could go into the stadium to find them. The Cross Keys were impassive and as hard as granite. 'Good try lad, now piss off before I whack your head'. Bernhard would eventually meet up with his pals and at half-time would spend the rest of their money on more *Hedamannsisse* or pretzels.

They always left the stadium with empty pockets. Bernhard had worked out his strategy to get back to Gröpelingen by visiting his Uncle Carl, married to one of Frieda's sisters, who kept a *bierstube* nearby. He would drop in as the pub filled with Werder supporters and talk to his uncle about the game. Carl would then talk about how he used to attend the games and mention the ice cream was always particularly good and how tempting it was to spend the tram fare on it. Bernhard always left with a handful of change to get them all home.

Bernhard used to visit the cinema once or twice a week, again sneaking in, this time through exit doors opened by friends inside whenever possible. The cinemas were now limited to propaganda films or American 'B' features passed by the censors. As a consequence, the cinemas showing the latter films were packed, whereas the State films played before only a few fanatics. The party would try to cajole the citizens into the cinemas, people's favourite excuse at the time being they were unable to do so because they did not have their spectacles with them. The NS must have felt they were an unnaturally short-sighted bunch.

Bernhard would often sit with Frieda after the film and explain, in absolute detail, the plot. She was particularly fond of love stories and would weep into her handkerchief if the film had an unhappy ending. This amused Bernhard to the extent that he would make his account as dramatic as possible.

In the last year at school it became apparent that his ability would not win him a place at the Gymnasium. The last year also coincided with more dramatic developments in the education and social structure of Germany. Adolf Hitler had decreed, 'All the German youth in the Reich is now organised within the Hitler Youth. The German youth, besides being reared within the family and schools, shall be educated physically and morally in the spirit of National Socialism, through the Hitler Youth.'

Between 1936 and 1938 a number of laws were passed that affected the children of Germany. By early 1937 all teachers had to take an oath of loyalty to Hitler. *Rassenkunde* – racial science – was introduced as a major part of study and special Adolf Hitler schools were founded with specially selected students.

These schools took the most promising youngsters and from the Hitler schools they graduated to the *Ordensburgen* or Order Castles, which were based firmly on the ideals of the old Prussian military academies. The most fanatical and intellectually gifted of the young National Socialists were chosen and they embarked on a six-year educational programme of Nazi political science and philosophy, interspersed with military training. All the students had to complete their *Land Jahr,* a whole year working in chosen farm communities.

One of Hitler's major decisions on taking power was to solve the immense agricultural problems of the country. He had always advocated land reforms and developed a farming programme to give the land back to the peasants under his *Blut und Boden* – Blood and Soil –programme. Through various laws, all Aryan citizens who could prove a bloodline back to the 1800s could own their own farm and the restrictions of a heavy mortgage and taxes were written off. Every aspect of farming was controlled by the state in order to give the farmers better profits but, more important, to make Germany self-sufficient in food. The Government also had a great deal of labour for the farmers – the Hitler Youth.

The less gifted of the children were chosen for the *Land Jahr* together with the peculators of the *Ordensburgen* programme. This enabled youngsters from all walks of life and differing classes to work together on the same tasks. Bernhard left school and at the end of 1937 was selected for the *Land Jahr* programme and also to represent Bremen in the *Land Jahr* sports events, perhaps the main criteria in his case.

On his 14th birthday, three months previously, he had become a member of the Hitler Youth movement proper. Together with half a dozen others, another histrionic ceremony had been staged before the unfurled Nazi banners, and each boy repeated his allegiance to the Führer, receiving the organisation's dagger engraved with the words 'Blood and Honour'. The *Jugend* group met at his school, and the classrooms were used to teach boys of their role in the new German society. The lectures did not contain anti-Semitic ravings or any hostile references to other countries or cultures. They still concentrated on the Aryan characteristics of strength and invincibility and how these qualities were to be used for the good of Germany. Similarly, the camping and hiking trips continued to concentrate on survival techniques and an appreciation of self-discipline. The summer of 1937 proved to be the last one together for the Trautmann gang; their fates were now being controlled by the puissant minds of the men controlling a re-emerging German nation.

In early 1938 Bernhard travelled in a group of 50 boys from Bremen and Lower Saxony on the long train journey to Görlitz in Eastern Germany. From there they were taken to a *schloss* – a small castle – at Schoebersdorf, next to the farm on which they would be working. After a speech of welcome from the *Land Jahr* leaders, they were shown to the dormitories, given a tour of the *schloss* and then taken to meet the large, ruddy-faced man for whom they would be working, farmer Henning.

The regime the boys were now under became tightly organised and more militaristic. A reveille was held at 5.30 each morning and the khaki uniforms of the Hitler Youth were replaced by harsh grey working uniforms with short trousers. After the flag had been raised they ate breakfast, usually sausage, cheese and bread, before being allocated duties for the day. Their names were chalked on a large blackboard, each under a specific heading. The majority were allocated to farm work with others given kitchen duty, cleaning chores or guard duty.

It was a small farm, around 200 acres, and was surrounded by woods and streams. Around the perimeter fencing, sentry boxes had been erected and each boy had to do a stint of guard duty split into two shifts, from six in the morning until two in the afternoon and from two until ten o'clock at night. They were marched in single file, with spades on their shoulders substituting for rifles, to take up their guard positions. They were subject to inspections at any time.

The farm was devoid of any mechanisation, Bernhard had to walk or travel by horse and cart to work. The main crops were potatoes, oats and wheat and the planting and reaping were done with horse-drawn wooden ploughs or hand ploughs. Bernhard thrived on the farms, his years of terrorizing the farmers in Bremen turned to a natural accord with the land. The *Land Jahr* boys were protected by regulations, however. They were not allowed to work over seven hours a day and were not to lift anything over 20 kilos. The work on the farm covered everything from painting and repairing the fences or poultry houses, to feeding the pigs and milking the cows.

Each Saturday morning the boys assembled in a classroom and were given lectures on NSDAP philosophy and German military history, but the rest of the weekend was taken up with sport or on visits to other parts of Silesia. Ten of the Bremen group, who had been selected for their sporting attributes, took part in athletics, handball and football matches against other *Land Jahr* groups, and Bernhard visited Prussia and, ominously, the Polish border areas. The Bremen team eventually qualified to represent the Silesia region, after winning the area championship in Frankfurt Oder, at the national championships in the Olympic Stadium in Berlin.

They arrived in Berlin in June 1938 and were accommodated in the athletes' village. The stadium was the best-planned and largest ever built, and some of the participants were overawed on the first sighting. Trautmann displayed a remarkable composure and was far more interested in the accommodation he shared with three others. It had its own kitchen and bathroom and, after the spartan conditions of the *schloss,* he revelled in the luxury and atmosphere. This was the place his sporting heroes had stayed two years before. Possibly Owens, Fischer, Chicque or Jack Lovelock had slept in one of the beds.

Trautmann recalled later that there were no great expectations by either the boys or the organisers for them to emulate the champions. They were seen only as the best young athletes from just one of many groups who used the stadium. Anyone with any interest in sport had the benefit of coaching. For only 50 pfennigs an individual could join a discus or sprint coach and the whole facility was used for the benefit of all, even those with a limited ability were encouraged.

The Bremen team came second overall and Bernhard also came second in the individual placing. He had competed in the 60 metres sprint, long jump and javelin, which he won, and came second in the shot put, using a three-kilo ladies' shot. The games were visited from time to time by party officials, mainly from the sports ministry, but none of the leading political figures appeared. Indeed, during their visit no rallies were attended or NS propaganda meetings arranged. The teams toured Berlin and were escorted to military museums and academies. Bernhard's box-camera recorded the statue of Frederick the Great astride his horse and the wide-open spaces of the streets and parks. They were taken to the new Reichstag building and surveyed the new Government structures that were appearing in the city. But they had very little contact with the population and were herded back to their quarters at the stadium by seven each evening.

They resumed the farm work with increased vigour and manoeuvres had now been introduced on some weekends and evenings, using the woods and fields around the surrounding villages. Many picnics were surprised by hordes of screaming teenagers appearing through the trees with broom-handles and sticks.

Bernhard was not allowed to return to Bremen for a visit. He wrote once a week to Frieda and Carl, noting a brief outline of his activities, and received from his parents an equally brief letter in reply. He was not missing his home or parents at all. His comradeship with the boys was close and meaningful, while his relationship with Henning and his wife was warm and fulfilling.

The most unpopular part of life proved to be kitchen duty. This mainly consisted of peeling potatoes or cleaning tiles and stoves. Even sweeping the grounds was more welcome. Allocation of kitchen work was now used as a punishment, and Trautmann was soon to suffer banishment to this hellhole.

Part of the *schloss* had been converted to a theatre, where visiting dignitaries would lecture the boys on the importance of their work, and it was also used each month to perform concerts. The local farmers and the village officials would be invited to attend. The normal format involved the boys singing NS songs or reciting poems and stories of tribute to the Führer. The audience were soon bored by this repetitive rubbish and did not have the same obsequiousness for Hitler that the leaders hoped for. In an effort to bolster the show's content, the organiser asked the boys if they knew any jokes. Bernhard offered to tell some and was bundled on to the stage.

Tunnes and Schuel were two mythical inhabitants of Cologne and had passed into German humour as the main characters in jokes. Thus, Tunnes and Schuel, tired of a Texan bragging about the ability of his state to build large buildings quickly and efficiently, were asked how long Cologne Cathedral had been around. 'I don't know', they replied, 'but it wasn't there yesterday.' The audience laughed and, encouraged by this success, Trautmann decided to tell another joke he had heard a couple of older boys laughing at in the village. Tunnes and Schuel were hungry and went to a monastery to get something to eat. Tunnes sent Schuel to see one of the monks and he came back with a bleeding nose and fat lip. 'What happened?' asked Tunnes. 'All I said was please give me something to eat, you look such a kind and warm brother.' The audience roared with laughter and shouted the punch line at each other. Unfortunately, Bernhard was bundled off the stage and the curtain closed before he could tell his appreciative audience any more gags. The literal translation of warm brother is 'warm bruder' and is a term applied to homosexuals. The Nazis had long tolerated homosexuals in their ranks and many scandals had resulted. Bernhard, in his innocence, had told a joke about one of the most sensitive issues to the NS. He spent the next week peeling potatoes.

His happy and fulfilling life in Silesia came to an end at the beginning of 1939 and, after saying a sad farewell to the Hennings and to the youth leaders, the group returned to Bremen. Bernhard had mixed feelings about his return to his family. He was pleased to see Frieda, to sleep on a real mattress again after 11 months on straw bags and to experience home cooking. He had returned a strapping, bronzed lad of 1.8 metres, and Frieda could not disguise her astonishment at the change in his physique. Karl-Heinz was completely indifferent to his return. Somehow, Bernhard felt that Carl looked on him as a man and for the first time took an active interest in his life. A major decision now had to be made. It was time for Bernhard Carl Trautmann to start his working life and a suitable career had to be found.

# LIVING AND WORKING IN THE THIRD REICH, JOINING THE LUFTWAFFE 1939–1941

*No one who has not lived for years in a totalitarian state can possibly conceive how difficult it is to escape the dread consequences of a regime's calculated and incessant propaganda.*

WILLIAM SHIRER

CARL SAT down with Bernd, as he was known to the family, and discussed with him his plans for the future – the first time father and son had a serious discussion. Carl, like his own father before him, had a certain amount of influence at his work, which would enable Bernd to start at Kalle or one of the other companies around there. The circumstances were now different, the economy and the nation were strong and opportunities for youngsters were variable and many. Carl also respected Frieda's unhappiness at Bernd being the third generation of the Trautmann men going into the docks, and he also had no particular wish or ambition for the line to be continued.

Bernd's neglect of his work during the last year in school meant he had left his education without any qualifications, not an insurmountable problem in finding a job but certainly restricting in his choice of work. At the end of their discussion it was established that Bernd should work in the engineering industry and, with his father's help, he applied to Henschel, the large locomotive company based in Berlin, for a place on their apprentice training programme. Unfortunately for Bernd, Henschel required education certificates, in some cases their apprentices needed to have passed the *Abitur* (matriculation examination). With such a rich amount of talented school leavers applying to work for them, Bernd's application was rejected.

Bernd was accompanied by Carl to the local Labour Office, where he was required to complete a number of written tests and to undergo manual dexterity exercises. The result of these tests was an offer of a four-year apprenticeship with Hanomag, a large diesel truck manufacturer with a maintenance depot in Bremen. Trautmann cycled the 20-minute journey to Hanomag to be interviewed by the manager, Herr Budde. He was a powerful intimidating man, who ran the depot with the aggression of a Dobermann chewing a leg. The younger interviewee was suitably intimidated, but recovered his wits enough to pass the interview and was employed as Hanomag's first apprentice at the Bremen garage.

He started work in March 1939 on a wage of three marks a week plus one mark for the cost of having his overalls laundered. Each Wednesday he was required to attend the technical college where he would be taught the theory and workings of diesel engines. His step into adulthood began.

The momentum of the Nazis' anti-Jewish brutality had begun to manifest itself more in Bremen at this time. While Bernd had been in Silesia he had heard of the horrific 'Crystal Night' in November 1938 when, throughout Germany, Jewish businesses had been smashed up, looted or burned. Numerous Jews had been killed or maimed while crowds stood and watched, doing nothing to stop the Nazi thugs. The victims were portrayed to the Germans as the parasites of society and enemies of the state. The NS were now able to focus that hate without any form of rebuttal. Trautmann well remembered the tirades against the Jews and conceded that his comprehension of the vile malice was both limited and clouded by the Nazi influence.

The Jewish community in Bremen were subjected to the appalling treatment as much as the rest of their race in the country, and on his return Bernd had noticed the effects of the anti-Semitic campaign. The Jews were the merchants and money lenders in the port and had a major influence in building up the prosperity, but their houses had been gutted by fire and their businesses vandalised and closed. A number of families had simply disappeared and many joined the exodus from Germany to other parts of Europe, some to Northern England, to escape the incessant persecution. Trautmann recalled with clarity a number of incidents from that period that were just accepted as the Reich's supreme decision, but in his later life would never allow his judgement of a person's race or colour to be prejudicial to friendship.

Despite the massive upturn in the German economy, it was now being geared for producing the machinery of war. Food and luxury items were still limited and diets were relatively sparse. The purges against any form of resistance to the Government and the propagation of the hatred of the Jews had become willingly accepted or, in some cases, was genuinely not known about.

The slogans of the Nazis continued relentlessly. 'Guns before Butter' was a particularly effective one from the Propaganda Ministry. The markets in Bremen had always been among the most plentiful in terms of variety, but that variety was now limited and queues began to form for food. Bernd saw horrific treatment dealt out to Jewish families in these queues. They were dragged out of line and sent to the back time and time again. In one particular obscene confrontation, the Brownshirts hacked off the beards of two elderly Jews in front of a laughing and jeering group of NS thugs. He also witnessed acts of violence by the blue-uniformed *Geheimi Staatspolizei*, the Gestapo secret police, who piled off the benches of their trucks to kick-in doors and cart people away into the night.

Every citizen was frightened of the secret police. The informers' network was wide and fearsome, and any form of criticism was, therefore, muted. The stance of the German people was being weakened each day, as they became supplicants before the hegemonic state.

Individual strength of character was only accepted if it was for the good of the machinery of the Reich. Bernd Trautmann, at the age of 15, was an important and essential part of that machinery. When Bernd started work at Hanomag, Hitler had achieved the *Anschluss* of Austria and had marched against Czechoslovakia. Much more was being planned.

The Hanomag building was a 100-metre long, single-storey structure set among a small housing complex. It had a spacious forecourt with two huge wide doors leading into the garage workshops. The owner of Hanomag Bremen, Herr Poppe, employed 25 mechanics in addition to Budde and a couple of office staff. Their function was to maintain fleets of haulage vehicles and the considerable amount of farm vehicles and tractors in the area. Machines of 20 and 36 horsepower required servicing and maintenance. Bernd was apprenticed to one of the most experienced men, Carl Wegenhaur.

The two were to work together during the apprenticeship, Carl teaching Bernd the practical skills of diesel engines. The conditions in the garage were always pristine clean, although the work was obviously dirty and smelly. The floors of the workshop were white concrete. Each day the oil stains had to be cleaned and the general debris swept up. Bernd's first duties were to ensure the workshops were clean. He had to spread sawdust around the work areas to absorb the oil deposits and sweep up the residual mess after each job had been completed. He was the subject of all the normal jokes that apprentices had to endure, sent for 'skyhooks' or 'elbow grease'.

'Hey Bernd, go and find me a duckdo.'

'What's a duckdo?'

'Quack, quack.'

Bernd got on well with Wegenhaur and most of the other mechanics. He progressed quickly from filing blocks of metal, using a file without any teeth, to more constructive tutoring. Wegenhaur taught him how to strip and reassemble engines with some short cuts to the more rigid theory being taught at the college. As the apprentice, though, each Saturday morning he had to clear up the general litter caused by mechanics during the week, so he spent his time cleaning window sills and ramps of tools and other equipment until he finished at one o'clock. The rest of the weekend was his own, revolving totally around his sporting activities.

He had progressed through the junior teams with Tura and had developed into an aggressive, tough centre-forward with the youth side. He still watched Werder when he could, although he now took the tram both ways and paid to get into the stadium. His friends, Richard and Herbert, had gone their own ways and were working in other parts of Bremen. Although Bernd saw them on the odd occasion at handball matches, the closeness of the friendship had gone. It was hard to maintain any real friendship at that time with so much change going on in people's lives, and to a certain extent Bernd was feeling a little lonely and solitary.

His involvement with the Hitler Youth was less enthusiastic and he rarely bothered to attend any meetings. The *Jugend* had become an absurd dilemma anyway. Conscription to the armed forces or to the labour force had been introduced in 1939, at the time he had joined Hanomag, and all children and teenagers of 10 to 18 were compulsorily required to become members of the Hitler Youth groups. Parents who tried to prevent their offspring joining were subject to heavy prison sentences or were warned that the child would be placed in care or foster homes if they did not comply.

The youth movement was now eight-million strong. Parents were registering their youngsters as members but not forcing them to attend any meetings. The organisation was now enormous and the Government, masterminding its invasion plans, the *Land Jahr* programme and labour force volunteers, merely ensured that all other youth organisations were discarded. The size of the *Jugend* and *Jungvolk* meant there was no effective control at grass roots level. Trautmann lost interest and could not remember Karl-Heinz attending any *Jugend* or *Jungvolk* activities at all.

As a party member he was, however, contributing to the Reich with blind obedience to most law and decrees and, like his family and workmates, accepting the arguments for war. For six years the Germans had been fed lies and half-truths and, as August 1939 progressed, they had read in the papers or heard on the radio the Führer's appeasing tones in his approach to Poland. The men at Hanomag discussed the problem over meal breaks and most of them were in agreement, Hitler's stance was more than reasonable. Carl and Frieda were of the same opinion that nobody wanted war, but if it was necessary then so be it. All agreed, however, that Poland was the aggressor and that, frankly, England would not carry out her threat of war with Germany.

On 27 August rationing was introduced with immediate restrictions on the purchase of coal, textiles, shoes and soap. By then even the most obtuse realised war was imminent. By 3 September Germany had invaded Poland and was at war with England and France.

Trautmann was excited and stimulated by the speculation and rumours in Bremen. Some of the older boys at Tura had been recruited into the forces some months before and turned up for matches in their uniforms, proud and willing soldiers, instilling envy in the younger players. Their stories of the life and glamour in the services encouraged several more to join up and the ambition of Bernd was to one day become a pilot with the *Luftwaffe*. The image of war to a 15-year-old was unrealistic and frustrating. Nothing happened. Germany seemed invincible and life carried on as normal, and Bernd had to face each day the more mundane prospect of working at Hanomag.

Bernd's hands were now cut and scarred and his fingernails blackened by his job. Every replacement component seemed to have to be tooled. He would have to mix up chimney soot into a black paste, used for imprints, and the cutting or filing work was to exact millimetres. Cold water was used for washing. He used glycerine for cleaning his hands, which were stripped of layers of skin. Life revolved around crankshafts, injection pumps or transmissions.

His job was not always dispiriting, however. Budde and Poppe were a shrewd twosome when it came to gaining some reward for themselves. The restrictions on various foodstuffs caused them little hardship because the means of production of the Lower Saxony farmers were linked to their tractors and lorries. If an urgent repair was necessary, the farmers would telephone Hanomag and ask for a mechanic to be sent out. Budde would always look forward to the farmer's distress calls. Of course, he realised the importance of the repair or spare parts, but surely the farmer was aware of the other more important jobs Hanomag were working flat out on? He would try as hard as he could to get a mechanic out as soon as possible. When he assessed the level of difficulty of the work, Budde would drag Bernd from his work and drive him out to the farm. He would be effusive and apologetic to the farmer for bringing only an apprentice, who was all the labour he had available, but Trautmann was the best apprentice Hanomag had and he could be relied on to do the job. The fact that he was the only apprentice Hanomag had was beside the point. The farmer was overwhelmingly grateful and promised Budde he would be looked after. Bernd was left to complete the work before he was driven back in a vehicle laden with fresh farm produce. After the spoils were split between Budde and Poppe, Trautmann was often rewarded with fresh vegetables to take home to Frieda, which rivalled some of the loot Carl was bringing home from the docks.

After a year with Hanomag, Bernd became more than the only apprentice they had. Three more were taken on and he was placed in charge of them. Each apprentice was placed under the supervision of a licensed mechanic, as Bernd was with Wegenhaur, but he was responsible for showing them the ropes and organising the cleaning duties. Bernd was now the leader of a gang again. He was able to delegate some of the more unpleasant jobs to the younger lads. Rationing meant that the soap they used to wash with was a horrible, grey carbolic substance that was more abhorrent than glycerine, and Trautmann became less hand conscious as the others became afflicted with dermatitis.

The apprentices all attended the technical college together. Bernd was a year ahead of the rest and was less enthusiastic than the others in his attendance. In the past he had often skipped classes for a day by the river or a morning in bed, without any form of retribution. But he realised that with three others from the same workplace attending the same college he was always open to some sneaky so-and-so reporting him to Budde for not being where he should be. As the senior apprentice, he had a certain power or influence, and as the rest became less interested in lessons they displayed the willpower of lemmings in being persuaded to take a day off, particularly on a baking hot summer's day.

Trautmann organised a day by the banks of the Weser, fishing, swimming and lying in the scorching blaze of the sun. They all awoke about the same time in the late afternoon. Although not pasty youths, each one had been burned bright red by the fierce rays and one unfortunate, who had fallen asleep on his side, looked like a piece of white bread spread with strawberry jam. They cycled home, and Bernd had an uncomfortable supper as Frieda, Carl and Karl-Heinz stared at their guest tomato. The group of apprentices appeared at Hanomag the next morning, representing the Austrian flag. By an unhappy coincidence, Budde had telephoned the technical college the previous day to check on the progress of his hapless quartet, only to be told that, by an equally strange coincidence, none of them appeared to be in attendance. They were called into his office and asked for an explanation.

The three others showed remarkable solidarity in apportioning the blame to Trautmann. Budde lost all control and produced a broom-handle ready to pulverise Bernd into pulp. Bernd, in turn, ran a 100-metre dash across the workshops that, even in his heavy boots, would have brought first place in the German athletics championships. The three lemmings could not find a cliff to throw themselves over and metamorphosed into quivering hamsters in the corner of Budde's office. Budde eventually calmed down as the mechanics hooted with laughter at his rage, and Wegenhaur managed to act as peacemaker in the dispute, Budde eliciting a promise from Bernd not to skip lessons again.

Bernd was a popular lad and a good worker, which even Budde had to concede was an asset to his workforce, but it was not by any means Bernd's only run-in with him. One of the apprentices called Alphonse was a particular rival of Trautmann's. Although younger, he was a few centimetres taller and always fancied his chances at taking on Bernd. He was a particularly lazy boy and often skipped cleaning duties, always sorting for the mechanic he was working with to 'arrange' important assistance on urgent jobs, which meant Alphonse would be unavailable for other work. The apprentices resented the extra 'shit' patrols they had to undergo because of Alphonse's lack of effort, and eventually matters came to a head when Bernd could stand no more of his laziness.

By now, Saturday duties were being extended to late in the afternoon with three people doing the work of four. Trautmann's patience snapped, and he walked over to the bay where Alphonse and his senior man were changing the gearbox of a large diesel truck. Alphonse was sitting in the cab of the truck and when Bernd asked to speak to him he was told to 'Fuck off'. Bernd, livid with frustration, gathered the other two outside after their work was finished and waited for Alphonse. When he came outside, Trautmann laced into him and was in the process of rearranging the boy's face when Budde suddenly appeared on a creaky old bicycle and caught the one-sided scrap. He screamed at Trautmann and the apprentices showed, once again, their complete cowardice by jumping on their own bikes and disappearing in different directions.

Budde chased Trautmann for kilometres before losing him in the allotments where Bernd had begun his indoctrination into the *Jungvolk*. Young Trautmann returned home after three hours and went straight into the bathroom for a long, hot soak. Within minutes of his tired body being immersed into the water, the sound of a large diesel truck was heard pulling up outside the building. Budde had turned up at the house and was complaining to Carl about Bernd's behaviour. Carl was particularly amused by this escapade and took Bernd's side in the dispute, backing his son all the way. At the same time he pacified Budde, who agreed not to take further action on the understanding that Bernd would try harder to control his wayward spirit and try to show more responsibility in his job. Carl, at the end of the day, was pleased Bernd was a 'real lad' and advised him to always stick up for himself if he believed he was right. Bernd and Carl Trautmann were becoming closer.

Karl-Heinz was still a loner, sitting in his room making models. He had now left school and was working as an apprentice carpenter, a skill that perhaps suited his insular nature, but he in turn was excited by the war and joined in the family discussions about the German victories.

Bernd was, at this time, supplementing his earnings by doing extra work with Hanomag. Poppe and Budde would arrange some urgent servicing on Sundays, on a cash-only basis, and Wegenhaur would be asked to complete the work, often receiving a week's wages for a day's work. He, in turn, would ask Trautmann to come in and assist for cash in hand. During any holidays or days off he was also working in the docks, where he unloaded barges, again for cash. He was developing a canny instinct for money and was not afraid of hard graft to get it. The extra payments were saved or used to pay for new sports equipment.

It was about this time that Bernd's ambition to join the Armed Forces became more pronounced. Frieda became particularly agitated about the subject, no mother wanted her son to take up arms, regardless of the fact Germany was pulverising the rest of Europe with the immense power of its *blitzkrieg* and was winning all the battles.

From a career point of view, Bernd was now enjoying his job and the older men regarded him as a character and a tough lad, who had grown in stature and confidence since his first, hesitant introduction to working life. To a certain extent, some of the mechanics were a little bit scared of the boy, whose refusal to suffer any intimidation brought a lot of respect. They also knew his reputation as a footballer and all-round sportsman. This gave him a certain amount of celebrity status and they spent hours discussing sport in general.

The inevitability of his involvement with the Forces became more imminent each day and the majority of his friends of 18 had been called-up. He discussed with his parents and workmates the advantage of volunteering into a branch of the Forces he fancied rather than suffer the lottery of call-up. He remembered the family discussions well, with Carl recounting his own experiences as a soldier. Carl recalled the imagery of the mud and despair of the 1918 débâcle and the suffering and humiliation of defeat. He made the point that this new *Wehrmacht* was strong and a winner. The Führer had proved that the weakness of the enemy would lead to a quick and easy victory for the Germans, and Bernd's ambition was encouraged. The valour and bravery of the Great War would be rewarded by the Reich's restoration of the losses of the earlier war and then peace would be restored. Adolf Hitler had said so.

The first British aircraft had flown over and bombed parts of Bremen by this time. As a port of economic importance, it was a strategic target. The raids were, however, sporadic and did little damage, other than to the morale of the people, who had been told they inhabited an impregnable fortress. Gun batteries and

34

searchlights were becoming more prominent, and Bernd picked up many pieces of shrapnel, always a cobalt blue or pitted deep-grey. He kept them in the bedroom among Karl-Heinz's wooden aircraft.

His first step to enlist involved a visit to the *Luftwaffe* recruiting office where he offered his services as a cadet pilot. In a similar way to the RAF, the *Luftwaffe* was based on elitism and the old school tie, and in all reality Bernd did not have anywhere near the qualifications or intellect that was required. He signed up with the air force as a wireless operator, at least he would have the opportunity to fly, and in March 1941 began his part in World War Two.

From the day he signed his papers to joining his unit, Trautmann had a gap of three weeks in which to settle his personal affairs and say his farewells. At Hanomag his great protagonist, Budde, wished him well, with the offer of a job when the war was over. The other apprentices all stated their own intentions of joining up as soon as possible. Some of the mechanics had also received call-up papers by now, and the workshop was to have a depleted workforce over the next few months.

Bernd's going-away party was held at his Uncle Carl's pub, attended by his family and friends from Hanomag and Tura. Carl and Frieda laid on the food and he was given the freedom of the bar. His inexperience of booze determined him to keep a clear head, and he chose to drink an innocent looking liquid kept at the back of the bar, much to the concealed amusement of the others. It was *Crème de Menthe*. He was legless by the time he made his farewells to everyone and convulsing like a vomiting dog on the journey home.

The following afternoon Frieda helped him pack his clothes, and he left early the next morning for Schwerin-in-Mecklenburg, 60 kilometres from Hamburg, to begin his training as a wireless operator.

His arrival at the barracks, together with another 20 or so recruits, was tinged with excitement. They were all eager to begin their lives in the Forces. The enthusiasm was short-lived. Most of them had received basic training in the youth groups, but none were prepared for the immediate rigours of the *Luftwaffe*. They were shouted and sworn at, pushed around and subjected to early cold-water showers before two hours of square-bashing. After the morning drills, preparation for them to become proficient wireless operators was more daunting.

The theory of the Femca codes was taught in a drab, grey classroom with the walls covered in charts and diagrams. At first the codes seemed easy to learn and the recruits quickly developed their speed in deciphering and transmitting 30 letters a minute. The *Luftwaffe* were in a hurry, however, and the average increased to 40 and then to the required standard of 50 to 60 per minute. The pressure on recruits was intense and Trautmann was finding it tough. Regardless of how hard he tried, he could not achieve more than 40 letters. He was not alone. Several were still achieving only 30 a minute and stories of mental breakdowns were circulating. At least one suicide was known and two others rumoured from another class.

After an exhausting 14-hour day, the young men retired to bed at 9.30pm and were normally all sleeping within minutes. On many occasions, the merciless instructor would crash into their quarters half an hour later and force them to put on headphones at the side of each bed. He then returned to his office and tapped out signals for two or three hours.

Within a month it was apparent a number of them were not going to make it, but Bernd had to accept he would be among the failures. After an interview with the commandant and instructor, in which he expressed his wish to stay with the air force, Bernd was told of a new regiment that was being formed in Berlin and asked if he would be interested in becoming a paratrooper. His main concern was still to be involved with aircraft and he willingly volunteered. In later years he rued, 'If I'd known I'd have to jump out of the bloody things, I might have reconsidered.'

At the end of April 1941 he was transferred to the Standeau-based paratroop regiment in Berlin. The training of the *Odenwald* unit at Standeau made that at the wireless base seem like a picnic, but the concentration on physical fitness for a natural athlete like Trautmann was a great boost to his confidence and he responded with enthusiasm. The paratroopers were a new phenomenon of modern warfare, each of whom became a specialist within the group. In the first basic training sessions they were taught to handle weapons and camouflage and survival techniques, and for Bernd this seemed very much a grown-up version of the *Jugend*.

The concept of the paratroopers in the minds of the public was limited, the essence of romanticism and the spirit of true heroism had been epitomised by the submariners, whose action in their U-boats in the North Sea and Atlantic Ocean had done so much to destroy the Allied shipping and disrupt supply lanes. To the Germans they were true heroes. A new breed of hero was created while Trautmann was under training: the battle of Greece had begun in April, and the capture of Crete the following month by an airborne assault division meant the paratroops were now represented as the crack force and gained a glamorous and forceful image. For the recruits at Standeau this was just the stimulus that was needed. Each one of them basked in the vicarious glory of their colleagues in Greece and they were keen to emulate them in battles to come.

Trautmann's training programme was extensive. He learnt to drive every possible type of vehicle from motorcycles to half-tracks. His time at Hanomag gave him an extra skill and his knowledge of engines was suitably noted. The unit were to be used as sabotage and back-up troops and, through instruction, they had to fully understand the use and types of mines and handle the explosives and other tools of destruction of a hit-and-run outfit.

Training to jump out of aeroplanes began by learning to fall and roll on the coconut matting in the gymnasium. From this they progressed to a tower and, secured by harnesses, began to practice falling from 30, 50 and then finally 60 metres. After six days they were ready for their flight in a decrepit old Junkers training plane. Each recruit was required to complete six jumps before being considered ready for combat. The highest fall was from 1,500 metres and was the first to be carried out, progressing to the shortest distance of 700 metres. Each jump was carried out in absolutely ideal conditions, very little wind and clear skies, and

Trautmann felt the exhilaration and excitement that only parachutists know. Unfortunately, no one pointed out that the conditions of war would be different and that the short-lived euphoria would never be repeated.

Bernd had little time to make any close friends in the unit; the training schedules were such that they excluded any time for recreational activities other than sports as part of the physical instruction programme. Unfortunately for him, football was the least of the priorities of the *Luftwaffe* and handball and the odd game of völkerball were the main sporting outlets. Bernd's skill at both these games was immediately obvious to the instructor.

By the end of May 1941 Trautmann and the others were given their paratroopers' wings and were deemed ready for war. Their destination was to be Zamos in Poland. After two days' rest and recreation in Berlin, the unit were transported to their new base. The hundred or so fit and enthusiastic young men arrived at the camp without any knowledge of what they would be doing there. Unknowingly, they were part of an army of occupation. The Poles had succumbed to the power of the German forces and in the rest of Europe they had complete control. Hitler was about to instigate Operation Barbarossa, the invasion of Russia.

The paratroops were confined to their immediate environment in Zamos. They had no contact at all with the Polish people and boredom soon set in. The days were spent maintaining equipment or unloading supplies that came into the compound at every hour of the day. Impromptu football games helped relieve the tedium, and Bernd played handball against other regiments in the area. They felt completely cut off from the war and frustrated at their lack of action. Some of the older, more experienced troops advised them to be patient, they would lose their innocence and naivety soon enough.

Rumours of impending action started in early June, and it was obvious from the amount of equipment being stockpiled that some sort of move was imminent. The officers gave nothing away and the men could only speculate on where they would be going. Russia was mentioned, but the Germans had negotiated a pact with Stalin, the Russian head of state, and as such the possibility of war in the east seemed remote to the unit. Still, with Adolf Hitler as leader, you could never tell.

At four in the morning of 22 June, Trautmann's unit, after being in a state of alert for days, swept across the Russian border and headed south towards the Ukraine. Hitler had declared war against the Soviets and his immediate aim was to secure the vital industry and grain harvests in the south and also the Crimea, which was a vital strategic area for the Germans to gain access to the Caucasus.

The vanguard of the German attack were the SS *Einsatzgruppen* in units of 3,000. The SS had orders to liquidate any form of resistance, which they did with ruthless efficiency. The attack on Russia was so swift and successful that any partisan groups that had not been killed re-formed, and found themselves behind the German lines. The paratroops came in behind the SS and mopped up any remaining defences. Bernd Trautmann's war had begun.

# THE RUSSIAN CAMPAIGN

*So many things I want to tell you, I'll forget most of them. I want to tell you that a soldier gives so much to get something back. From the day of a child's birth he is taught by every circumstance, by every law and rule and right to protect his own life. He starts with that great instinct, and everything confirms it. And then he is a soldier and he must learn to violate all of this – he must learn coldly to put himself in the way of losing his own life without going mad.*

JOHN STEINBECK

FOURTEEN days after the invasion of Russia, Trautmann's unit set up a base at Berdichev, south-west of Zhitomir. The advance through the Soviet countryside had been made over particularly rough terrain and the speed of the attack had left the supply convoys a greater distance behind than they should have been. The condition of many vehicles was such that urgent repairs were needed for the advance to continue. It was decided to send transport to Warsaw to collect spares, a journey that would take around 10 days. In the meantime, orders to continue the advance were received.

A number of drivers and mechanics were left behind to stay with the vehicles needing repair, Bernd among them. They would be left without serviceable transport, all the truck engines had been broken down for the advance units and, in effect, the group were stranded. The sergeant left in charge was not particularly happy about this, and Trautmann was taken to one side on the night before the main force continued. He was persuaded to alter the timing of a small Ply Opel car to prevent it from starting the following morning. Bernd, impressed by the sergeant's confidence in him, duly obliged before retiring to bed. To his amazement the car was not there the following day, and he received a severe reprimand for not doing the job properly.

Around lunchtime, the driver of the car walked wearily into the camp causing Bernd and the sergeant to exchange puzzled looks. After a cup of coffee and food, the driver told the conspiratorial duo that he had been unable to start the Opel so it was towed out of the camp by one of the trucks with a Staff Sergeant sitting on the open bonnet and tinkering with the engine. Unfortunately, the engine had somehow caught fire, severely burning the Staff Sergeant's arms. After the flames were extinguished, the car was left abandoned and the driver told to make his way back to Berdichev. Trautmann and the sergeant hitched a lift out to the car and persuaded a driver from another *Luftwaffe* unit to tow it back for them in exchange for a carton of cigarettes. After a few hours' work the little car was serviceable again and was to prove invaluable.

The food stocks were basic rations and the men yearned for a change to their boring diet. The 10-day estimate for the arrival of the spare parts was wholly unrealistic, and it was soon apparent that it would be over two weeks before they arrived. Trautmann's group were in a relatively safe area, free from partisan attacks and far away from the Russian Army, and so they decided to enjoy their little holiday.

Surprisingly, the local people were not all hostile to their presence and were actively involved in exchanging farm produce for army rations and that great international currency of war, cigarettes. The Opel was used to charge about the countryside to collect fresh food supplies, eggs, sugar and bread being the most sought after commodities, but the men yearned for the favourite meat of the German diet – pork.

Trautmann heard from a passing truck driver of a farm 30 kilometres away that had pigs among the livestock, and he quickly passed on the news to the sergeant, who rapidly organised a 'pig-possession' party. Bernd and two others piled into the car and drove to the farm where they managed to bargain for two piglets. They set off back to camp with the two animals trussed up in the back, while Bernd's stomach rumbled at the prospect of crackling and roast pork.

By this time the car was in a pretty sorry state. It had been maintained as well as possible, but the clutch needed replacing and the brakes were as efficient as a one-armed archer. As the car approached Berdichev, it had to travel down a steep hill. Halfway down a squealing piglet escaped its bonds and jumped out of the car, which could not stop until the level road at the bottom of the hill. With the remaining piglet under guard, Trautmann and the other member of the pig party ran up the hill to find the runaway. After a manic chase lasting nearly three hours, they managed to recapture the animal and arrived triumphantly at their base. One of the drivers had been a butcher before the war and slaughtered the piglets before an expectant audience. The smiles of the men soon turned to distain as he opened up the stomachs. 'Sorry lads, the little bastards are diseased.' The group had an unhappy supper of canned meat and beans.

After 17 days the spares finally arrived from Warsaw. The men worked continually for three days to get the vehicles serviceable again and then a further five days to catch up with the main unit. Bernd had been bothered with a stomach problem for a few days before reuniting with the main force, but within a couple of days he was bothered by something far more serious.

The sergeant involved in the car episode with Bernd had told the driver what he had done. When he rejoined the main force, the driver immediately told Staff Sergeant Glockner, who had received the burns. Glockner reported the incident to Oberleutnant Bergenthum, the commanding officer. Trautmann and the sergeant were arrested on charges of sabotage and a court-martial was held at Berdichev aerodrome, which at the time was the headquarters of the *Luftwaffe* fighter squadrons.

Bergenthum was a good commanding officer. He realised that the sergeant's influence on Bernd had been considerable and intimidating, and he argued long and hard for Bernd. He stressed his youth and inexperience and pointed out the crime was more of a jape than an act of rebellion. Trautmann was sentenced to nine months' imprisonment, later reduced to three months after Bergenthum's insistent protests.

Remarkably, Trautmann was allowed to rejoin his unit, by now advancing rapidly towards the Black Sea. By the time he caught up with them the terms of his detention had been worked out, and within days he was escorted north again to begin his sentence in Zhitomir prison, some 500 kilometres distant. Zhitomir was a bleak Russian prison that had housed many political prisoners during the Revolution. It had been controlled by the OGPU, the predecessors of the KGB, and Bernd was overwhelmed by depression as he entered through the huge black doors. His cell was deep in the bowels of the structure and, as he descended the stairs, a shroud of despair enveloped him. His cell was about six metres long by two metres wide, with the floor under several centimetres of stagnant water. Duck-boards had been laid down, but they were covered in slime and rat droppings and were treacherous underfoot. There were three planks set against the walls, which acted as beds, each with a stinking, damp blanket. As the heavy, steel door clanged behind him, Bernd adjusted his eyes to the dim light and his nose to the pungent odours.

Two unshaven, red-eyed men greeted his arrival with the offer of a cigarette and an official welcome to the cesspit. The men were both SS soldiers, held on charges of murdering a Russian civilian they had shot on suspicion of being a member of a partisan group. Considering the gross brutality of the SS *Einsatzgruppen* in Russia, this was rather like charging Caligula with indecent exposure. But, for some reason, these two had been sentenced to three years' imprisonment.

Desperate for company and conversation, the SS men kept Bernd talking for most of the night until he collapsed on his plank in a fitful sleep. The pain in his stomach had increased considerably by now and as the doors of the cell opened at five in the morning he dragged himself into the urinals to relieve himself and have a cold-water wash. They exercised in the prison yard for half an hour, breakfasted on tepid coffee and black bread and were led back to the cell. Bernd collapsed on to his plank, doubled up with pain.

The SS men realised that he had a serious problem and called the prison guards, who in turn called the prison commandant. In Trautmann's own words, 'I suppose in most war films you will have seen the arrogant, blustering German Officer. The commandant of Zhitomir prison was just that.' He asked, 'What's wrong with you, you little turd?' Bernd explained his problem through tears of pain. 'I'll get the doctor, but if you're pretending, I'll treble your sentence.' One of the SS men was far more succinct about the commandant: 'If I could get him on his own for two minutes, I'd kick his balls so hard he'd have three Adam's apples.'

Within an hour Bernd was transferred to an army hospital and diagnosed with appendicitis. The doctors whipped out the useless part of his stomach just in time. He was told later that he was within hours of death. His recovery was painfully slow and, to a certain extent, his lack of enthusiasm to return to the prison encouraged the odd relapse, but he managed to complete his sentence in the relative comfort of the hospital.

The field hospital dealt with some of the more serious injuries, and men had been ferried back from the lines to have guts removed and limbs severed. The doctors were young and reminiscent to Bernd of the MASH units he saw romanticised in later life. The medics wore T-shirts and rubber aprons. Sometimes he helped to wash off bits of gore and blood. He was allowed to watch operations and, in effect, became an auxiliary nurse. He became hardened to the macabre humour, and his experience there helped him to overcome the grotesque sights he was to see on the battlefront.

Bernd rejoined his unit in October 1941, coinciding with the onset of the Russian winter. Trautmann's war had lasted six months, which had been spent training, waiting, being in trouble and hospitalisation. He had yet to return fire on his enemy. Still, it could have been worse, he could have been a wireless operator being shot down over England during the Battle of Britain.

Bernd rejoined his unit at Dnepropetrovsk, some 500 kilometres south-east of Zhitomir. The Russian winter had started early and the greatcoats of the division had been worn for a couple of weeks. The wind roared from the north and each morning the frost was thicker. Bernd arrived back in time for the first snowfalls. The cold weather, arriving surprisingly early, had found the great German Army totally unprepared. This mighty war machine of efficiency was caught without adequate clothing and, already, the men were chilled to the bone.

To make matters worse, the attack on Moscow was floundering. In addition, rumours that Field-Marshal von Runstedt had resigned and that the German Army had retreated from Rostov were circulating (both of which were true). Von Runstedt was trying to capture the Russian oil fields around Kiev, but the Germans had totally underestimated the strength of the Russian Army. More and more reserve divisions seemed to appear from nowhere. More important, the Germans had no answer to the T34 tank, which was almost impregnable against German shells and was far more heavy duty than the German tanks. The snows stopped and the temperature rose, resulting in heavy rains. The roads and countryside turned into a quagmire, and Trautmann's unit were bogged down in filthy brown mud. In early November the snows returned, the ground froze over and temperatures plummeted.

Trautmann's unit were now deployed on hit-and-run raids throughout the area, but were also destroying oil and ammunition dumps to prevent them falling into the hands of the advancing Russian Fifth Army. Bernd had by this time killed for the first time, returning fire against some anonymous grey figure who dropped like a stone. That was it – no feeling of revulsion or guilt, just nothing. The mixture of fear, self–preservation and fatigue whittled down normal sensibilities to a detached pragmatism.

The camaraderie and comradeship within the unit was good. The bravery and common suffering of the men had forged great loyalties among them. Bernd had formed a great attachment to Peter Kularz, and they were to remain close friends throughout the Russian campaign. Their main problem was the diminishing stocks of supplies and, for the officers, the low morale this was causing. The black market continued to flourish and the paratroopers would often venture into the city of Dnepropetrovsk to negotiate for goods. A number of Italian units had been deployed in the area and these men also seemed to have more goods than the shops. Bernd, Peter and the rest of the unit were regularly involved in brawls with the Italians, and often great hauls of cigarettes and booze would be liberated for the use of the German forces. The men's bond with the officers was also good; the rigid formality of the Forces was being replaced by a brotherhood concept. The officers were also young and related well to their men. They did not disguise their feelings at some of the inexplicable orders emanating from the general command. After one particularly difficult action against the Russians, Trautmann and the others were called to see their captain to receive new orders. Half expecting to be sent towards Stalingrad to reinforce the beleaguered German troops, they were staggered to find they had been selected to play a handball match 100 kilometres away from the front.

The weather got worse; Trautmann remembers temperatures of -35 degrees in early December. The ground was so hard that graves for the dead could not be dug and hundreds of frozen corpses were left in grim rows. The paratroops were now concentrating all their efforts on keeping vehicles and their equipment moving. The low temperatures had frozen half-tracks and tanks, the oil in the vehicles had become viscous and it became a losing battle to keep the supply trucks going. The regiment began cutting oil drums in half and used them for fires, which would be placed under vehicles to defrost them, and also for the men to keep themselves warm. The forest, at least, provided the wood for the fires, but also contained a number of partisan groups, who were getting stronger by the day and were more used to the awful conditions. Even though the main Russian counter-offensive was also frozen-in, the partisans would always be a threat. They operated independently from the Russian Army and were generally formed by bandit groups, who were always on the lookout for loot during the conflicts. Trautmann's unit were involved in a number of skirmishes with these groups and, as the war progressed, they were to prove a formidable force.

By the spring of 1942 there was little action on the battle fronts as both sides sought to replace equipment and bring in fresh troops to replace the exhausted armies. It was necessary to bring in new vehicles and parts, and Trautmann's regiment were actively involved. This was perhaps one of the main problems with the German war machine. They had so many different types of tank and trucks, whereas the Russians used just one or two different types. It was easy for them to utilise parts, and with their factories geared to the production of the same engines and spares the Russian forces were never stranded through lack of parts. The German factories and those in newly conquered countries were constantly upgrading and redesigning. There was always a new tank, vehicle or gun in production and, consequently, the forces were never able to utilise their stocks or spares properly. Different cylinder heads or gaskets meant more and more vehicles had to be left behind through lack of the correct spares and an inability to improvise, as the Russians were doing. The problem with equipment was further compounded by acts of sabotage carried out by the factory workers in the occupied countries, whose factories were producing for the Germans. During the early spring some of Bernd's colleagues had been despatched to Mechelen in Belgium to supervise the loading of trains carrying new vehicles and to act as guards on the long journey back to Russia. When their train unloaded, many of the vehicles were found to be useless; sand had been placed in batteries, sugar in petrol tanks and cylinder heads were damaged.

Somehow things managed to come together again, and by the beginning of June the German forces were ready to resume the offensive once more. With the terrain firmer and unhampered by the snow they were able to hold their ground against fierce Russian attacks, and in many cases began to gain ground again.

As the war gathered momentum once more, the Germans were determined to gain the oil fields before the end of the summer, while Stalin was equally determined to secure them. The 35th were still being used on hit-and-run missions and sabotaging Russian supply routes. At other times they were used to back other units or to support the Waffen SS, who were always sent in where battle was thickest.

The Waffen SS were altogether different from the thugs of the *Einsatzgruppen* and were known as the 'fire brigade' by the rest of the forces. These were the elite of fighting men with the best equipment and the best rations. They were also men of immense bravery and often held or secured forward positions where others had failed. Bernd would always remember the acts of heroism of these men and, in later life, defend their reputation. Bernd, who had been promoted to corporal in the spring of 1942, had now become hardened by the rigours of the war. The dependence of the men on each other was so absolute as they felt increasingly isolated. The field mail carrying news from Germany was irregular and heavily censored, as were the men's letters home. The only news they heard was the ceaseless propaganda of the German radio, which they loathed and treated with cynicism. Leave was rare and the married men with families took precedence over the single soldiers.

Bernd had managed to get back to Bremen for a couple of weeks in March, but the journey home was fraught with danger, discomfort and de-lousing. The journey back would always be on freight trains or cattle trucks through the huge forests of Central Russia and invariably his old enemies, the partisans, would want to interfere with the train timetable. They were now regularly blowing up trains and track, and each soldier, going or returning from leave, travelled with a rifle, pistol and ammunition. Trautmann, describing the journey, said, 'At various points down the line there were blockhouses occupied by German pioneers, who had a thankless and near-hopeless time of relaying the track every time it was blown up. As soon as they left the blockhouse they would be machine-gunned by the partisans, who were experts at hiding in the forest, which came right up to the railway track on each side. Railway engines were blown up regularly and soldiers going on leave had to wait while another was sent from the point of departure and the stretch of track re-laid. And while they waited they fought off the partisans. Coming back off leave, it was not unknown for our soldiers to be called from the train to reinforce a battalion some 70 kilometres away, where the Russians had broken through. Yet our soldiers were prepared to go through all that just to get away from the Russian battlefront for a while.'

If and when the train finally reached Bialystok on the Polish border they were able to connect with a passenger train for the last part of the journey home. Before being allowed on to this train, they had to undergo de-lousing and were stripped naked while their bodies and clothing were cleansed. They were given a special card to be carried with their other documents, which signified de-lousing had been carried out.

Once at the border, the troops were presented with the 'Führer's Parcel', a 10-kilo package containing flour, a succulent sausage of *Mettwurst,* cooking oil and other things, which would be of immense use to their families. Bernd presented his to Frieda on his return to Gröpelingen. Despite rationing and the sporadic air-raid, life in Bremen seemed as normal. Carl was still working hard at Kalle, Frieda put up with her lot, while Karl-Heinz concentrated on his joinery. It was during this leave that Bernd discovered his family knew little of the conditions in Russia or the way the war was going. To them the forces were victorious everywhere and the huge losses of men and territory were hidden from them by propaganda broadcasts. They listened with disbelief as Bernd told them of the hardships the troops were enduring and the shortages of supplies.

At the same time Bernd had to admit he knew little of the advance on Moscow and Leningrad, but he suspected from the stories percolating back that the troops were not having an easy time. He became more confident that victory would eventually be achieved when he read the official reports in the Nazi Press of the progress now being made, although some of the accounts of the areas he had been in seemed somewhat dubious.

It was an uneventful leave. He caught up with the few friends that had not yet been called-up, visited relatives or had a few beers with his father. But his two weeks were soon over and he started the long journey back to the Russian Steppes, little realising he would not be seeing Bremen again for many years.

On his way back to the Ukraine it was noticeable that the pioneers had started to cut down the trees by the side of the track to a distance of 20 or 30 metres, a tremendous feat of endeavour, which eventually lessened some of the damage being inflicted by the partisans by reducing their cover.

Bernd arrived back in Russia as the Germans began the big summer offensive in 1942. More generals had been replaced and a number of new faces had joined the regiment during Bernd's leave. Bernd caught up with the news from Peter, who told him some of the junior officers were out to make a name for themselves. He noticed that immediately when he was torn off a strip for not saluting a lieutenant. The relaxed discipline of a small unit was being replaced by old Prussian values.

During the summer of 1942 the German Army regained lost ground in the south, and by August they had reached the Volga, just north of Stalingrad. The paratroopers were used to secure bridges and keep open important roads, a task they performed with immense professionalism. The Russians were, however, proving to be tough and resilient fighters, and the German armies, used to having it fairly easy, were becoming frustrated by the depth of the Russian defences. Trautmann had a more intimate encounter with the Soviets than he had bargained for.

During a routine patrol near Zaporozhye, they were attacked by a Russian machine-gun post after the driver of the truck lost his way. Trautmann and seven others were captured and taken to a command centre nearby. They were treated surprisingly well by their captors, who immediately put them to work repairing damaged buildings that the Russians needed as billets. Trautmann discussed the situation with the others and they agreed the Russians would probably execute them when the work was finished. It was a gut reaction rather than from any implied threat, but these soldiers were a fighting unit and would have no time for prisoners when their next battle commenced. After three days Trautmann and two others took the opportunity to slip away by taking advantage of a disinterested guard. Under the cover of darkness they just crawled away and the following morning flagged down another paratroop group who got them back to their lines.

The intense pressure on the commanders and the troops continued to build from the Nazi leaders. Victory in Russia was to be achieved at all costs. Despite promises of more men and more equipment, very little appeared. Officers who questioned commands were recalled or demoted under a decree made by Hitler, part of which read, 'The Führer must be in a position to force, with all means at his disposal, every German, if necessary, whether he be a common soldier or officer, to fulfil his duties. In cases of violation of these duties, the Führer is entitled, after conscientious examination, regardless of so-called well deserved rights, to mete out due punishments and to remove the offender from his rank without introducing prescribed procedures.'

By the autumn of 1942 the German armies had not achieved their military objective and, as the winter set in, the Russian armies began their massive counter-offensive. The Germans were forced back on all sides, their Sixth Army was surrounded at Stalingrad and Hitler would not allow them to fall back. Thousands of troops froze to death and the war was turning against them. More important, the morale and incredible discipline of the German forces was collapsing, but still the Nazis poured out slogans and propaganda instructions urging the men to stand firm, while ignoring the utter hardship and overwhelming odds they were up against. Trautmann recalled one slogan, 'Wheels have to roll for the final victory', which quickly became, 'Heads will have to roll after defeat'. The truth was now transparently obvious to the men, Germany, to quote one of Bernd's colleagues, was 'getting stuffed'.

In an effort to bolster the retreating armies from Moscow and Leningrad, the paratroops were transferred to Smolensk. The unit spent a wretched two weeks aboard a freight train that made a tortuously slow journey north. They arrived in early December and were ordered to patrol the main railway lines outside the city.

The bitterly cold conditions, lack of news, frost-bite and hardly any rations had brought the unit to the lowest point of its campaign. On one patrol two of the men slipped down an embankment and fell into a small lake. The holes were iced over within 30 seconds and they were lost. The others returned to the camp in a distressed state, their bodies and uniforms in filthy condition. One of the new officers immediately ordered a kit inspection. This man had no experience of the Russian war; he had left the army college just a few weeks before and was determined to repair the ragged discipline the men were now showing. He recoiled under the barrage of abuse and threats from the men, and then retreated in panic from the hostile stares of battle-hardened veterans with an average age of 21. The officer was 20 years of age.

On Christmas Day in 1942 each man was given extra rations and bottles of liquor. Trautmann chose a bottle of *Kummel,* a particularly potent liquor. They retired to their hut and proceeded to get roaring drunk. Bernd drank his whole litre of booze quickly and crashed out on his bunk for a couple of hours, awaking to find the party in full swing. Peter Kularz, who was teetotal, gave Bernd his bottle of *Kummel* and a grateful Trautmann proceeded to pour this down his throat just as a Staff Sergeant came in and barked out some instruction or other. Bernd never did discover what the sergeant said, but, with the effects of the alcohol and the frustration and anxiety building up, his temper erupted and he threw a punch that Max Schmeling might have envied. The Staff Sergeant was knocked out cold. Kularz and the others bundled Trautmann outside into the freezing night. Someone shouted, 'Try and sober the stupid bastard up.'

Nearby was a two-metre-deep pit used for storing potatoes and his colleagues decided it was a good place for Trautmann to go. They tossed him in and went back to the prostrate sergeant. The temperature outside that night was 35 below zero and within 20 minutes Bernd was dragged out, frozen and sober. Fortunately, the Staff Sergeant had been with the unit from the beginning, and he accepted the incident as a release from the pent-up emotions they were all feeling. Trautmann apologised and nothing more was said about it. The desperate winter continued with the Germans falling back irretrievably, kilometre by kilometre. The Sixth Army was annihilated in Stalingrad and only a third of that army still survived.

In the *Odenwald* unit only 300 of the original force of 1,000 were left. They were now concentrating solely on destroying their own munition dumps, equipment and airfields to prevent them falling into the hands of the Soviet forces. One of the German airfields at Wjasma, just north of Smolensk, was in immediate danger of being captured. Trautmann and his group arrived just before midnight to lay mines around the hangars, fuel tanks and runways. During the rush, Bernd crashed into a munitions store, tripped over a packing case and fell on to a huge bomb. He lay in eerie silence on the metal casing, his heart thudding like a jackhammer. He giggled idiotically as he pushed himself away, his nerves stretched as taut as piano wires. Then he ran like the wind. The airfield was destroyed just in time because the Russians moved in the following morning. It was his last major participation in the war on the Eastern Front, and Bernd left Russia for another theatre of war. He was 21 years old.

# THE WESTERN FRONT AND CAPTURE

*In the army vocabulary the word 'fart' had been in favourite use from time immemorial and in the main this honourable title was bestowed on colonels or senior captains and majors, and it indicated a degree higher than the commonly used term 'Bloody old man'.*

*Without the adjective 'bloody' the appellation 'old man' indicated friendly appreciation of a old colonel or major who blew his top a lot but at the same time was fond of his men and protected them from other regiments, particularly when it came to other patrols rounding them up in pubs when they had been given extended leave. An 'old man' looked after the interests of his soldiers and insisted their messing was in order, but he always had some kind of bee in his bonnet, was always on about something – and so he was an 'old man'. But when the old man gave the officers and men a lot of unnecessary hell, thought up night operations and other things like that, he became the 'bloody old man'.*

*From the 'bloody old man' if he attained the highest degree of bloodiness, bullying and blockheadedness, he became a 'fart'. This word was full of meaning, and great was the difference between a 'fart' in civilian life and 'fart' in the army.*

JAROSLAV HASEK

*Adolf Hitler suffered from meteorism – uncontrollable farting.*

JOHN TOLAND

FOR THE first time in nearly two years Trautmann was required to jump out of a plane again, and he landed in France. The old men in Berlin were preparing to defend against the Allied invasion in Western Europe. Bernd had been promoted to sergeant just before his unit left Russia with the remnants of the *Odenwald* paratroopers, and they grouped together at Melun, some 60 kilometres south of Paris. The regiment had been decimated in Russia and a new unit was to be formed with an eclectic group of displaced forces personnel.

Peter Kularz had been dreadfully injured in Smolensk and had been taken back to Germany for treatment. Now only 90 of the original unit remained. The reinforcements included youngsters of 17, *Luftwaffe* crews who no longer had aircraft to fly and anti-aircraft units with no guns to use, all under the command of non-commissioned officers with little experience. The new *Odenwald* unit were moved to Dijon, where they all completed the six required jumps, with Trautmann again completing a basic training. This time they completed jumps in darkness as well as day and the conditions were both blustery and dangerous. In the rush to finish the training, a number of the men were involved in accidents which took them out of the war completely.

In May 1944 Trautmann found himself in St Valery-sur-Somme and in the same vicinity that his father had fought 27 years before. The German forces were forming the 'Atlantic Wall' in preparation to repel the Allied invasion. The general staff in Berlin were divided in their opinion about if and where the invasion would begin. The Sixth Army under General Dollman were expecting it to start around the Pas-de-Calais area, but the bulk of the German forces were grouped further south stretching east and west of Le Havre.

The *Odenwald* established defensive positions at St Valery and faced out to the English Channel. The beaches were covered with 'Rommel's asparagus', huge wooden poles buried in the sand, which rose two metres above. Barbed wire had been run along each piece and mines placed to complete the awesome fortification. The Germans waited for the invasion to begin.

In the meantime, the activities of the French Resistance groups were stepped up, and for a short time Trautmann was captured again. He was being used as a despatch rider at the time. The Resistance were operating under the cover of the dense woods. Bernd caught up with some of his colleagues, who were out on patrol to counteract the French, when they were attacked and captured. They were bound and gagged and left under guard without food or water for 30 hours. Trautmann, slowly but surely, loosened his bonds and once again slipped away from his captors. He arrived back just in time for the invasion of 6 June 1944.

The Germans fell back under the fearsome barrage from the sea and air and once again a retreat began. The officers began to panic and, again, those old men, with Hitler the main culprit, could not accept the reality of the situation. As a result, delays in sending Panzer divisions to meet the attackers meant the German forces became fragmented. They retreated in chaos, and by July Bernd and what was left of the paratroopers were desperately trying to find some orderly chain of command that could give them some direction. They were left bitterly critical of the inexplicable blockheadedness of the officers, and the 'fart' syndrome gathered momentum. The 'bloody old man' was Adolf Hitler.

For months, stories of new 'miracle' weapons were initiated by the high command and promises of new men and equipment had been made, but as none appeared and reinforcements did not arrive the men became more and more *Chokker* (fed up) and *Nasevoil* (pissed off). To make matters worse, the German radio was broadcasting news of an attempt to assassinate Hitler and rumours of a *coup d'état* in Berlin were prominent.

By August the German forces had lost half a million men, dead or captured, and most of their arms and equipment had been destroyed on the Western Front. On 25 August Paris was liberated and the Germans were being pushed back to defend the Fatherland.

In September 1944 Montgomery's British and Canadian troops were pouring through Belgium and Holland, and Trautmann's unit were sent across the border to bolster the defences. They joined up with two Waffen SS units, who were just outside Arnhem. Montgomery had decided to establish a bridgehead there, just as the SS and *Odenwald* units were grouping.

The carnage was indescribable. The Allied paratroops fell out of the sky to be greeted by one of the most devastating and experienced German forces. Trautmann captured a number of allied airmen and the imagery of the helpless men hanging in the trees then being shot came to haunt him. The bravery of these men and coming face-to-face with his contemporaries from the other side left him with little appetite to go on fighting, and the futility of the war was now having a profound effect on his comrades.

By the end of September the Allied advance faltered, in a similar way to the German attack on Russia. They had to wait for spares and supplies to catch up. The Germans once again fell back and regrouped to defend the Rhine. Trautmann was taken away from the front line for a while, to rest in the small town of Kleve, which was the main thoroughfare for what remained of the German supply convoys. It was remarkably untouched by the fighting and a good place for the men to relax. Trautmann had been there for three days when the air-raid sirens started. Most people thought it was just another practice drill until, within minutes, the sky was filled, as far as the eye could see, by planes of every description and the bombs started to fall. He recalled, 'Along with hundreds of civilians and German soldiers, I dashed into a cellar under the local school. Almost immediately the school suffered a direct hit and the whole building collapsed on top of us.'

Bernd and another soldier had dived into a small broom cupboard, used by the school caretaker, just as the building collapsed around them. He came around after a few minutes to discover his body trapped in the rubble. By some miracle his head was free and he could feel, at intervals, air coming into the cavity. His eyes, nose and mouth were choked with dust and he had to gulp in the air as it wafted its way through to the air-pocket. He heard the groans of his companion and through the eerie stillness and pitch darkness he could hear the sounds of the rescuers digging above. With great difficulty, he eventually managed to push an arm through the debris and removed some of the dust from his mouth. He tried to shout out to the rescue teams, but the attempt only caused more dust to fall into his mouth again. The rescuers came closer and he became more confident of being freed. In all, he was trapped for three days before he and his comrade were lifted to safety and taken to another cellar to recuperate. He gulped down hot, sweet tea and biscuits and washed the debris from his body before covering himself with a blanket. He heard from his saviours that most of the town had been destroyed and hundreds had been killed. Bernd and the other soldier were the only two found alive at the school.

As he lay under his blanket, he took in the unhealthy surroundings through the dim light. Just above his head were a number of shelves crammed with jars of preserved fruits, and thoughts of a rich, sweet meal began to manifest themselves. Rather inopportunely, an unexploded bomb detonated a few hundred metres from the cellar and the shockwaves sent the shelving crashing down around him. He became an avant-garde artist's delight, a human fruit salad. Although he felt relieved to come through the ordeal without serious injury, the incident in the cellar was to have a lasting and considerable effect on him in a few years' time. Within two days of being rescued he was on the move again, firstly helping to transport evacuees from Kleve and then rejoining the paratroopers at Kraneburg on the Dutch border. Almost immediately he was recovering from another trauma.

A stray grenade blew up as they were organising equipment, and Bernt suffered a number of small, fairly superficial shrapnel wounds. When he recovered from the stunning force of the explosion, he saw, to his utter horror, that one of his colleagues had been terribly injured. Heinz Berger, who had been with Trautmann since leaving Poland, had taken the full force and was lying unconscious with his intestines hanging out through his shredded uniform. Bernd tore at a birch tree and made a makeshift stretcher. Then, with immense courage, he drove through the battle zone to get Heinz to a field hospital. Inexorably, he was losing his friends.

The 'bloody old man' enclosed in his bunker was now sending out a stream of decrees or communiqués to the beleaguered German forces. The stream of messages included such gems as: 'Certain unreliable elements seem to believe that the war will be over for them as soon as they surrender to the enemy. Every deserter will find his just punishment. Furthermore, his ignominious behaviour will entail the most severe consequences for his family – they will be summarily shot.'

At the same time, other messages were arriving each day from other 'bloody old men' urging the troops to fight harder with the promise of eventual victory if they did so. The German forces were running scared from the Allies and the 'farts'.

There was a further blow to the morale of the men as news of Rommel's death filtered through the chaos. This great hero, who had been implicated in the plot to assassinate Hitler, had died, according to the official sources, from wounds received in an air attack, but he had in truth died under more dubious circumstances.

In December 1944 the last Christmas of World War Two was approaching and the last great counter-offensive was launched by the desperate Hitler. The Allies had resumed their push towards the Rhine at the end of October and, despite superior forces, they had not yet broken the brave and stubborn resistance. Bernd's unit were pulled back to take part in the new initiative the Germans planned.

The American Army had captured Aachen and were poised to penetrate along the Rhine deep into Germany. The Germans planned to attack through the Ardennes, force their way to Antwerp and try to capture this most strategic of ports. They assembled a huge force of men and advanced on a frosty, foggy night through the hazardous snow-covered hills of the Ardennes forests. The *Odenwald* unit found themselves once more alongside the Waffen SS and this amazing fighting force initially took the US Army by surprise. They made their way to just a few kilometres from Spa, the headquarters of the American First Army, and then onwards towards a huge supply of oil. Yet again, they had been let down by back–up petrol stocks and the capture of the fuel was imperative for them to continue.

The Americans eventually managed to regroup and launched a devastating air attack on the Germans. The advance was abruptly halted by the aircraft ripping apart thousands of men, tanks and supplies progressing through the narrow passes in the hills. Bernd's Christmas was again spent under the most appalling conditions. It was apparent they would not reach their objective. They began what would be their final retreat.

At the end of January Bernd formed part of a detachment at Krefeld near the Dutch border, and he had to organise an incredible hotch potch of 'reinforcements' from 16 to 60-year-olds. The 'farts' were running out of steam and had sent in the Hitler Youth and the Home Guard. He spent most of the February teaching them how to lay mines and methods of sabotage and the rest of the time watching the inexperienced replacements being blown away in their first engagements with the enemy.

Bernd's war was about to come to an end. He escorted the new recruits to a larger detachment gathered between Wesel and Emmerich. It was here that Bernd's bitterness and the unrelenting pressure of the awful situation exploded, to his intense shame and regret. One of the last remaining men from the Russian Front still around was Heinz Schnabel, the nephew of a renowned German pianist. Heinz was a few years older than the others and was regarded as a confidant and father figure. An incredible rapport and closeness had been established between them and, as their numbers diminished, the comradeship was particularly special. The men shared everything; enduring the same hardships and shortages had brought about an acute awareness of their common survival.

They were sent out with a reconnaissance patrol one morning and were almost immediately attacked by some American Thunderbolt aircraft. The group dived for the nearest cover and the great survivors found themselves sheltering in an old sewage pipe down the road. They emerged, covered in filth, to find huge craters in the road with torsos and limbs scattered around them. Bernd asked Heinz for a cigarette, and, as they stared into each others empty eyes, Heinz said, 'Sorry, I only have one.'

These were the men who had shared everything. In the past they had broken cigarettes in half so they could have a smoke, or stuck a pin into smouldering last millimetres of a cigarette and shared that. Bernd slapped Heinz and walked away. He did not speak to or see him again[1].

The chain of command was now totally severed. The few officers remaining stood around twiddling their thumbs and were doing little to try and reorganise their men. Desertions were now commonplace as the soldiers desperately tried to get back to what they believed was the comparative safety of their homes. Further orders were issued in an effort to stem the tide of justifiably frightened men. The SS were being used to exterminate any soldiers with doubtful leave papers or other travel documents. They were shot or hanged on the spot. The order to execute soldiers was then extended to any Germans who said they had been separated from their units. Trautmann had found himself in that situation several times during the

[1] Author's note: Trautmann tried unsuccessfully to contact Schnabel through the Red Cross after the war. He never had the chance to apologise or enjoy a reunion with his friend.

war, this time he had no unit left to try to find. He spent the early part of March avoiding the SS and the advancing allied troops, and he then made a decision to try and get back to Bremen, several hundred kilometres to the north. He had no transport and only his P.38 pistol. His clothes were in tatters. Walking aimlessly, he came across a fairly isolated farmhouse where his need for food and water overcame any thoughts of danger. The farmer gave him some ham and bread and a mug of milk. He then told him that he had a number of wounded German soldiers in the barn. Parked beside the structure was an ammunition lorry, pock-marked with bullet holes. The six men aboard the truck had all received wounds but had had a remarkable escape as the vehicle was loaded with grenades and explosives.

Bernd and the farmer unloaded the cargo and laid the men carefully into the lorry. The farmer's wife found a white sheet on which they drew a crude cross before fixing it to the canopy. Trautmann intended to drive the wounded men to an army hospital, which the couple said was a few kilometres along the road in the village, and then drive the truck on to Bremen.

As he drove along the road Bernd passed a number of American troops who were completely unconcerned about the makeshift ambulance. They knew the war was nearly finished and the Germans had accepted any further resistance would constitute provocation against the conquering Allied armies.

On the approach to the village, Bernd heard the last pockets of resistance still going on. As he passed the sign for Arminchel, a barrage of heavy guns obliterated the village before his eyes. The hospital, an old country house, had been excluded from the destruction, but the access road was totally impassable and Trautmann left the lorry and his wounded passengers to seek help. It took three hours to move the men into hospital, the stretcher bearers had to negotiate shell craters and rubble to deliver their charges to the medics.

The lorry still had a considerable amount of fuel in its tank, and Trautmann decided to make his dash for freedom. What he did not know was that back in Bremen any form of authority or control had, like the battlefront, ceased to exist. The Allies were already on the outskirts of the port and, appallingly, Hitler had ordered the destruction of his own towns' and cities' manufacturing plants and food stocks. He planned to march all the population to the centre of Germany and let them die together. These last orders were thankfully ignored. Back in Bremen, Carl and Frieda were looking at a country in a worse state than when Carl returned home in 1918.

Trautmann drove away from the village as darkness fell and was soon hopelessly lost along the narrow lanes. Road signs had disappeared and so had Bernd's sense of direction. Unbelievably, he found himself back at the farmhouse he had left several hours previously. The place was in darkness and he could get no response from banging on the doors and windows. He returned to his vehicle and drove a few hundred metres up the road to another farmhouse, but this was also deserted. By this time he was racked with fatigue and hunger and salvaged the remains of food given to him earlier.

He sat wearily against the truck and devoured the scraps. As he ate he heard voices and saw lights in the distance. An overpowering loneliness lured him towards them. This source of activity was yet another farmhouse, but just as he entered through a gate he realised too late he had walked into an American position.

He instinctively drew his gun before being flattened by a couple of hundred kilos of GIs. Fists and boots hammered into his head and body as his gun sailed away into the long grass. He was dragged semi-conscious into a barn and regained his senses in front of a young American captain, who, Trautmann was convinced, was only about 13 years old.

The captain spoke fluent German and immediately demanded to know from Bernd where the rest of his unit was. Bernd in turn recovered his composure, giving only his name, rank and number. The captain's interrogation turned into a summary of the Allied position and left Bernd in no doubt that the war was over. He decided that Trautmann had no useful intelligence to provide and ordered two guards to take him outside. The guards were massive, both over two metres tall, and almost dwarfed the not inconsiderable size of Bernd. They pushed and shoved him menacingly and intimidated him with their hand machine guns into the now bright, moonlit night. He was taken behind the barn and forced through an uncultivated field towards a large tree. The Americans gesticulated for him to raise his arms and as he did so the moonlight caught his shadow, which elongated for metres in front of him. At each side the daunting shadows of the two giants stretched even further.

After all the hardship and pain, the suffering and bravery, Bernd did not want to die with his face in a pile of cow dung. His mind raced as he looked for some escape. Did the Americans shoot prisoners, or were they a unit operating on their own under unforeseen circumstances?

His captors were now shouting something, but in English. How the hell could he understand? His arms were becoming heavier and he felt them slowly descending involuntarily towards his sides. Perhaps it was his imagination, but hadn't the GIs stopped walking? More shouts came, but more distant this time, and as his arms dropped a huge surge of adrenalin made him bolt for his life. No shots slammed into him, he ran like a hare and his ears throbbed with the sound of his blood pumping through his body. Bernd ran and ran through fields and hedges, and he climbed stiles and fences until he could run no further.

He collapsed into a sweating heap, gasping for breath, and could feel the bile rising as he tasted, at the back of his throat, what could have been his last supper. He rose slowly with his head held towards the sky, gulping in air. Some 100 metres away was a hedgerow, which Bernd slowly trotted up to before throwing himself over. He landed at the feet of a British tommy peeing in the bushes. 'Hello Fritz, fancy a cup of tea?' Trautmann learned his first few words of English. This time his captors were a British telephone unit. He was taken to their commanding officer before being led to another barn containing several other German prisoners. Without bothering to introduce himself, he slumped into the straw and fell into a deep sleep.

The following morning they were lined up by a field kitchen, given food and cigarettes before facing more interrogation. Small groups were then transported to holding camps. Trautmann was there for three days until he was escorted to a colony of humiliated German troops on the Dutch border at Weeze. They were detained in a circle of tanks and trucks. As Bernd arrived, some of the men were trying to dig for water from underground streams. The British were trying to stop them for fear of a cholera outbreak as the ground had been contaminated by the dead of five years of fighting.

For two days Bernd and almost 3,000 others were contained within the captive ring and the stench of unwashed bodies and raw sewage was overpowering. Eventually huge tarpaulins containing fresh water arrived and the men were able to wash and drink. The main communication came from the German officers who were unable to answer the one main question: 'What was going to happen?' All they could say was to wait and see. In reality, the British were still awaiting in-structions and just let the prisoners speculate.

A strange peacefulness settled on the camp, men caught up on sleep and were left alone in their thoughts. Bernd's were in Bremen, with his parents and Karl-Heinz, Tura Werder and Hanomag, and he even managed to smile as he thought of his great adversary, Budde.

That evening, towards the end of March, news came through that became a babble of noise as they heard their destination – St Forte, just outside Ostend in Belgium, and then on to England. As the spring darkness set in, camp fires were lit and the dancing flames illuminated the faces of a pensive multitude. A beautiful tenor voice rose above the silence, singing an old folk song, and the soldiers joined in, hesitantly at first and then rising to a crescendo of defiant voices. The singer then stood on a hurriedly constructed stage of crates and tins and sang *Heimat Deine Stern*, an emotive and beloved song for the troops. The tears ran freely and Bernd's huge shoulders could not control his sobbing as hot salty tears poured down his cheeks. He was not alone, as the equivalent of a German banshee wail was induced by the lone voice.

Early the following morning they travelled to the Belgium coast, to the new camp. It was a disused brick foundry in a derelict state, consisting of a number of old drying sheds open at each end. The prisoners immediately called them the *hundertschaften*, as 100 men were crammed into each shed with only comfortable room for half that number. The men in the centre were sheltered from the English Channel breezes, but those near the open ends had to pack brick dust around their bodies to keep out the chill.

From the emotional singing in the circle of tanks, Bernd plunged into depression and he experienced the lowest point of his young life. His comrades were behaving at their most basic instincts under the crudest of conditions. Men were openly trading their medals and possessions for food and any other items essential to their needs. The rations were basic: a gruel of stew or soup and a hunk of bread. Regard for rank among the prisoners was disregarded as the villains among them formed cliques of thieves and black-marketeers. They stole rings, watches and lighters to exchange with the guards for extra food rations. The guards themselves gained perverse satisfaction by throwing down half-smoked cigarettes and watching men fighting to retrieve the discarded treasure.

Trautmann sought only one fight, to preserve his integrity, and said to himself, 'If I lose, I lose with dignity.' His inherent, stubborn nature and his own pride in his efforts for the German nation would not allow him to descend to the animal behaviour being shown by many of his countrymen. His contribution to the war, after his delinquent start, had earned five medals for bravery, including the Iron Cross (First Class) and two commendations for exemplary conduct. He was not going to give up lightly. He tried hard to analyse the implications of his capture. While accepting the conflict was over, he had come to terms with what this meant to his life. His fate was now in the hands of other 'bloody old men' in a country he knew little about or, indeed, cared. At the same time, the fear of death and the effects of death and destruction of people and habitat had, to his mind, now finished. He would wait to see what fate had in store.

Before the prisoners of war could be shipped to England they had to undergo de-lousing again. The lice were vile, in the hair and pubic regions and under the skin. The men were painted with Gentian violet, sprayed with DDT and blue unction applied to the most intimate parts of their bodies. Trautmann felt no humiliation, rather the opposite; there was some semblance of order now after the total breakdown of the German efficiency. In a way he felt more looked after by his captors than the terror that had been directed against the troops by his own side. He boarded the landing craft at Ostend and, a few hours later, disembarked up the Thames estuary at Tilbury.

Bernd Carl Trautmann had arrived in England, not as a conqueror but as a vanquished foe.

# A PRISONER OF WAR

*In the industrial areas one always feels that the smoke and filth must go on for ever and that no part of the earth's surface can escape them. In a crowded, dirty little country like ours one takes defilement almost for granted.*

GEORGE ORWELL

KEMPTON Park Racecourse at Sunbury-on-Thames in Middlesex had been used as a transit camp for German prisoners since 1944, when the Allied invasion resulted in prisoners being sent back to England in great numbers for the first time. By April 1945 over 200,000 German and Italian troops were being held in camps and hostels throughout the country.

The scale of the atrocities committed by the Nazis in Europe became more prominent each day, and pressure on the military intelligence service was considerable as they sought out war criminals and extreme Nazi supporters. Many of the men changed identities and the difficult task of uncovering these people involved lengthy interrogation procedures to which all German prisoners of war were subjected. The British Government also had the huge problem of implementing a re-education programme and de-Nazification process. This presented a great dilemma in assessing the attitudes of the men. They had not experienced any form of democracy for many years, and while the civilian zealots and party officials could be dealt with easily the practical aspects of re-educating soldiers on a massive scale demanded great resources and a good knowledge of the German mentality.

The primary assumption of the intelligence service was, apart from a small proportion who were bitten by the NSDAP bug, that the captured troops' attitude to Nazism was essentially practical in the professional sense rather than the political. They were content to accept its existence in so far that it provided them with good materials for their jobs as professional soldiers but disliked the fanaticism as well as its interference. In this connection, however, it was important for the interrogators to distinguish between practical sense and political faith. When discussing the effects of the Nazi regime with them it became simple to classify an individual as pro-Nazi when he was perhaps being merely objective. Nazi youth training did a lot to develop the tactical initiatives of the German recruits, while a romantic faith in Hitler stiffened morale.

The view held by many in British intelligence was that nationalism was still the most dangerous emotion. Many soldiers had discarded the NSDAP philosophy only because it had lost the war. It became necessary to devise classifications for the men, so specific groupings were devised and clear definitions were constructed. Thus, a Nazi was one who, by reason of political association or business connections with the Nazi regime, would be considered potentially dangerous to the revival of democracy.

Similarly, a militarist was one who, by reason of his professional military knowledge, would be considered potentially dangerous to the Allied cause. The German prisoners of war were classified in accordance with political opinion, being consigned to one of three categories, A, B or C.

The A grouping were convinced anti-Nazis who had always been opposed to the ideology, but they had to provide proof of this and it was difficult for most of them to do so.

The B grouping were essentially non-political and non-Nazi, who were disinterested by politics and only lukewarm to the NSDAP conditioning by considerations of expediency.

The final C group was aimed at the young German soldier who, from the age of seven, had not known anything but the Nazi way of life and who had only now just experienced democracy. The main bulk were SS and paratroopers. Bernd Trautmann was classified as a Nazi.

The interrogation procedures established whether the soldiers had been conscripted or had volunteered and went on to the next stage of investigation, the man's decorations and promotions achieved. It was reasoned that an obviously good soldier, distinguished on the field of battle, who had entered the war with enthusiasm and took easily to military life would, therefore, view with some regret the prospect of disarmament and the submergence of Germany as a great military power[1].

One of the tricks the interrogators used was to make a provocative or derogatory remark about the NSDAP and look for a reaction. They would also ask about the men's views on Adolf Hitler or the Jews. More often than not, the intelligence officers found the Germans exhibiting a great deal of bitterness about losing the war. The overwhelming emotion felt by them was one of deception, and the most common phrase heard by the interrogators was '*Wir sind betrügen und belügen*' – 'They told us lies'. They found it inconceivable that Germany had lost the war and the British found it disconcerting that, in many cases, the soldiers did not renounce overwhelmingly the NSDAP. The use of psychology was introduced for the re-education of the prisoners as a matter of great priority.

At Kempton Park, Trautmann was accommodated in an army bell tent with seven other fellow prisoners. Medical examinations were carried out and further de-lousing before the first interrogation. A number of German prisoners were on the staff, acting as interpreters, and sat with the British officials when each prisoner was interviewed. Trautmann discussed his role and his career in the forces and gave

[1] Author's note: Trautmann, in this rigid philosophy, had to accept the pre-emptive grading. Things were further complicated by some missing records of his from 1943 to 1945.

an honest account of his involvement with the *Jungvolk* and the Hitler Youth, promptly being categorised a C prisoner. The mood at the racecourse camp was muted as the German men came to terms with their capture. There was little communication in Trautmann's group and, consequently, little to do within the camp. They queued for food, which they ate in groups without any deep conversation. The German interpreters had told them they would be sent off to other camps within the country where some would be set to work for the English, while others would be confined within the camps. By this time they had been issued with old brown English uniforms, with a light brown, round patch on the back and a yellow diamond on the left arm, to replace their ragged battledress. Bernd stayed at Kempton Park for a week before being told he was to be transferred to a camp in north-west England at Marbury Hall in Northwich, Cheshire.

The group of north-bound prisoners boarded a special train with an armed escort of British tommies. As the green fields of the south receded the Germans were amazed as they approached the industrial Midlands. Trautmann remembered the washing hanging on the lines and tightly packed red-brick houses. He had the feeling of going back in time as the industrial landscape unfolded, and with a sense of amusement he now knew where all the bricks had gone from the factory in Belgium. The captured troops were all incredulous of how such a backward country could have won the war. As the army lorries transferred them from the train to Prison Camp 180, Trautmann found his self-confidence returning. His captors had shown little hostility towards them and the few civilians they had been in contact with showed little interest in their guests.

The Northwich camp contained 3,300 prisoners, all German, under the command of Lieutenant-Colonel Fisher. The commanding officer welcomed the new arrivals with a speech outlining the geography of the camp and then gave a general lecture on the meaning of freedom and democracy. Fisher concluded by telling the men that normal army discipline would be applied. Only the officers retained any rank, albeit on a more relaxed basis then they were used to. However, there would be a German officer who was the camp leader – 'That is part of your punishment,' said Fisher. Bernd was led off to a hut containing 25 two-tiered bunks. In the centre was an old iron stove, the rest of the hut was bare. The camp was divided into the East and West zones, with the anti-Nazis in the East and Bernd, because of his C classification, with the pro-Nazis in the West camp. The East camp had been organised into working parties who were driven out each day to work on farms or repair roads. Bernd and his fellow 'Nazis' were confined within the boundaries and just sat around all day.

After roll-call each morning the men ate their breakfast and then either played chess or kicked a football around. The camp had a library, but few German language books could be found that did not contain some element of Nazi propaganda, resulting in the stock of books being limited. Handball and football became the main recreation and eventually matches were arranged between the East and West camps.

Trautmann's recollection of these games was vivid. 'The camp football ground was in the East section so, of course, the West had to play their games away. We used to march to the ground under a strong escort and on arrival were booed and hissed by our fellow countrymen, who regarded us as criminals no doubt. There were shouts of "Pigs, murderers and Nazi bastards". I felt my blood boil with indignation because in my case, and a number of others, it simply was not so. True, there were a number of hardliners in the camp, but they were kept together by the authorities and we had little contact with them. Needless to say, I'd never played a match under such extraordinary conditions. It was difficult to tell who were the more excited, the players or the spectators, and there were plenty of fights both on and off the field. I used to feel sorry for the referee, who was always a British soldier. I can't imagine him ever volunteering for the job. Maybe it was an alternative to spending 14 days in the glasshouse!

We had several good players in our team and one of them, Günther Rackow, later became a famous sports writer back in Germany. I played at left-half in those games and the West camp only lost one of the many games we had against our compatriots across the road.'

The West camp prisoners were required to register their skills with a local labour officer, with a view to integrating them into the labour groups as their classification was reviewed. In Bernd's case he was allocated B status fairly quickly and a number of his colleagues were transferred to the East camp. By a quirk of fate, Bernd's destiny was about to change again. All the drivers in the camp were required to put down their experience and various qualifications and were then given driving tests. Trautmann had not bothered on the grounds that the older men got preference for any driving duties over their younger colleagues. Trautmann sat around with a couple of his cronies as some of the drivers went through their tests under the supervision of a bad-tempered and foul-mouthed Scottish corporal, who would have made a Gorbal publican blush. Most of the English the Germans were learning were profanities and colloquialisms.

To Bernd's amusement, a driver was put into the cab of a 1500cc, six-cylinder Bedford Truck and proceeded to crash through the gears and kangaroo it along the service road. The corporal saw Bernd laughing, kicked the hapless driver out and dragged Bernd to the truck, effing and blinding about useless Krauts. Bernd drove the truck around the camp roads with all the skill and self-confidence that he had gained from his enormous knowledge of vehicles, leaving the foul-mouthed Scot virtually speechless, an achievement in itself. A few days later Trautmann was told he was to be transferred to another camp, a few miles further north in Lancashire. Incredibly, he had been assigned to be the driver for the officers' pool at Camp 50 at Ashton-in-Makerfield.

Bernd arrived there at the beginning of June 1945 and was billeted in his own room in the English zone at the camp, that is to say outside the fences. He was allocated to drive for an officer called Ireland, who Bernd, with his limited English, called Sir Ireland.

Trautmann's room was in the general staff area, near to the quartermaster's store. He could not believe his situation. He was the only German at the camp, the rest were all Italians.

The camp was situated at Garswood Park (just opposite another racecourse, Haydock Park), which was under the command, at that time, of Colonel Prattely and had around 1,300 Italian inmates, who were all allocated to local farmers on work projects. One of the intelligence officers had written a report about the camp and described it as one of 'the dreariest and most depressing in England'. While the camp itself was surrounded by fields and the racecourse, the local town, Ashton-in-Makerfield, was part of a series of towns in south-east Lancashire whose sooty, back-to-back houses stretched in an almost straight line along the Liverpool to Manchester road. Their very names were synonymous with the dirt and grime associated with the North-West: Wigan, Newton-le-Willows, Eccles and Salford. Most of the southern-based intelligence officers received the same first impression of the north as Bernd had as they arrived at Wigan station and were driven to Camp 50 through the drab streets. Trautmann, however, was not based in the towns, but in the relative beauty of the outskirts. Bernd was also discovering the warmth and kindness of the local people as his driving duties enabled him to come into contact with non-military English people for the first time on a regular basis.

His brief encounters with the local population at Northwich had seen the locals throwing up the two-fingered V-sign as the men were driven to camp. Within Camp 180 a few civilians were employed and made the odd remark about 'Hitler Kaput'. Trautmann was now suddenly given an unexpected freedom to meet the locals and he liked what he found. They were particularly friendly to this handsome young man. He adapted to his surroundings as quickly as he did to driving on the wrong side of the road, and was treated with respect and courtesy by the officers he drove around the area. Without any formal lessons, Bernd was picking up the English language, albeit with the flat vowels of Lancashire.

Bernd Trautmann also had time to reflect again on his life, he accepted his privileged position with gratitude and was now getting news from Bremen. He had received his first letter from Carl and Frieda in which they described the conditions at home. They were not too good. Any semblance of order had broken down at the time of Bernd's capture in Belgium. It was the survival of the fittest over there and the Trautmann family, with Carl's determination to survive, were getting through. Carl was under investigation as a Nazi, his involvement with the Kalle band being the reason. Karl-Heinz was home but had been arrested and imprisoned for an offence under the military law imposed by the Allies on the citizens of Bremen. The offence, a minor one, was not carried into his civilian life. Frieda sent her love and affection to her son.

He realised his new surroundings in England were more secure than he would achieve back home and, in reality, he was starting to enjoy his life again.

At the end of the summer of 1945, the Italian prisoners were repatriated and replaced with German prisoners, who soon organised themselves with typical thoroughness. Within days they had organised sports groups, specifically handball and football, and a camp newspaper appeared – the *Aufbauwille*. The men also responded to the English lessons the camp administrators were organising on a formal examination basis.

The British organised lectures that were compulsory for the men to attend. Bernd often met visiting lecturers at Wigan or St Helens stations and drove them into Garswood Park. He would then sit with the rest of his countrymen and listen to the academics deliver long and boring lectures on the 'Constitution of the British Empire', 'The future of the skilled worker' and 'Nationalism', all interpreted by an uninterested official translator. Most of the men had realised by now, through common sense, that the NSDAP were frauds.

More traumatically, the British showed films of concentration camps, and the horrors of Belsen and Auschwitz did more to dispel any feelings of loyalty to the Third Reich than anything else. The Germans were as sickened as the rest of the world at what they saw. Again, *'Wir sind betrügen und belügen'* – and they meant it. Any hardliners had been spirited off by the British and the remaining prisoners were rediscovering decency and pride in themselves. They were all trying to rebuild their lives and accepted the hatred of the Nazis as reasonable and just. They also knew that they would have to accept a certain amount of the retribution for the very fact they were German, and so bear the nation's collective guilt and, in their case, shame. It was their good fortune that they were in an area where the local people accepted them as men and not criminals. There were two reasons for this, firstly the immediate area around the camp was a coal-mining and agricultural community and to an extent most of the men had been excluded from conscription because they were involved in essential war work. Secondly, the German prisoners proved themselves to be hardworking, industrious and trustworthy. A labour office was attached to the camp under the administration of Mr Maynard, whose job was to provide the local farmers with labour from the camp. Maynard allocated the same number of Germans to the farmers to replace the departed Italians. Within days they were reporting the allocation of workers too high – two Germans were doing the work of five Italians.

Their main duties on the farms were to make land arable again, and so they were engaged in removing anti-aircraft batteries and breaking up bunkers, or generally helping on the farm. The pay was six shillings a week for their labour in the form of plastic discs, each imprinted with the value, from a halfpenny to a shilling. This was spent in the camp shop where they had become addicted to the sugary slab cakes, which they devoured by the kilo. Any luxury goods had to be bartered for, cigarettes, clothing or chocolate, but these were also in short supply in civilian life. The men applied their ingenuity and cunning in the most constructive ways.

The whole area was influenced economically by the Burtonwood American Air Force base, and the level of black-market activities there made Sergeant Bilko seem like a sweet stealer at the 'Pic-and-Mix' at Woolworth's. The Americans had everything and the whole of Lancashire seemed to be involved one way or another with the unfettered villainy on the military budget of the US Treasury. The Americans sold everything that could not be nailed down and the black economy thrived. The German lads were determined to become beneficiaries of this rich source of goods. Trautmann still had delighted amusement, decades later, at the outrageous thieving, pilfering and petty corruption.

The prisoners were now allowed out of the camp and were confined to a three-mile radius, a limit established by the authorities, although this was never enforced to any extent. The relationship with the camp guards was comradely and warm and, with their collusion, raiding expeditions for various swag were actively encouraged. 'I remember,' Trautmann reminisced, 'some enterprising bugger had managed to get a small lathe into one of the huts and was knocking out various knick-knacks that were being sold to the locals. You have to remember we were all, in the main, honest men, but any form of control over their activities was non-existent. When the Italians were at Camp 50, as fast as one of the old three-wheel Scammel lorries was unloaded, stuff would be disappearing out of the back door with the wink of an eye. We were told by the CO how much he could trust us with camp stores, which was true; the only thing we used to nick was soap. But we were desperate for various bits, our shoes had holes and our clothes were in a bad way.'

They started to make picture frames from old treacle tins and queues were formed outside the gates by people trying to buy them, or swap other commodities. The men were bringing back sacks pilfered from the farms and these were dyed and fashioned into clothing. But the holes in their shoes were letting in water.

The Burtonwood base, some 20 kilometres away, had the basic material for shoe repairs – rubber. Nice, thick rubber. The source of this came from tank tracks. Trautmann organised a clandestine visit to the base, and, in scenes reminiscent of his visits to watch Werder, they ran all the way from Garswood and carried back their purchases with unconcealed delight. The camp shoe repairer's last was as busy as a flea on a dog's backside for days after.

Just opposite Camp 50 at Haydock Park, the Americans had stored hundreds of gliders in huge packing cases. They were raided on a regular basis and various parts from the gliders were utilised for everything from building cupboards and shelves in the huts to providing wood for stoves. The American guards at Haydock were to vigilance the equivalent of the captain of the *Titanic* to navigation.

The relationship with British and local civilians became closer and closer as they all strove to recover from the traumas of the war. Trautmann was slowly but surely picking up his English, although still a little uncertain with 'nowt' and 'luv'. Bernd's first Christmas in England was approaching, and he thought back with sadness at the awful experiences of the previous four. Once again the English people displayed remarkable kindness to the German prisoners, and a number of invitations were received from the locals for them to spend Christmas Day with English families. Bernd and a fellow inmate, Egon Warmeil, found themselves sat with the Staniforth family for Christmas lunch. Unlike the Americans, the lads had long come to terms with brussel sprouts and devoured them eagerly with the turkey. They both positively glowed with the warmth and company, and Egon and Phyllis Staniforth, the only daughter, flirted outrageously. Bernd and Egon rolled back to camp full of good feeling for the English, with Egon desperately in love with Phyllis. (Egon and Phyllis married two years later. They moved to Germany in the late 1970s.)

As 1946 progressed, life at Garswood Park Camp 50 caused the prisoners of war to have mixed feelings about their incarceration. On the one hand they were in the country perceived by their own nation as the enemy just a short time ago, and now they were receiving such kind treatment and succour that they could not believe it. 'It was difficult for us to understand,' Trautmann said in retrospect, 'here we were, prisoners of war in a country that was still under severe rationing, and yet every man received the same amount of rations as the civilian population. We had the same amount of meat, eggs and other basics, our treatment by the British was to our minds unbelievable.'

At the same time the morale of the men was not too wonderful. While they appreciated the welfare being provided, news from Germany was not good, and irregular. The destruction of German towns and cities and the occupation of the East by the Soviets gave them much cause for worry. News from their families was limited and the news they had received was of extreme conditions as the Allies tried hard to restore some order to the ravaged country and at the same time keep the Soviets at bay. Bernd, in his own mind, was content to let things continue as they were for a while, at least he knew his own family were safe and he was better off in the UK for the time being.

In an effort to instil some *joie de vivre* into their lives, the sports organisation became increasingly important. Bernd had made friends with two particularly energetic men, Rudolf (Rudi) Hering and Bubi Staudinger, who, together with Rolf Stankoviak, had been busily building up the sports activities within the camp.

During the summer there had been an influx of prisoners from the US and Canada. These men, who all had distinct red patches on their prisoners' uniforms, had been loaned by the British to the North Americans to work in the cotton fields and to harvest the wheat crops. Their arrival brought a rich vein of sporting talent.

To Bernd's delight, two former members of the Tura team were among their number, and there were also a few others from the Bremen area. He had an enjoyable reunion with his home-town people. Regular competitive sports for the men helped considerably to build up their flagging spirits. Again, with typical Teutonic organisation, they lined out pitches for handball and football, made themselves goal posts from materials that should have been enabling American gliders to soar, and they had enough players to form a league of a very high standard at the camp.

Garswood Park Camp 50 formed a rectangle, taking up around a third of the total area. The remainder was open to the civilian population and the only area where the full-size pitch could possibly be situated was outside the camp perimeter. The authorities agreed to this without fuss. Around this time, some of the Germans had taken to swimming at the nearby Carr Mill Dam, where they had come into contact with a number of local people enjoying the same facility. In the course of conversation one of the prisoners-of-war mentioned that Camp 50 had organised themselves into a couple of useful football teams and the idea of a game against one of the area teams was first mooted. The first Anglo–German fixture was arranged against the Haydock Park side.

The PoW team began to train in earnest. Trautmann, who was playing at centre-half in the camp games, had sustained an injury and asked the goalkeeper if he could play in goal for a while until the injury healed. (Bernd's teammate who agreed to change places was Günther Luhr, who went on to have a distinguished career in German football). Bernd did not mind playing in goal, what the hell? You were always goalkeeper as a kid if you couldn't do the business on the pitch, or if you needed a breather for a while you stuck yourself between the coats acting as the posts.

He found, to his amazement, he enjoyed being in goal and his ability to the rest of his teammates was obvious. From the moment Günther agreed to the positional swap he became the unwitting catalyst for a man who was to reach the very heights of excellence. Bernd became the undoubted first choice in goal.

Bob Leyland had just been discharged from the army, and on his return to Lancashire he helped to re-form the Holy Cross CYMS football team, as secretary. He watched the match against Haydock on the King George playing field and immediately formed the impression he was watching the most skilful and sensational of goalkeepers. Bob contacted the commandant at the camp to arrange a match against Camp 50, and in October the Holy Cross team lost 4–2. In January 1947 they returned to Garswood Park and were defeated 3–1. Bob's great wish was to take the German team to the Holy Cross ground at Parr in St Helens.

Lieutenant-Colonel Glendenning was an immensely popular commandant, with both the English and the German contingent. He received Bob Leyland's request for the men to travel to Parr with immediate sympathy and tacit approval, subject to red tape and the government officials also approving. With typical rigidity, the powers that be pointed out that a journey to the St Helens district would exceed the three-mile limit and the men were not authorised to use public transport. This was of course nonsense, the men had been ignoring these restrictions from the beginning and nobody had really cared about it before now. Glendenning and Leyland arranged their way around these problems with suitable cunning, and the team from Camp 50 found themselves at Parr Stocks in St Helens playing against the Parr XI that Bob had organised from Holy Cross and some other local sides. He had also organised considerable publicity for the game and arranged for any proceeds to benefit the Red Cross.

Leyland's memories of that game are remarkable. Bob played in the game and he recalled, 'We expected a fair crowd but, in fact, more than two thousand spectators turned up, including the superintendent of police and his deputy. It was a good entertaining game and the score stood at one each with about 20 minutes to go when Parr were awarded a penalty. All eyes were on Trautmann, and the penalty taker, a chap called Les Lynan, placed the ball on the spot. Everyone wanted a good view of this exciting moment, and the crowd from the opposite end of the pitch surged forward to form a huge semi-circle on the halfway line and along the touchlines. There were good-natured problems behind Trautmann's goal because we didn't have goal-nets at the time. Hordes of small boys were jostling about for a good spot, much to the annoyance of Trautmann's minder. The goalkeeper of course was well over 6ft tall but the minder must have been 6ft 8in. He patrolled behind the goal in every match the PoWs played in. Les Lynan hit the ball with the power of a two-year-old and the ball trickled its way into Trautmann's hands. Camp 50 scored again shortly afterwards and won 2–1.'

This was the first of many charity matches and the three-mile limit was regularly extended to play in various parts of Lancashire, raising thousands of pounds for the funds of the Red Cross in the process. As each game was played, however, it became apparent that the goalkeeper in the team was proving to be the star attraction. Bernd Trautmann's ability was bringing him to prominence in local football circles.

# FROM BERND TO BERT

*And, therefore, I was doing evil in enjoying something that was good in one situation, bad in another, and my fault lay in trying to reconcile natural appetite and the dictates of the rational soul.*

UMBER TO ECO

A S 1947 progressed some of the prisoners at Camp 50 were becoming increasingly unhappy about the delays in repatriation. The men loaned to the Americans were particularly upset as they were under the impression their stay in England would be for just a few weeks. To be fair to the British the delays were not entirely their fault. There were two reasons for this, firstly, the interrogation of the prisoners and re-education programme had slowed down due to lack of interpreters and interest and, secondly, a number of forged papers or dubious compassionate appeals had gained early release for some without proper vetting. News and information from home was still depressing, particularly from the Russian zones where it was apparent that Germany was to be permanently divided as far as the Soviets were concerned.

Trautmann thought carefully about his own repatriation, and when the opportunity came he volunteered to stay on in England and continue to enjoy his life here, which he certainly was doing. The relationships with the local people, the camp guards and officers, with one or two exceptions, were becoming more friendly each day. The guards would always tip them off about camp inspections so that any unusual merchandise or prohibited materials could be stashed away. In terms of cleanliness and order, the German huts were always immaculate. Part of Bernd's driving duties included tours of inspection by British officers of the numerous hostels around the area. These were inhabited by former SS and C-graded men. Invariably, the CO would just sit around and drink tea and chat to the men without bothering to make any rigorous inspection. He told Trautmann: 'There is no need to worry about looking around, I know I will never find fault, nor do I want to'. A sergeant at the camp named Block, formerly Herr Bloch of Berlin, had fled from his home in the early years of the Nazi's rise and settled in England, joining the British Army at the start of the war. As well as interpreting, his main duties were to visit the local farmers to ensure the prisoners were not being exploited and were receiving adequate provisions during the working day, or adequate quarters where the men were being billeted. The farmers wrote reports on each man, which were taken to Maynard at the Labour office. The farmers were, in most cases, more than happy with the Germans, whose work-rate was incredible in relation to the Italian prisoners they had taken over from. Block's main interest in the visits, however, was to procure a free meal or provisions. The man had an appetite like a dray horse and developed to perfection the 'water trick'. Trautmann explained, 'The bugger knew the friendliness of the farmers, and particularly the kindness of their wives. He would get me to go round to the kitchen of the farmhouse and ask for a glass of water. Invariably, the farmers' wife would ask if I was hungry. Block and I were then invited to sit at the table and tucked into mounds of food that resembled a scale model of Ben Nevis.'

Bernd was still making trips to Wigan station to meet visiting dignitaries and lecturers and also interrogators from military intelligence. Bernd's temper was about to get him into trouble again. One of the intelligence men was Jewish and his undisguised hatred of the Germans brought no objectivity to his handling of the interviews. Trautmann met him at Wigan and drove in silence to the camp. Most of the passengers made small talk or some attempts at conversation and Bernd, in his halting English, would try to make conversation the best he could. Bernd could feel the man's hate burning into him as he sat in the back of the car with his feet resting on the front seat next to Bernd's head. The Jewish officer was at the camp all day making life as uncomfortable as possible for his interviewees and also alienating some of the British. In the evening Bernd was detailed to drive the man back to Wigan station.

Trautmann, as a man, had accepted the collective guilt of his nation for the Nazi's genocide, he had no excuses to make and like the majority of his comrades felt shamed and was horrified. There was nothing, absolutely nothing, that they could do except bear that guilt. Even the half-hearted insults of 'Nazi' and the rendering of *Hitler Has Only Got One Ball* song by the locals had been accepted as a justifiable stricture, but no one had considered the searing wrath that the Jews had for any German. As Trautmann drove him back, the officer started to insult him in both German and English. 'You slimy Nazi bastard', 'You horrible German pig'. Unable to endure any more, Bernd slammed on the brakes, picked up the officer and threw him out of the car. He drove back to Ashton-in-Makerfield in a bitter rage.

He was dragged from his bed at two in the morning by the 'King of Kirby'. This was the huge Staff Sergeant from the King's Own Regiment, whom Bob Leyland had remembered as Trautmann's minder. The 'King of Kirby' was so called because he was in charge of the nearby Kirby PoW hostel, which he ran with an iron fist. He was accompanied by two of the camp guards, both Scousers, with whom Bernd had been on friendly terms. Both were impassive as they escorted him to the detention room. The Staff Sergeant informed Bernd he was to be charged with assaulting an officer and was to appear before the CO at ten o'clock that morning.

As one of the guards closed the door he remarked, 'Sorry mate, you know what a twat he is', further enlarging Bernd's English vocabulary.

He faced Lieutenant-Colonel Glendenning as the 'King of Kirby' barked the charges. Glendenning listened to Bernd's explanation with a certain amount of sympathy, while explaining to him the need to control his feelings under provocation of anti-German sentiments. It was, unfortunately, an unpleasant reality he would have to live with for quite a while.

Glendenning was an astute and endearing man and the old school, gentleman officer. Trautmann, on a military charge yet again, had found another Oberleutnant Bergenthum. The CO had also felt intimidated by the intelligence officer, but at the same time he had the responsibility of giving out some form of punishment to one of his own drivers. Bernd received a custodial two-week confinement within the camp, to the obvious displeasure of the 'King'. Glendenning's empathy with his charges was first rate, and he showed remarkable tolerance to their escapades. Trautmann, Bubi Staudinger and Rudi Hering were regularly escaping to take part in the pursuit of their interests, while the wheeling and dealing in goods, plus the football matches, were bringing more and more people to Garswood Park. The men had two main escape routes out of camp. The first was to climb over a low wall that divided the perimeter fence, after which they scooted across the road into Haydock Park and then made their way into Ashton-in-Makerfield. The second escape route was more bold. At the far end of the camp were the officer quarters, consisting of a number of stone bungalows. The escapees used to sneak around the back then make their way through the bushes, which brought them on to the main road. One morning at roll call Glendenning faced the men and said he had a request to make: 'I know damn well that you are going out of camp at night, but, one small point, don't make so much bloody noise when you pass by my quarters.'

The Germans continued to be amazed at the kindness and generosity they were experiencing. As well as receiving the same ration coupons as the impoverished English, they were also receiving clothing coupons. Trautmann was developing an obsession about clothing. He was desperate to discard the shapeless and uncomfortable prisoners' uniform and he saved his coupons, together with any cash he made from various transactions, until he had enough to kit himself out with smarter attire. The paucity of his clothing was always a concern to him.

On one occasion a German, who had been released from one of the camps in Southern England, turned up at Camp 50 with huge wads of clothing coupons that he had obtained from some dubious source. He was now making a living travelling around the camps like a tinker peddling his wares. Trautmann was one of his best customers for a while, until news filtered back that the man had been caught and was now in prison with a few other spivs.

When the men escaped the confines of the camp at night they changed into their 'civvies' for their excursions into the local towns. Rudi Hering was an enthusiastic dancer and often went into Wigan once a week. The men were now allowed to travel by public transport so Rudi went by bus to his rendezvous at the dance hall where he waltzed and tangoed the evening away. Getting back was always a problem as the last bus back to Garswood Park left before the dance finished. Taxis, because of fuel rationing, plied for trade by filling the cab with different passengers travelling in the same direction, each paying a set fare. One particular evening Rudi was comfortably seated next to the driver when a distinguished-looking man in a dinner suit squeezed into the back where the others were already squashed together. Hering felt a tap on his shoulder and turned to face Glendenning. 'I say, aren't you one of the men from the camp?' 'Yes sir,' sheepish Rudi replied. 'Climb in the back there's a good chap, I'll have your seat.' Rudi paid Glendenning's fare as the CO bade him a cheerful goodnight.

This night was one of the few times Glendenning had not used his official car, with Trautmann driving the green Hillman. The job, in reality, had given Trautmann a great advantage over the others in terms of social contacts, but shyness was his big problem, not helped by his still limited English. Bernd, who had not attended the formal lessons at the camp, was learning from radio, newspapers and, of course, the English themselves. Many years later, Trautmann heard a story of a particularly arrogant German who bragged he had no need to learn formally; every bit of English he had learned was from British soldiers. 'I have stored every single word,' he said pointing to his head, 'here in my asshole.' Bernd laughed with delight at this tale but was never sure if it was a joke or a true story.

His knowledge of cars and engines was a great asset to the English and a number of camp staff asked for his advice when purchasing private cars. He was once taken to Manchester by one of the officers, who wanted him to check out a Triumph Dolomite car, which he eventually bought. The particular officer was a French major who had been attached to Camp 50 when the Italians were there. He was an unsmiling man who only spoke when necessary. On the journey to look at the car the man opened up a little to Trautmann, who had been trying to make conversation. The Frenchman told Bernd both his parents had been killed by the Gestapo in France and, as a result, he had harboured an intense hatred for Bernd's countrymen. Bernd was stunned into silence. The Frenchman smiled at him and said, 'You lot have done a lot to help me change my mind about the Krauts.'

All the repairs on the trucks and cars were done at the camp, and Bernd was invariably asked to help fix problems with the officers' private vehicles. He was always paid cash by them or received payment in kind from the quartermasters' stores.

As the restrictions at the camp became more and more relaxed, the influx and contact with the Lancashire people became increasingly close. The football team's attraction and novelty value were influencing people starved of entertainment by the austere conditions they were still suffering as a result of the war. The German men were also attracting a lot of female interest.

The local girls had been seduced and courted by the Americans at Burtonwood, by the lifestyle and the seemingly unlimited supply of nylon stockings, booze and money. The Germans were different; they were poor but had a much greater attraction. While the Americans had provided some corporeal and material needs, the sexual attraction of the Germans was overwhelming and they were treated with profound salaciousness by the local lasses. The girls had always been used to local men's working-class attributes, their bad teeth and the pale skin of the mining and industrial communities, but these German men were different, always seeking the sun, statuesque and as fit as fiddles. The girls gathered *en masse* to get at them.

Bubi Staudinger was one of the main attractions for them, although he was not the stereotype German profile. He was quite swarthy with dark hair, almost Latin in appearance. He also had that Latin instinct for homing in on a woman. Bernd was always very confident within the environment of the camp and his sports, but in the presence of female company he was painfully shy and tongue-tied, a sexually ignorant young man in the company of sexually interested young women.

As Bubi and Rudi regularly made their conquests, Bernd was merely polite and unassuming. Bubi began to see one girl on a regular basis, but unfortunately for him she always had a friend in tow, who did not particularly relish her role of chaperone.

Marion Greenall was a local Ashton-in-Makerfield girl, who had been attracted to Bernd from the first meeting. It was Marion and her friends who transformed Bernd's christian name. The pronunciation of Bernd in German is similar to 'Burnt', but try as they could the Lancashire accent could not master it and Bernd became Bert.

Bubi tried hard to persuade Bert to start a relationship with Marion, based on a selfish desire to have his own girlfriend more to himself. Slowly Bert overcame his shyness and began to see more of Marion on his own, firstly walks and visits to the cinema. The inevitable happened, Bert, at 23, and Marion, at 19, both had their first sexual experience. Bert Trautmann's first girlfriend became pregnant shortly afterwards.

His social life was increasing all the time and football enlarged his circle of acquaintances. By this time he had watched his first English professional game at Goodison Park, where he was immediately impressed by the ability of Everton goalkeeper Ted Sagar.

He now realised his ability as a goalkeeper was far greater than his skill as an outfield player, which itself was excellent, and with typical thoroughness he started to work hard to improve his goalkeeping skills. He studied Sagar's every move and position, absorbing mentally the various angles and anticipation. One thing Trautmann had over Sagar was an immense natural fitness and gymnastic athleticism. As the number of games Camp 50 played increased, Bert knew that the first team was a good side. He ventured to suggest that at the time they would have held their own in the Third Division, a claim not disputed by many of the spectators who attended those games.

A number of professional footballers were now returning to the north after their time in the forces, older and sadly unable to regain their former eminence. They had come home to start their lives again, and, in football terms, they drifted towards the number of semi-professional and amateur sides now re-forming. The standards of the local leagues immediately improved, and for the spectators the matches were now greatly enhanced by the skills of the returning athletes.

Haydock Football Club, as the Camp 50 immediate neighbours, were – along with the Red Cross funds – the main beneficiaries of the skills of the team. The Germans had in turn made many friends among the Haydock players, and they had been entertained at tea and social functions by the club, with an increasing number of local girls attending the games.

Bubi and Rudi loved the attention while Bert, with his worries over Marion on his mind, was trying to concentrate purely on his football. He now had to think more of his future and felt unsure of what to do. When he reflected back on his life, from the age of nine he had been organised into a pattern of life, from the *Jungvolk* through the *Luftwaffe* and paratroops to his situation here as a prisoner of war. Everything he had done had been influenced by totalitarianism or by enforced confinement. He had become used to corrupting influences over 14 years, and at the end of that period he had absorbed so many different ideas and restrictions in such a matter-of-fact way that he found it difficult to confront his problems as the spectre of reality loomed at him like a beckoning skeletal finger. His release into democracy and freedom from restrictions meant he had to learn to think for himself again and to decide what was best for Bert Trautmann in a selfish sense.

Marion lived with her parents in one of the small back-to-back terrace houses in Ashton-in-Makerfield. They were now putting pressure on Bert and Marion to marry so that the social disgrace of an illegitimate child would be averted. The affair, as far as Trautmann was concerned, was a casual romance that he had experienced as a consequence of his attraction to Marion, but he did not love her and did not see his future living with a wife and child in a tiny red-brick terrace.

Marion's parents complained to the CO, who asked Bert what he was going to do. But he applied no pressure, just explaining to him the moral dilemma Bert was facing and that the decision was his alone. Bert's decision was not to marry his girlfriend, to the chagrin of the Greenall family.

It was his inexperience of women and of life that he discussed with Rudi, who was now his closest friend. Rudi loved his time in England; he liked the people and the way of life. He was far more worldly than Bert, who was naive in many ways and his chronic shyness at the time made him seem withdrawn to some people and aloof to others. Rudi knew Bert did not love Marion. A number of enforced marriages had resulted from the liaisons of the Germans and English girls that were not particularly successful, and he supported Bert's decision not to marry if he did not want to. Bert, in turn, needed the advice from his friend and was grateful for Rudi's support. His feeling of guilt about the relationship bothered him intently, but he had a stubborn nature at times and this streak further alienated the Greenalls from the man they now regarded as untrustworthy and cruel.

As 1948 progressed, most of the prisoners of war had been released and returned home. The government offered some of the men contracts to stay on for a while to work within the UK under military or governmental control.

Garswood Park Camp 50 was due to close in April 1948, and Trautmann was offered work on a farm further north. The government had made a promise to repatriate all prisoners by the end of August 1948 if they so wanted, and Trautmann had spent the last few months saying fond farewells to his friends. Bert, Rudi and a few others were staying and were soon let loose into English society, carrying their Aliens Registration cards. Lieutenant-Colonel Glendenning had already left, and the French major was left to wind things down. He was genuinely sorry to see the German lads leaving, a great tribute to their contribution to the area. Bert felt a sadness at leaving, and he had a last tour of the deserted camp, remembering with pleasure and amusement some of the good times he had experienced. He passed the bakery, which had been installed some time after his arrival, and thought of the aroma of freshly baked bread that filled the camp in the early mornings. Bert passed the detention cells where he had been placed by the 'King of Kirby', who had probably now taken a job as a Genghis Khan impersonator, and finally to the sports area where the Germans had done so much to integrate with the locals through their sporting endeavours. These sporting links were not going to be severed, however, and Bert had the chance of playing for one of the local teams. During his contact with the Haydock footballers he had become friendly with Cliff Knowles, whom he had met socially at pubs or visits to other football clubs. Cliff had recently joined St Helens Town in the Liverpool Combination and had mentioned the Camp 50 team to the manager.

Most of the teams in the league were factory or social club sides – UGB, the initials of United Glass Bottlers, Prescott Cables and Marine formed from a pub side. The standard of the league was high, with the influx of good players returning from the forces, competition was keen and large crowds packed into tiny stadiums. There was a great local rivalry between the teams representing the knot of towns with their close communities. When Knowles moved to St Helens a huge amount of interest had been generated by the goalkeeping of Bert Trautmann and, together with another player called Marschallek, he was invited by the club to have a trial. They both impressed immediately and were asked to sign.

The problem for Bert was his new job. He was to start work at Bila River in Milnthorpe, Westmorland, and was to be accommodated at the farm. It was quite a distance to travel each Saturday to play football. He was a little apprehensive about moving away from the area where he had received so much kindness and made so many friends. This influenced him more than anything else, but St Helens would have to wait a while. Bert Trautmann had his official release from prisoner of war status in February 1948 'for temporary work in Agriculture or Domestic Hostel Employment approved by a County War Agricultural Executive Committee'.

# ST HELENS, RETURN TO BREMEN AND A CHANGE OF DIRECTION

*I knew a youth who went to the house of his girlfriend in South Lancashire where they heartened to Rugby League results then turned the wireless off when the soccer results were about to begin. His father was astounded to hear of such malpractice and gravely counselled him to extricate himself. 'You don't want to get mixed up with that class of folk'.*

*DON HAWORTH*

ST HELENS took its name from a medieval chapel at ease, standing at the crossroads that led to the developing port of Liverpool, 10 kilometres away to the west and 30 kilometres away from the busy textile city of Manchester, to the east. The town had become synonymous with glass-blowing and glass-making and developed a vigorous coal-mining trade.

By the early 1920s the Pilkington Glass works dominated local industry, being the main employer in the town, employing the majority of the working population from the 110,000 inhabitants, followed closely by the National Coal Board. St Helens was not associated as a footballing enclave, its claim to fame in sport were the mighty Rugby League side, The Saints, and huge crowds massed to watch them play at Knowsley Road in one of the toughest of sports. The people were in essence the archetypal tough, no-nonsense Northerners but who exuded warmth and friendliness to those they considered mattered.

Sara Winstanley lived with her daughter, Clarice, at 106 Marshalls Cross Road, a short distance from the rugby stadium and just opposite the cottage hospital. She was a strong-willed and sometimes cantankerous woman, who had invested some of her money, left by her late husband, into a hairdressing salon that was run by her daughter.

When Clarice met John Tradwell Friar, Sara did all she could to disrupt the association with the grocer's assistant from St Helens' Co-operative Wholesale Society. John was of course called Jack in the peculiar way most people of that given name are so nicknamed. He had started work with the CWS as a flour boy, delivering to the local bakers on a huge bicycle. Jack was full of ambition and determination which, together with his keen intelligence, enabled him to work his way up through the promotion system, and he had his sights set on a management job.

With equal determination, Sara tried hard to convince her daughter that Jack Friar was not good enough for her. After his work at the CWS he studied late into the night for the Society's promotion examinations and then gained a place at Bangor University where, after three years, he gained his degree in Economics.

Despite all Sara's opposition, Jack and Clarice married and Jack moved into the roomy terraced house in Marshalls Cross Road. Sara Winstanley did not speak to her son-in-law for three years, always referring to him as 'he'. 'What time is he home?' she would ask Clarice. When Jack was present Sara always spoke through her daughter, 'Will he get some coal in?'

Friar displayed the patience of an angler fishing in the polluted Mersey towards Sara. He was indeed a man of great humour and character and slowly but surely won over his antagonistic mother-in-law. She, in turn, recognising with reluctance her poor judgement of him, confided to friends: 'His stock has improved,' but she still, on occasions, practised her sharp-tongued venom on him when she was in a mood. Jack remained unmoved and bore any of her outbursts without concern.

On 16 February 1930 the Friars became parents, naming their daughter Margaret. Clarice gave up the hairdressing business to become a full-time mother. Jack, by this time, had reaped the rewards of his hard work and had become a branch manager at the largest 'Co-op' in St Helens, a considerable position in the town. He had a good standing within the local business community and became an active member of the Masonic Lodge.

Margaret Friar was growing up to be an exuberant girl, and a little precocious, much to the annoyance of Granny Winstanley. Just before her seventh birthday, Margaret met with a most unfortunate accident while playing with friends in a local park, when they discovered a huge iron roller used for flattening out the cricket pitch. The handle of the roller was spring-loaded to help with the tremendous weight the groundsmen had to manoeuvre. Some of the older children were swinging on the handle and they released it. The handle swung up and over violently from their hands and smacked resoundingly on to Margaret's skull, pole-axing her into immediate unconsciousness. It was three days before she came round again, remarkably without any fracture or obvious damage. Granny Winstanley was to repeat many times over the years, 'That girl was never right int' head since the accident.'

On 20 August 1940 Clarice gave birth to her second child, another girl, whom the Friars named Barbara. The increasingly eccentric Sara happily accepted her role as matriarch to her enlarging family. Jack was still, however, 'he' and she still regarded Clarice as a young girl, chastising her for perhaps having a button undone on her cardigan or for picking at food with her fingers. At the same time, she was of great help to her daughter in rearing the two girls and she was a great influence in their lives. Sara was also becoming increasingly, and surprisingly, proud of Jack.

When Barbara was born he had become the general manager for the St Helens CWS, his love and commitment to the family was absolute and his reputation in the town was second to none as his selfless and good-natured character developed. Granny Winstanley now levelled her criticisms at 'his bloody football'.

He had always enjoyed his games at school and at university, but his job gave him little time to play anymore and his ageing joints did little to encourage him. Jack's interest in sport was still strong, however, and he became involved with a number of local businessmen in reviving St Helens Town Football Club. Along with George Fryer of 'Fryers Tyres' in Mill Place, Tommy Lloyd, a haulage contractor based in Alder Hey Road, and two or three shopkeepers, arranged to buy some land adjacent to the main Liverpool-Manchester railway line in Hoghton Road. St Helens Town had been active since the turn of the century, playing at Park Road (which eventually became the greyhound racing track), but were wound up shortly after World War One. Any local football talent was, therefore, being lured to other teams in the Lancashire area, who had more than 'park football' to offer.

With Friar and Fryer to the fore, the consortium purchased the former site of the Sutton Cricket Club from Pilkingtons. A great deal of work was needed to cultivate an acceptable playing area, while changing rooms and refreshment huts were built from materials supplied by the local Bold Colliery, which adjoined the Hoghton Road ground. With these basic requirements and a various assortment of players, St Helens Town were accepted into the Liverpool County Combination. The eventual objective was to gain admittance to the English Football League.

George Fryer became the team manager and had fierce ambition. Jack became secretary and Tommy Lloyd, the club president. More importantly, a thriving supporters' club was established, bringing in regular funds to the fledgling football club.

By 1948 the supporters' club managed to purchase a timber structure from RAF Haydock, which they proceeded to transform into a lucrative social club, and a small stand was built to accommodate around 200 spectators. The overall capacity of Hoghton Road was 10,000, mostly on the cinder terracing.

Bert Trautmann was working hard at the Bila River farm at Milnthorpe. He was billeted in a hostel with a number of other German volunteers, being supervised by Ministry of Agriculture officials. To his mind, he had really swapped one prison camp for another. Although he had lost his prisoner of war stigma and uniform, he was now restricted in far more ways than in Ashton-in-Makerfield. The farm was isolated and he did not have much contact with local people. The farm work involved more labouring in making the soil arable again, and Bert missed the company of Rudi Hering and Bubi Staudinger.

On 28 July 1948 Bert received news that Marion Greenall had given birth to a daughter, whom she called Freda. The paternity suit against him was to cost 10 shillings a week. Bert was still playing in kick-about matches after work, but he sorely missed the organisation and collective talent of the old Camp 50 side. One of his workmates at the hostel had made contact with Bill Shankly, then with

Preston North End, who said he would arrange for them to have a trial at the club. The pair waited in vain, nothing was heard from Deepdale. Bert decided to accept the offer to play for St Helens and travelled south on the train each Saturday. Bert received one pound expenses for each game, but the return rail fare was 28 shillings! Bert reminisced of his first visit to Hoghton Road: 'The pitch looked like a ploughed field, this was at the beginning of the season remember, and I did not relish the prospect of diving around as the season wore on. There was an old hut to the right of the pitch, which the supporters used, and another containing a huge concrete bath. At one end was a training area, on the far side a row of terraced houses and at the far end the Bold Colliery, where a lot of supporters worked. The club had a great feel to it, I could see how committed everyone was and their great enthusiasm for the game. The people, more than anything, made me sign.'

After the first game for St Helens against Lomax, he won the hearts of the crowd with his bravery and incredible reflexes. In September the first crowd of 2,000 had assembled, many of the newcomers attracted by this star goalkeeper, whose reputation had spread to other clubs in the league. Trautmann was enjoying the limelight, and, more significantly, he felt more at home in the area than at Bila River and was developing a good friendship with Jack Friar, the club secretary.

He and Jack formed an immediate attachment, and a natural empathy was established from their first meeting. Jack became his confidant, protector and, crucially for Bert, a father figure. As their friendship developed Trautmann became more and more frustrated at having to travel down from Westmoreland and this isolation from his friend in St Helens was becoming unbearable for him. Two weeks before Christmas 1948 Jack took Bert home for tea at Marshalls Cross Road, a decision that would have far reaching effects on the Friars, but in the short term caused the varying, fiery female temperaments in the house to explode every which way. Margaret, just coming up to her 18th birthday, was an extremely attractive young lady. She had developed into a fiercely independent person, with dramatic mood changes and a complex behavioural pattern. She had become an amalgam of the Friars and the Winstanleys, Sara's fierce temperament, Jack's fun-loving philosophy and Clarice's placid calm, but Sara's idiosyncrasies were inherent in Margaret. Margaret had been schooled at Cowley Grammar School, her place there influenced more by Jack than her scholastic ability, but she had left with little qualification from her education. Margaret became a shop assistant at Boots, the national chemist chain, much to her own enjoyment and Sara's unhappiness at her granddaughter becoming a common shop girl. Despite her Granny Winstanley moods, Margaret had a keen sense of humour, which was finely attuned to Jack's. Jack once filled Margaret's lunch-box sandwiches with hair rollers, one of which she offered to her shop manager. Jack had to pay for a new set of false teeth.

Margaret stated that she did not like Germans, and she had no particular reason, she just didn't like them. When Jack told his family he had invited one for tea, Margaret announced, 'If he comes into the house, I'm going out,' and she did. Bert arrived at the house to be greeted warmly by Jack, indifferently by Sara, noncommittally by Clarice and ecstatically by Barbara, who at eight years of age fell in love at first sight with Bert. When he sat down on the settee she jumped on his lap and would not budge, to Jack's amusement and Clarice's disapproval. Granny hovered in the background glaring or crashing around cupboards to let everyone know she was there. Bert liked this slightly potty family and was pleased to be invited back in the New Year. In the meantime, he had a number of personal matters to settle and the beginning of 1949 was a busy time for him.

He arranged for a transfer from Milnthorpe and was allocated to a bomb disposal unit at Long View Lane, Huyton, just outside Liverpool and only a short journey from St Helens. In January 1949 the British Government granted leave for any former German prisoners working for them, and they also offered to pay for the fares home. Trautmann decided it was time to go to Bremen.

On Saturday 11 January, before leaving for Bremen, he played for the town in a league match, where he conceded two goals directly from corner-kicks; he was annoyed, but not as much as the spectators. The pitch, as usual, was heavy. A small army of volunteers had helped to drain away the water before the game. He had never been worried by heavy pitches before and he was angry with himself at losing concentration and costing St Helens the match. His teammates were understanding and put it down to his preoccupation with his visit to Germany. Trautmann was due to leave for Germany the following Tuesday, and as he was leaving Hoghton Road one of the supporters' club committee asked him if he could meet up at a local café the following day.

Bert was intrigued and turned up at the appointed time on Sunday evening. The café was packed with smiling supporters and they broke into applause and cheered his arrival. Bert was presented with a large trunk packed with foodstuffs. 'I was absolutely amazed, this thing was huge and must have weighed thirty kilos. Inside was sugar, cakes, hams and tinned foodstuffs. They had gone without their own food ration allocations in order to give me these things. Then they handed me an envelope containing 50 one-pound notes. I was completely overcome and stuttered out my thanks while my eyes filled with tears. It was only when I was leaving that it dawned on me that I would have to carry the trunk all the way.'

Trautmann boarded the boat-train to Harwich and then crossed the North Sea to the Hook of Holland before catching his train to Bremen. The train was crowded with ex-soldiers returning to North Germany, some for good, but Bert felt little excitement for his reunion with his family. It was seven years since he had last seen them on his brief leave from Russia, and as the train pulled into Bremen station he felt a little apprehensive. Bert was shocked by the devastation. He knew from Frieda's letters that the port had been badly damaged, but the city he had grown up in had gone. In his book *Steppes to Wembley* Trautmann commented: 'You good people have cried over your ruined towns and cities in England – I cried over mine. Friend or foe suffered alike and how much better off for it are they? Not one bit.' He struggled from the station with the trunk and manoeuvred it on to a tram heading for Gröpelingen. Frieda fell into Bert's arms and held him tightly as she sobbed out her welcome home. Carl smiled, shook his hand and slapped him on the back. Bert and Karl-Heinz shook hands politely and stared at each other.

His former home had been damaged by the bombing and the brothers' bedroom had taken most of the impact. Most of the belongings in there had been destroyed, including Bert's certificate from Hindenburg. Frieda wanted to know when he would be coming home permanently and was distressed to hear her son had no immediate plans to do so. Karl-Heinz was interested to know what the English were like, and he had a strange conversation with Bert who said, 'They really are the kindest and warmest people; look at the things they sent for you. If you fell over in the street you would be wrapped in a blanket and sipping a cup of tea within a minute.'

'I don't believe you,' said Karl-Heinz.

'It's true,' replied Bert.

'Well you're a bloody Englishman now anyway.'

To an extent Karl-Heinz was right. Bert did have a sense of Englishness, he found little in common with his family and neighbours, and he found himself strangely homesick for England. It was the start of a great conflict within him that would last all his life, a loyalty for two countries.

Bert spent some time trying to locate old friends and former colleagues from the forces. He had a few beers at Uncle Carl's pub and went to visit his old club, Tura, who promptly asked him to play in a couple of games to bolster their depleted teams. Like the rest of sports clubs in Germany, they were starting from scratch. The Nazis had controlled all sport at the height of their power and now, with only limited resources, Tura were trying to regain some of their former status. Bert received a couple of favourable Press reviews from his games and he enjoyed his outings with the club, even though they were defeated in both games.

He visited the docks where Carl was still working for Kalle, who were also in the process of rebuilding. Bert was particularly upset by the damage in the area. Some of the old warehouses dating back centuries had been blown to pieces and people huddled around fires made from the rubble. He knew that there was little to come back to Germany for at this time, and his resolve to stay in England became more determined when he realised that any immediate prospects for work and a decent standard of living were not good.

Bert said goodbye to his family and returned to England, arriving back in Huyton on 22 February. He immediately returned to work with the bomb disposal unit. The *modus operandi* of the unit was for Bert and his colleagues to dig a shaft around the unexploded bomb to clear a way for the technicians to defuse it. They were mainly working around the dock areas of Manchester and Liverpool, always in filthy conditions, constantly wet and cold and covered in damp clay. Not surprisingly, this troglodytic existence took a heavy toll on his health and his appearances for St Helens were becoming limited. Shortly after his return from

Bremen, Trautmann was taken ill with a chest infection and laid up at the Huyton hostel for two weeks. Jack Friar became increasingly concerned for his health and, after consulting Clarice, he asked the officials at Huyton if Bert could convalesce at the Friar house.

Trautmann moved in with the Friars sharing Barbara's bedroom, an arrangement not considered unusual in the late 1940s. Her sister, Margaret, suddenly developed a twinkle in her eye and a mutual attraction with Trautmann began to develop. From her distant and disdainful attitude to 'the German', she became concerned and sympathetic towards him. To Jack this was another new side to Margaret's contrary character, but he was a little worried about the development of any relationship between Bert and his daughter. He liked the man immensely, but recognised immediately that Bert could be fiery and Margaret wilful. The other problem was that Margaret was seeing another member of the St Helens team on a regular basis.

Bill Twist is a deeply religious and articulate man, whose football ability was such that Liverpool had signed him just before the war. The ramrod-straight centre-half was an excellent prospect for the First Division club and they were optimistic about his development. Bill was called up to the Army and spent most of his war in Egypt. On his return, he had not played any competitive football for almost two years and persuaded Liverpool to release him to his local St Helens team so he could build up his stamina again, and also to concentrate on his market garden business. Twist never returned to Anfield as a player.

He first met Margaret through one of the supporters' club dances and was soon escorting her to regular dances at the CWS Hall each weekend. Some of Margaret's friends described her as flirtatious, others as 'flighty', but all agreed she liked to be the centre of attraction. As Trautmann's fame was growing locally, she became more attracted, but the less she showed it to Bert. She had told him Bill Twist was not a serious boyfriend, at the same time telling Bill that Trautmann did not like him very much. This rivalry between the two men was being orchestrated by Margaret.

After treatment from the Friar family GP, Dr Chisnall, Trautmann's health improved and he moved back to the hostel at Huyton. But the seeds of a clandestine affair with Margaret had been sown and a confrontation with Bill Twist was imminent. Curiously, Sara Winstanley became a staunch ally of Trautmann and was beginning to have a great deal of affection, in her own way, for the blond German boy who had 'such nice manners'. Indeed, his confidence was built by his celebrity. He was also exuding an incredible charisma, particularly with the female supporters. Bill Twist recalled, without any rancour, one match where Trautmann was buried under an avalanche of girls at the final whistle. 'You couldn't see Bert at all, the rest of the players just looked on with awe as several nylon stocking tops were glimpsed as the girls tried to get at him. He was eventually rescued by the referee. Bert emerged with his hair all over the place, lipstick marks all over his face, and a 21-inch smile. In terms of the first pin-up of football, he pre-dated George Best by 15 years.'

Twist and Trautmann had a good relationship on and off the field prior to the problems arising from Margaret. They often enjoyed a beer together at the Junction Inn, where many of the players and supporters met up after a game. Bert often joked with Bill that he was the only player he knew who needed a huge lunch before the match to sustain him, saying that if Bill had not eaten well he would not play well. As the centre-half and captain, Twist was an influential figure on and off the field. Matters came to a head between the two of them one day when Bill called around to the Friars to see Margaret. Bill had his suspicions that something was going on, in his own mind he was convinced Jack Friar was encouraging his own relationship with Margaret as a front to stop gossip about her relationship with Bert. When functions were held at the football club Margaret would ignore Trautmann completely and often make disparaging remarks. If she passed him in the street with her friends she showed no recognition of his presence and looked the other way. Barbara remembered Bill Twist turning up at Marshalls Cross Road where Sara opened the front door. Normally, he would be permitted to sit around chatting until Margaret arrived home. Sara greeted Bill with a face like a crushed walnut and told him to go away as he wasn't welcome. Bill was devastated by this barrage of old lady's venom and replied in kind before retreating to the bus stop, where he waited to be transported home. Later, he saw a laughing and cuddling Bert and Margaret arrive and go into the house. Shortly afterwards Margaret came out of the house and told Bill that Bert had said a number of uncomplimentary things about him and she did not want to see him again.

After the next home match Bill and Bert squared up to each other outside the Junction Inn. Bill was more concerned with the alleged remarks about him than the obvious association between his former girlfriend and the goalkeeper. His pride had been hurt by Margaret's story, and he grabbed hold of Bert as he came along from Hoghton Road. Trautmann was bewildered by Bill's aggression, he was normally such a mild character, but at the same time denied making any remarks towards Twist. In truth, Margaret had concocted the story to keep up the rivalry. Trautmann and Twist were separated by other players but their relationship was irretrievably severed.

As the football season progressed it was apparent that the Town had developed into a fine team, in the main stemming from Trautmann's brilliant displays. They were holding their own in the League and progressing steadily through the rounds of the George Mahon Cup, the major trophy competition in the area.

Bert enjoyed his football at Hoghton Road. They trained each Tuesday and Thursday under the disciplined control of George 'Bow' Thomas, a former boxer. Bow introduced vigorous physical training exercises and banned smoking on match-days. He was a popular man with the team and tried to cushion them from burgeoning rivalries between the committee men and supporters' club that were unfortunately developing. A number of disagreements were going on, mostly concerning money and the allocation of club funds on hospitality for the committee members.

The supporters' club itself charged £2 a year for membership and many thought this entitled them to travel free on the return bus for away matches. George Fryer argued against this with Jonty Smith, a bookmaker's runner and supporters' club official, who then hit out at the committee, accusing them of only being involved with the club for what they could get out of it. Smith fuelled stories of wholesale fiddling by club officials, none of which were substantiated, but the Town supporters adopted a 'no smoke without fire' attitude. Certainly on the committee side the fusion of strong characters was causing friction. George Fryer was envious of Jack Friars' relationship with the team star and annoyed at the interference of team selection by the gushing president, Tommy Lloyd. Lloyd bragged increasingly about his role in the Freemasons. The real masons at the club duped him in to false handshakes and signs. They watched, smirking, as he put four fingers over his crotch or gave convoluted handshakes.

Lloyd's business had benefited greatly from the generosity of the Burtonwood Camp. He had built up his haulage fleet nicely from the acquisition of 'second-hand' trucks for as little as £50 from the GI's, and he liked to boast of his business skill and his role as a self-made man. He was a particular flatterer of Trautmann, and liked to invite him and other players to his home. He always introduced Bert to his other guests as a real German soldier, not like the bloody SS animals. Bert once introduced him to two German colleagues from the bomb disposal squad who charmed and entertained Lloyd for hours. He commented to Bert at their next meeting what pleasant men they were. 'Yes Tommy, they are, they used to be in the SS.' Lloyd's red face could have been used as a stop sign for traffic.

Trautmann's reputation preceded him into games, and on more than one occasion George Fryer asked referees to 'look after the boy' when anti-German insults were shouted at him. Bert's short fuse caused him to be sent off in a game against UGB on 12 April 1949. This was to be the first of a number of controversial incidents in his career. In his early days he had a habit of holding on to the ball waiting for his teammates to move away from his area, wherein he would dispatch the ball with a powerful throw up the field, a feat that had the crowd in awe. Many referees penalised him for delaying the game.

Against UGB he had let in some soft goals and the Town side were being outplayed in every position. Eventually, Trautmann was again accused of holding on to the ball for too long and the referee awarded a free-kick against him. Bert exploded and gave the official an astonishing array of expletives. Bert was the first player to get into the concrete bath, while the remainder of his team lost six goals to one. He received a weeks' suspension before returning to the side in time for the Mahon Cup semi-final against the previous years winners, Burscough. He had an inspired game; Town won by one goal to nil and were in the Final against Runcorn, which was played at Prescott on 7 May.

The *St Helens Reporter* noted that a record crowd, estimated at 9,000, had packed into the ground 'many of whom hoped to see Town's spectacular goalkeeper pull off his incredible repertoire of saves'. In fact, Trautmann only had to handle the ball half a dozen times, including retrieving the ball from his net as Runcorn went into a 1–0 half-time lead. In the second half Bill Twist equalised with a disputed penalty, and in extra-time Ally McAnn scored the winner for St Helens. Bert had an unremarkable game by his standards, but was a proud man as he returned to Huyton with his first medal in football and having completed a wonderful season for himself and St Helens FC.

His joy was short-lived. On his return to the hostel he discovered that he was to be transferred to another bomb disposal unit in Bristol.

It was a shock to all concerned. Margaret cried herself to sleep the night Bert broke the news, while Jack had to think quickly to try and resolve the problem. It was decided that Bert would go ahead with the move south while Jack used his influence in St Helens to arrange a move back to the town. This influence proved to be powerful and effective.

Trautmann arrived at the 7A bomb disposal hostel at Long Ashton at the beginning of July. It was a good summer and the work at Bristol docks was not as difficult as his experience in the North-West. More interestingly for Bert, among the German contingent were a number of skilled footballers. He met Karl Krause, an electrician at the hostel, who had been based at Camp 50 at one time, and another former inmate, Alec Eisenstrager. Both men had signed amateur forms with Bristol City and had been playing in the reserve team at Ashton Gate. Bristol were due to start training later in the month for the 1949–50 season, and Karl suggested that Trautmann go along for a trial. He reminded Krause that he was committed to St Helens and was keen to return there as soon as possible, but Karl was persuasive and he agreed to go along and try his luck.

The cleaner air and surroundings in the West Country did wonders for Bert's health. He regained a healthy tan again, and he spent hours playing football or just walking along Clifton Downs. At the end of July Bert turned up at Ashton Gate with Krause and Eisenstrager. They asked the trainer to give him a game but were astonished to hear that, 'We are OK for 'keepers at the moment.' Both Preston North End and Bristol City had now missed out on the goalkeeping discovery of a lifetime.

Back in St Helens, Jack Friar had not been idle. The Member of Parliament for St Helens was Sir Hartley Shawcross KC, who was the Attorney General in the Labour Government and had also been a member of the prosecuting counsel at the Nuremburg Trials. Within a few days of looking at Trautmann's case, he had arranged for a transfer back to Huyton in time for the new season at Hoghton Road.

St Helens Town had not been slow to capitalise on the success of the previous season. They had been elected to the Lancashire Combination and, with money raised by the supporters' club, had built a new grandstand. This ambitious little club were on their way.

Events were also taking place within the Friar household. Jack had accepted a new job as General Manager and Buyer for the Stockport CWS and, in order to be nearer to his work, he had rented a flat in the area. He was leaving St Helens early on Monday morning and returning late on Friday. He continued as secretary with the Town club, but his time and energy were now limited and most people expected him to relinquish his position before the season was over. Most supporters did not expect Trautmann to be with St Helens either.

Rumours of Trautmann's impending departure had started from the opening day of the season and the Town supporters joked that the League scouts at the games were doubling the attendance figures. In the opening games representatives from Grimsby, Doncaster, Burnley, Everton and Liverpool watched Trautmann and several more clubs had reports on his performances. Burnley contacted Jack Friar and made arrangements to talk to Trautmann at the beginning of October. Bert trusted Friar implicitly, and he agreed not to make any decision unless Jack agreed. Jack had two things to consider, firstly that Trautmann, as an alien, would only be allowed to play on a part-time professional basis and, secondly, his amateur status would not bring a transfer fee to St Helens unless he could persuade the successful club to arrange a donation to the Town funds. Jack agreed to take Trautmann to Burnley's Turf Moor ground on 8 October, but in the meantime Jock Thompson had contacted him on behalf of Manchester City. From hereon a web of total confusion and deceit dictated the proceedings and a series of charges and counter charges were to begin. During this period Trautmann had gone down with influenza again, but he had got up from his sickbed to play for St Helens against Bangor City in an FA Cup preliminary round. Over 5,000 spectators turned up at Hoghton Road, all convinced that they were watching Trautmann's last appearance in the Town goal. Bangor won the game 3–0, and Trautmann, feeling wretched, took refuge in Marshalls Cross Road where he fell into his bed in Barbara Friar's room.

The spectators were correct in their assumption, this was Trautmann's last game for St Helens and a huge controversy was to begin.

# MANCHESTER CITY FC –
# A CONTROVERSIAL TRANSFER

*Each member of the Jewish community is entitled to his own opinion, but there is no concerted action in favour of the proposal to end their support of Manchester City FC. Despite the terrible cruelties we suffered at the hands of the Germans, we would not try to punish an individual German who is unconnected with these crimes of hatred. If this footballer is a decent fellow, I would say there is no harm in it. Each must be judged on its merits.*

DR A.ALTMANN
Communal Rabbi
Manchester, 1949

WERE FOOTBALL supporters asked to name the most eccentric and erratic football team in the English Football League, their answer would be, unequivocally, Manchester City. Even their former stadium, Maine Road, was, for some unaccountable reason, named after a state in the US. The stadium was vast, over 84,000 had watched an FA Cup tie against Stoke in 1934, which is still the record English attendance for a game outside Wembley Stadium.

In terms of eccentricity the club had no rival. What other club had a Welsh miner who devastated opponents with his wing play while chewing on a toothpick before reputedly cycling back to Wales? Billy Meredith had passed into soccer legend from his exploits.

Could it be possible for a professional football team to have an amateur captain who was not only a Cambridge triple blue but also a Wimbledon doubles champion, who never trained with his professional colleagues? This talented sportsman was Max Woosnam.

Dare it be mentioned that this club once had a bespectacled goalkeeper on the staff who once walked off the pitch before the end of the game by mistake and allowed the opposition to score into an open goal? Well J.F. Mitchell did.

This was just the players; the board were capable of committing the most outrageous blunders. Back in 1905 they were found guilty of making illegal payments to the players after the 1904 Cup Final win and as a result lost virtually all their playing staff overnight. Even in success the club dropped resounding clangers. In one of their most successful pre-war periods, City reached the FA Cup Final twice, finished in the top five on three occasions and their run of success culminated in winning their first Championship in 1937. They were promptly relegated with remarkable contrast the following season.

Wilf Wild, who was the secretary-manager during that period, was in charge of a Second Division club when League Football commenced after the war. In common with other clubs, they had to start from nothing because only three players from the first team that were relegated remained. The war had taken its toll of the playing staff and most of the players were unable to compete again in first-class football because of their age. War injury reduced the staff also, Arthur Kelling had been killed and another player, George Smith, was running around with a stump where his right hand had been shot away.

Wild worked hard to build his promotion team, but in December 1946 he was relieved of the managerial role, and the directors brought in Sam Cowans as the new team boss. City won the Second Division championship and returned to the First Division with optimism.

Sam Cowans resigned during the close season after clashes with his chairman, Bob Smith, and the board hired Jock Thompson as manager on 13 November 1947. The club finished a creditable tenth in their first season back and seventh the following year.

The attendances at Maine Road in those early years after the war were massive. Manchester United, who shared the stadium with City for a short time, experienced three 'gates' over 80,000, while City, as a mid-table side, were attracting crowds of over 60,000. As the money poured in Thompson was hopeful of strengthening his side in the transfer market, but his immediate problem was Frank Swift's decision to call it a day. Swift was building up his business interests in the industrial catering industry and had become a director with Smallmans Catering. His retirement announcement had caused a bitter row with the not particularly endearing chairman, Bob Smith.

The goalkeeper lived in a club house that City had provided for him in the 1930s, and Swift had negotiated to purchase the property to make his future more secure. He bought the house at the cost price City had paid and earned a few hundred pounds in equity before promptly announcing his retirement. Smith was outraged at what he considered Swift's audacity and refused to speak to him for weeks. Smith was also aware of Manchester United's covert attempts to sign him. (Bob Smith held on to Swift's registration for three years to prevent him coming out of retirement and joining City's great rivals at Old Trafford). Jock Thompson's persuasive charm, fortunately for City, succeeded in Swift agreeing to open the 1949–50 season for the club.

Johnny Hart, a young forward from Golborne, had mentioned to the City training staff that one of his local sides, St Helens Town, had a goalkeeper who was building up quite a reputation and could prove to be a reasonable replacement, at least in the short term. Thompson dispatched his scouts, and as soon as he heard from them he made a hurried visit to Hoghton Road together with his trainer, Fred Tilson. On his return he quickly informed the board of his keen interest. Walter Smith was the City director who was the most involved with new signings, and he immediately backed

Thompson's assessment, and at the board meeting on 4 October he outlined the goalkeeper's history and, more importantly, his ability. Thompson, in the meantime, had contacted St Helens and from there events at times became clouded in secrecy, and to this day no one seems to have the full story. Eric Thornton of the *Manchester Evening News* claimed to have discovered the story first as far as the Press were concerned. The City board conducted themselves with total secrecy; it was vital they secured this gifted athlete without delay, and at the same time prepare the ground for the reaction of the supporters and Press when the signing was announced. It was normal practice for them to provide Thornton and Eric Todd on the rival *Evening Chronicle* with any news of impending transfer activity. Thornton discovered from a contact that City were rumoured to be on the verge of signing a German player from St Helens. He, strangely, did not seek confirmation from Maine Road but dashed off to St Helens with a photographer. In that evening's edition of the *Evening News* a hazy picture of Trautmann appeared together with the announcement that Manchester City were about to sign a former German prisoner of war named *Berg* Trautmann. Within hours the national newspapers had the story and all hell broke loose. Thompson was convinced one of the directors had tipped off Thornton and now valuable time was lost dealing with the Press and supporters trying to confirm the story. Walter Smith had by now contacted George Fryer and arranged a press conference at Hoghton Road on the evening of 6 October. In the meantime, Jack Friar had received a message at his office in Stockport to meet Smith and Thompson in the Kingsway Hotel that same evening. Friar sent a message to Trautmann not to sign anything until he could get back to St Helens. Trautmann, for his part, remained oblivious to the furore and was as miserable as a model with a cold sore as he lay in his bed. Jack Friar had driven back to St Helens to find out, 'What the bloody hell was going on', and he stayed the night at Marshalls Cross Road before driving back early the following morning, totally unaware of the Press conference at Hoghton Road that Thursday evening.

On Thursday 6 October the national and local Press met at the St Helens' ground waiting for Trautmann and the officials from St Helens and Manchester City to complete the signing. A message from the manager, George Fryer, told the assembled hacks that there would not be any signing that night, and the following day the *St Helens Reporter* recorded two statements attributed to Trautmann, he was, 'ill in bed and did not want to commit himself', and a statement from St Helens Town that, 'he wanted more time to think it over'. By this time Burnley officials were desperately trying to find out, 'What the bloody hell was going on', but could not contact any of the Town officials.

Trautmann actually signed for City on the night of 6 October. The Friar's telephone had been ringing all day and a number of people had arrived unannounced at the house. Had she the energy Granny Winstanley would have performed somersaults of annoyance. Shortly after eight o'clock, two immaculately dressed men appeared at the door and said to Clarice, 'Good evening Mrs Friar, we are from Manchester City and would like to speak to Mr Trautmann.' Mrs Friar, with little resistance, led them to his room and stirred Bert from his drowsy state to receive the two visitors.

Barbara was pretending to be asleep in her corner of the room when Clarice led Smith and Thompson in. The nine year old was quivering with excitement in her bed as the men talked to her Bert and the idolatrous child tried hard to catch what the men were saying. She drifted into a fitful sleep as the three men talked late into the night, with her mother bringing in cups of tea every so often, while downstairs she had been desperately trying to contact Jack. Granny Winstanley retired to bed muttering, 'It's not right you know, it's not right.'

Jock Thompson was always regarded as a gentleman, and he had a quiet, persuasive manner. Jock did most of the talking, while Walter Smith smiled benignly at the bemused goalkeeper. His hazy recollection was of Thompson saying what a big city club he would be joining, who enjoyed huge crowds and were a club going places, unlike some of the clubs showing interest. Thompson's paternalistic approach eventually wore down the defences of the increasingly fatigued Trautmann, who was also suffering from an acute personal discomfort while all the time hoping for Jack to turn up. At quarter to midnight Bert signed for Thompson's club. He was to be contacted the following day about reporting to Maine Road, and Clarice let out the jubilant men from Maine Road. Barbara recalled jumping out of bed after the City officials had left asking, 'Well Bert, did you sign?' He made her collapse into giggles as he replied in his German-Lancashire accent, 'Yes, becoz I voz desperate to go t' toilet.' Barbara jumped back into bed as he staggered off towards the bathroom.

Half an hour later an angry and tired Jack Friar burst into the bedroom. 'What's going on,' demanded Jack. 'I've signed for Manchester City,' replied Bert.

After a few seconds Jack's tired eyes looked into Trautmann's as the shock took hold. With great sadness he said wearily, 'Well you've made your own bed, now you'll have to lie in it.' Jack retreated slowly and sadly from the room. The signing had weakened any bargaining power Jack had hoped for, and now he had to face the Press and Town supporters to explain.

The first thing to greet Jack the following morning was a hand-delivered letter from Burnley, who had expected Friar and Trautmann at Turf Moor on 8 October. The letter from the chairman, George Tate, outlined the plans his club had made for Bert. At the time, aliens had to play part time for professional clubs and have another job outside football. With this in mind, Burnley had arranged an interview with the Ministry of Labour and the National Coal Board to provide him with work. Tate's letter went on, 'I had also arranged to settle the financial aspect for the St Helens club, yourself, and all concerned in the best possible terms. In addition, if so desired, I had arranged to provide a goalkeeper for St Helens. Whatever City have done for you, we could have done better if you could have given us the chance, and honestly I feel that if you had come to Turf Moor today you would have been very pleased and satisfied, and there would not have been any unpleasant publicity. I was relying on the assurance that you would not do anything except through Mr Friar or believe me I should have come over last night.'

Jack was unable to believe the speed at which the letter had arrived and how much Burnley knew about the signing. He had not, however, been party to the frantic wheeling and dealing going on in St Helens while on his wild-goose chase in Manchester. He also felt Burnley had left themselves open to misconduct charges in their references to generous terms and transfer fees, and payment for amateurs was strictly illegal.

The Friar's were being bombarded by telephone calls from newspapers and receiving abusive anonymous calls from irate Town supporters. The St *Helens Reporter* recorded the reaction of the St Helens fans. One said, 'He cost us nothing and as he's an amateur we can get nothing from his transfer. It's all loss and no gain for St Helens so why let him go?' Others expressed the view that he was far too good for the Lancashire Combination so why stop him bettering himself.

In the meantime, a rumour had started in the town that Jack and Bert had both received substantial payments from City, totally unfounded and untrue. George Fryer was quoted as saying, 'I'd never agree to keep a man who was good enough for a better class side. Trautmann wanted to get into higher-grade soccer and we decided not to stand in his way. Our only regret was that we did not have him on our books as a professional. He would have brought a good fee and at the moment we could do with the money.' The transfer forms for Bert's move to Manchester were signed by George Fryer.

Jack's main concern for Bert was to now try and protect him from what Burnley had described as unpleasant publicity. Trautmann remarked later: 'I don't think even George Tate foresaw the tempest of controversy and ill feeling that accompanied me to Manchester. I was so bewildered by it all I wish I never left St Helens.'

There had been a substantial Jewish community in Manchester since the early 1800s. Jewish pedlars had always been around the area as early as 1740, but it was 60 years later that shopkeepers from Germany, Holland and France set up businesses in the Cheetham Hill area of the city, and the community built up with the textile industry and became closely associated with the rag trade and finance. Eventually, Cheetham Hill was dominated in architecture by the Great Synagogue, and the entrepreneurial adventure and economic invention of the Mancunian Jews became renowned.

Gradually, the community had built up to over 40,000, and the Jewish area spread to Cheadle Hulme and Lower Broughton. As World War Two had begun, their ranks were swelled by an influx of refugees from Germany and other parts of Europe, who were escaping the poverty, exploitation and prejudice.

Within the community a number of Jewish Working Men's Clubs and Jewish Lad's Brigades were founded with football a significant part of their activities. In terms of support for the two professional sides in Manchester, they gravitated towards the protestant City rather than the catholic associations of United, and by 1949 Manchester City had a large number of Jewish supporters.

When the *Manchester Evening News* broke the story of the club's interest in Trautmann, letters of indignation were delivered by the sack load. In addition, the gentile ex-servicemen's club were equally outraged and the two groups formed an alliance to boycott City's matches if Trautmann was signed, while hundreds threatened to return their season tickets to the club.

In Salford a fight started at a pub between City and United fans where the local police had to call for reinforcements to break it up. The debate had spread through the country, and Eric Thornton at the *Evening News* had wires from several other countries, notably the US, who were interested in the story. There was no doubt that the city of Manchester was divided by the addition of a German footballer to the playing staff of one of their clubs. The letters to the newspapers poured in:

*'So the signing of a German goalkeeper has upset the sporting instincts of some City supporters. Well I think it a great idea and a bold move by the City directors. I have never had any distinct liking for the German race but my antagonism is not centred on this one individual. Good luck to him – and the team.'*

*'Leaving aside the question of racial prejudice and the advisability of including a German in our League soccer, the real issue is whether Trautmann can play better than any English substitute who Manchester City could have found and even if he can will the high feeling that is bound to be felt affect his form? It just needs an incident arising from a harmless rough and tumble for the German to be the centre of dispute and supporters' demonstration that will do neither the players, the club nor the British public any good. For feeling will be high and this sort of thing is simply playing with dynamite. Surely there are goalkeepers as good if not better than this St Helens discovery.'*

*'Some of my friends were killed in the war. Members of my family were in the services too. So was I. So I can understand to some extent the feelings of people who will criticise City's action, but indiscriminate condemnation on racial grounds is inhuman and absurd.'*

*'After all the dreadful nights we went through to when the dawn came, women and children being dug out dead from under bricks and mortar, City expect supporters to go and watch a German playing football with men the Germans tried to kill. If the players are proper men they will refuse to turn out with such a man.'*

*'Whether he be gentile or Jew, black or white, German or Chinaman, if this recruit plays the games in the sporting way Frank Swift did, he'll do for me. Until this bitterness is stamped out how can we expect nations to unite? Good luck Berg Frautmann [sic].'*
*'As a disabled serviceman from the last war I am writing with bitterness in my heart. To think that after all we in this country went through and still are going through due to that war, Manchester City sign a German. I have followed City up and down the country and will cease to follow my club if they sign this man.'*

*'Racial antagonism ought not to be perpetuated like this. Sport should be one of the means of reconciliation not of wider division – the protests of*

*some ignore the reality of what active service experience the two world wars proclaimed – that between front-line soldiers there is no real personal hatred. The German soldier and the British tommy were only obeying orders. Moreover what have racialism and past national antagonisms to do with this game of football – one would think that the player was the Belsen Camp commandant – when born a German he had to do his duty as a German.'*

Perhaps the most quoted and certainly the most famous letter to the Press read:

*'When I think of all those millions of Jews who were tortured and murdered I can only marvel at Manchester City's crass stupidity.'*

Bob Smith and his board were under siege at Maine Road. His grey jowls overwhelmed his directors as they discussed the mounting crisis. Smith had kept open only essential lines on the switchboard, Bob and Walter Smith (who, contrary to opinion at the time, were not related) did most of the talking, and the eventual decision was to issue a statement to the Press giving the board's views. Bob Smith was not concerned how the player himself would react, that was Jock Thompson's responsibility, his main concern was the club's reputation. In his statement to the Press he commented, 'One can understand the feeling of those who have suffered from the war, but we have to get down to the task of building a stronger team. A little while ago some supporters threatened a boycott because we were not getting new players, and now we're threatened with a boycott because we are bringing new players to Maine Road. It seems we shall be in trouble whichever way we go.'

The Football League also issued a statement. 'We do not make any condition of nationality about the registration of a player. If there was an objection the FA would deal with that.'

Bob Smith and the rest of the City board were using their influence in Manchester to gain acceptance of Trautmann's signing and to an extent orchestrating, through the supporters' club, some of the letters to the Press in support of the transfer. While this was going on, secretary Wilf Wild was looking at the more practical aspects of the signing. He was busy negotiating Trautmann's release from his contract with the War Agricultural Executive, arranging registration with the Football League and trying to organise a job for him locally. Alexander Altmann was himself a refugee from Hitler's Germany. His influence as the communal Rabbi in Manchester was considerable. When he issued his placatory statement about the Trautmann storm he did a great deal to pour oil on troubled waters. City had the stroke of luck they needed to help the storm subside, for the immediate period anyway. The goalkeeper had yet to play. Jock Thompson decided to give Trautmann his first game in a reserve-team match at Barnsley the following weekend, well away from Maine Road.

Back in St Helens, Jack Friar and Bert Trautmann were deep in discussion about the footballer's future and yet another chapter in his life was about to begin.

# MANCHESTER CITY FC –
# THE EARLY YEARS

*The rain is falling all around*
*It falls on field and tree*
*It rains on the umbrellas here*
*And on the ships at sea.*

ROBERT LOUIS STEVENSON

O N TUESDAY 11 October 1949, still weak and unfit from his influenza symptoms, Bert Trautmann travelled from St Helens to Manchester Victoria Station and continued by bus to Maine Road. Rain to Manchester is the equivalent of sand to the Sahara Desert in association for most people. Its geographical position in the North West is such that clouds become trapped by the backbone of the Pennines and as a consequence dump millions of gallons of rain on to the city. No exception was made for Trautmann as he splashed through the puddles towards the stadium.

Moss Side at the turn of the 20th century had been a reasonably well-to-do area, with wide thoroughfares and middle-class homes. As the affluent moved out to the leafy lanes of Cheshire, terraced houses appeared as the older mansions were demolished, and industrial workers moved in. The area around the stadium was a mass of cobbled streets with small terraced houses separated by cobbled alleyways filled with dustbins and dog muck. The football ground rose above the bleak surroundings, with the huge main stand dominating the vista. Coincidently for Trautmann, the ground had been built on the former site of a brick works, and he would always refer to it later as the Brick Factory.

He had visited Maine Road before as a spectator, on an excursion with Jack Friar, and had been impressed by the immense size of the place. Bert climbed the steps to the entrance, met Jock Thompson in the panelled reception area and was led off to the right into the dressing room. A number of first-team players were assembled as Jock introduced them to the new goalkeeper. Eric Westwood, the Manchester City captain, had been carefully briefed by Bob Smith and the most famous welcome in football had been well rehearsed. The newspapers all quoted his remark: 'There's no war in this dressing-room, we welcome you as any other member of the staff. Just make yourself at home, and good luck.'

The newspapers' football correspondents all reported that Westwood had fought on the Normandy beaches and had been mentioned in dispatches. On the premise that if it was alright with Westwood it was alright with everyone else, Bob Smith ducked out of any further comment and left any ensuing problems to his manager and players. Westwood, as a consummate professional, had done his job but in private had expressed his own misgivings about Trautmann's arrival. To his credit, they were not given to the rest of the players and the first official photograph issued showed a clumsy ensemble of players hoisting Bert on to their shoulders.

In one part of the City dressing room is the traditional goalkeepers corner, for the previous 16 years occupied by Frank Swift. After hanging his belongings on to the almost sacred clothes hook, Bert was led out to the pitch and placed himself between the goal posts at the score-board end for the first time. This earliest training session consisted of Westwood and two or three others hitting shots from various distances, and half an hour later it was over. Thompson told him to report to Maine Road on Saturday morning to meet up with the reserve-team bus, which would be taking them to Barnsley.

His debut for Manchester City reserves resulted in a 1–0 defeat before a smaller attendance than his final match at St Helens Town. There were no bitter protests, little barracking from the Yorkshiremen at Oakwell, and from a professional point of view he was playing while not being fully fit to do so, a state he would have to experience many times in the future. He was still weak from his recent illness and suffering two painful boils on his left arm, hardly helpful to any gymnastic prowess. Nevertheless, his professional colleagues were encouraged by his performance and the football journalists, who had crammed into Barnsley's limited facilities, were generous in their praise.

Eric Thornton wrote afterwards, 'He could become as good as Frank Swift,' while *The Times* wrote, 'Trautmann is going to be one of the goalkeeper discoveries of recent years.'

Bert returned to St Helens late in the evening that Saturday reasonably happy with his performance, while in Manchester Jock Thompson could barely contain his excitement, when hearing the good reports from Barnsley. He might well have found an adequate replacement for Swift, but would he be good enough for the supporters and the directors? Thompson decided not.

'He'll have to bloody emulate Swifty.'

'No, he'll have to be better than that boss,' said one of the more ebullient players.

Wilf Wild, in the meantime, was pulling out all the stops to ensure Trautmann's immediate future. Having obtained the necessary release from his work obligations to the Government, he contacted a long-time City supporter, Bill Proctor, who owned a garage in Hulme, a short distance away from Maine Road. Proctor agreed to employ Bert as a part-time mechanic and in turn Wild was able to register Trautmann as a part-time professional with the Football League.

He played four further reserve-team games before Thompson felt he was ready to play in the First Division, selecting him for the match against Bolton Wanderers on 19 November. Thompson knew after the first few games that City were going to have a difficult season and the team needed strengthening in key positions. Money for new players was not forthcoming but, to be fair to the board, extensive improvement work had to be carried out at the ground, much of it necessary from new legislation, which had been brought in by the authorities following the tragedy at Burnden Park. Three seasons previously a number of spectators had been killed when key structural parts of the stadium had given way under crowd pressure. Trautmann was now to make his debut at the scene of that appalling accident.

The team itself was a mixture of ageing international players and cheap local signings. The side had spirit and experience but needed younger and stronger legs. Eric Westwood, in particular, had seen his best days, and although a strong and inspirational captain his speed had gone, whereas wingers of the ability of Tom Finney and Stanley Matthews had retained theirs.

Trautmann arrived at Burnden Park with an outward display of confidence. The Press interest in the match was naturally keen and over 10,000 fans had made the journey from Manchester to support City. Within himself, Bert was taut with nervous tension, but his ascetic attitude helped him to cope with the pre-match attention and his nerves steadied as he came out with the team in front of 35,000 people. He was given a roar of encouragement from the City supporters, but they could not drown out the barracking from parts of the ground. Bert heard the first 'Heil Hitler' and 'Nazi' taunts that day that were to be heard throughout his career at every stadium in which he played in England.

The match itself was a disaster for City. Bolton had just signed Bobby Langton, the England international from Preston, and he gave Westwood a torrid time. Trautmann kept the Bolton forwards at bay for the first 45 minutes, but in the second half they increased the pressure and finished convincing 3–0 victors. Bert was disconsolate as he came off the field, he felt he should have saved the penalty awarded against City and could have prevented another goal. Already his need for perfection was beginning to assert itself and the almost manic self-critical analysis of his own game was taking hold.

Jock Thompson and the players all congratulated him on a competent debut, but he was still brooding when Frank Swift walked into the dressing room. Swift came straight to his successor, flashing a beaming smile, and shook him by the hand.

'Well done son, you'll do.'

Those few words brought Trautmann out of his depression and Swift's encouragement and advice in those early days were of great help to him.

The following week he made his home debut at Maine Road against Birmingham City. The anti-Trautmann lobby were still forthright in the Manchester area and many people were expecting a demonstration at the Birmingham game, together with a boycott by a number of season-ticket holders. The newspapers happily fuelled the rumours, and the City officials spent an anxious few days awaiting any developments. Trautmann was more concerned with proving himself as a sportsman to his detractors and becoming doggedly determined to do so. In the event, the threatened action by the supporters was limited, but a few supporters did stay away, a small group made a protest outside the stadium, while some season tickets were returned. The City supporters in general were concerned for their team and now this new player was a crucial element of that team, their fanatical allegiance and loyalty transcended any prejudice.

Trautmann was greatly encouraged by his reception from the crowd, and the team found its form, with an excellent all-round performance, by winning 4–0. He had little goalkeeping to do in the game. After the match he was introduced to a number of prominent supporters who made encouraging and complimentary comments.

The following Saturday Manchester City travelled to play Derby County at the Baseball Ground. The weather had been vile for most of the week, rain had come down in torrents and the pitch was a quagmire when the two sides kicked-off at two o'clock. The City football was as appalling as the weather. Without exception, each player gave a poor display and Trautmann found himself in a nightmare that would not end. The Derby forwards hit their shots as soon as the goal was sighted, and, with City's defence in its most philanthropic mood to the opposition, they smashed seven goals past the beleaguered and hapless Bert. To make matters worse his concentration was being distracted by the crowd as, when each goal went in, the jubilant Derby supporters on the terrace behind him were being expressly discreditable, the crux of their taunts being Trautmann's nationality. He left the pitch covered in mud and humiliated, and the team bus back to Manchester was cloaked in silence and brooding. Trautmann arrived back in St Helens distressed and desperate, but he returned to the fulcrum of his life, the Friars and Granny Winstanley.

Jack had forgiven Bert for signing for City and was doing all he could to make the transition to a major football club as smooth as possible. He was also assisting Bert to come to terms with the malice directed at him by the crowds and the letters still pouring in from all over the country. Criticism in St Helens was still being directed at the club, and accusations were being aimed at Friar and George Fryer relating to backhanders from Manchester City. The supporters' club was decidedly irate about newspaper stories, which indicated City had provided money for the Hoghton Road stand. The cost of £1,200 had been raised solely by the supporters themselves. The only agreement George Fryer had managed to negotiate was for City to send their first team to St Helens for a friendly match each season for the next five years. This was not a contractual obligation for the Manchester club, purely a verbal arrangement between Fryer and Walter Smith. The first of these games was to take place at the end of the season.

After Trautmann had signed the registration forms for his new club, Jack Friar was facing alienation from St Helens Town because of his loyalty to Trautmann and the difficulties of being away from his family during the week. In his own mind he knew his resignation from the role of secretary at St Helens was inevitable, with pressure from within the club making his tenure more arduous and also from his dilemma at the relationship between Margaret and Bert.

Trautmann was now living permanently at Marshalls Cross Road, although officially he was still registered at the Bomb Disposal Hostel at Huyton. While Jack conducted business in Cheshire during the week, Bert was the man in the house and the four females adored him in their own way. While Barbara wore her heart on her sleeve, Clarice found him more and more endearing and Granny Winstanley developed her own curious ambivalence towards the man. She adopted the same stance with him as she adopted with Jack, never referring to Bert by name, always as 'he' or 'him', but there is no doubt that she liked him enormously.

The immediate delight of their relationship was one of communication. Trautmann's ability to pick up English was influenced by his immediate surroundings; he adopted the language used by those who were closest to him. Unfortunately for Bert, Granny was Mrs Malaprop. Her misuse of words became legendary within the family. Looking at the steamed-up windows in the kitchen she would remark, 'Oh! Look at t'condecension.'

Once when Margaret and Barbara were looking through a prism, which Jack had bought for them, she uttered 'Beautiful, you can see all t' colours of t' rectum.' Trautmann used to mystify his City colleagues with his 'Winstanleyisms'. On one occasion, when the dressing room was decidedly raucous and chaotic, he declared, 'It's like Beddlington in here.'

His future was looking good, he was now feeling confident that he would be a success with City, the haven at Marshalls Cross Road made him feel secure and he revelled in the warmth of family life, an experience he had never felt in Bremen. He was also encountering something else in his life for the first time – he was in love. His relationship with Margaret had developed with great intensity. Poor Bill Twist had faded away and Margaret had despatched her other suitors with short shrift; Bert was now her only interest. The stigma of his relationship with Marion Greenall was none the less his blot on the landscape. As the relationship between Margaret and Bert had blossomed, the news soon travelled to Ashtonin-Makerfield. The Greenalls had turned up on the doorstep, with Marion carrying Freda in her arms, to confront Bert. The Friars and Granny closed ranks in front of him in a swirl of possessive skirts, but the incident left them all in fear of a scandal as Trautmann's fame developed. The Greenalls, for their part, also closed ranks to prevent any unpleasant publicity and both families came through the incident without vilification. The skeleton in the cupboard would always remain, and privately Jack and Clarice had expressed sympathy with the Greenalls.

In Trautmann's case, his prospects with Margaret overruled any hope for Marion to persuade him to honour his obligations to their daughter, and she faded into the background with her 10 shillings a week maintenance.

To a certain extent Jack Friar was fairly ignorant of the relationship between his daughter and Bert. He had accepted his responsibility of the son he had always wanted, while he had been established in Trautmann's mind as the father that Carl had never been. Jack's initial concept of the relationship between Margaret and Bert was as a purely platonic friendship, he knew his daughter's whims and moods and Bert's explosive nature, but he had a fearful apprehension of any long-term relationship, an intuition that would eventually prove to be an astute judgement.

Both men were now living a transitory life, travelling between their homes and their work in the same area. Jack knew that eventually he would have to uproot the family from St Helens to Cheshire, and with Bert also commuting to the area he began negotiations with the CWS for a suitable home there.

Trautmann was still subjected to intermittent checks or interrogation by the authorities, he was still subject to the Aliens Order of 1920 and was only accepted by the British Government as a denizen, his rights and freedom still answerable to the scrutiny of the state. His lifestyle was, therefore, fairly rigid and his job outside football a necessary requirement.

Bill Proctor ran his garage in Mulberry Street, Hulme, with the help of his wife and daughter. He had a small repair bay and two petrol pumps in the forecourt, where Trautmann was regularly seen filling up Austin Sevens and pre-war Vauxhalls. Motorists who supported City made regular diversions to the garage where Manchester's new sports celebrity worked. He was good for business for Proctor and the football club. He fitted in his work at the garage with City training sessions, consisting of the same, boring old routines, and certainly there was no specialised coaching. The players would lap the pitch for a prescribed number of times, run a few sprints and head to the gym for circuit training. The sporadic game of head tennis was played, usually organised by the players themselves, but no tactical innovations or ball skills were introduced.

Trautmann was a naturally fit man anyway, with great reserves of stamina, and he was never really exerted to any degree, but one serious problem suddenly materialised. Roy Clarke, the City outside-left and Welsh international, was becoming a great friend of the goalkeeper. During one training session Clarke and Trautmann were lapping the pitch together when the Welshman spurted the last few yards and turned to find Bert collapsed. Clarke, trainer Fred Tilson and the other players rushed over to find him hyperventilating and his heart beating at an alarming pace. Clarke recalled, 'There was a look of absolute panic in his eyes as Tilson tried to make him comfortable. He was gulping for air. I had not seen anything like it before and my immediate impression was that he had suffered from a heart attack.'

Trautmann was seen by the club doctor and then sent for a check-up at the hospital. No defects could be found, but during questioning by the medical staff Bert mentioned he occasionally found himself fighting for breath during the night and his heart would palpitate wildly. The symptoms would last half an hour or so and then subside. After further questions the doctors concluded the problem was a result of him being trapped under the rubble at the school in Kleve during his war service. His fight for life had triggered some abnormality in his breathing mechanism which, after any great exertion or stress, could bring on the symptoms at any time. There was no way of curing the problem, and it was something Bert would have to live with. The main concern for him and the club was the possibility of the phenomenon happening during a game. Over the years he learnt to recognise when an attack was imminent and through his own mental strength managed to contain the problem. Over his whole career he only found himself troubled in a handful of games.

Bert Trautmann, as a man, was now maturing into a confident and charismatic individual. Of his early days in Manchester he remarked, 'As well as the obvious problems of my German nationality, I was a little concerned initially about leaving St Helens for the less parochial atmosphere of Manchester and Salford with their combined populations of over a million people. In terms of the work I was doing, I could not believe my luck at the age of twenty-six being paid, albeit on a small scale, for doing something I loved. I had no doubt in my own mind I could make it as a professional and my confidence grew with each game, even though we received some awful results that first year. In a way it was no different from my time at Hanomag or in the forces. Men bitched about pay or conditions and footballers are no different in that respect. I couldn't understand at first the discontent, particularly of Eric Westwood, about pay, the older players were always whinging about that, but to be paid as a sportsman for me was wonderful. As the years went on, of course, I began to understand their complaints. At that time, however, I was as happy as a child in a sandpit. I loved the attention and despite the awful dirt and grime of the area the people were so incredibly kind to me. I also had the Friars and I was making new friends each day. I rather liked being a celebrity.'

From a playing point of view, Manchester City were going through another of their eccentric periods, and Bert still had to play his first game in London. The club had gone into the Christmas games lying in 21st position in the First Division after a 1–0 defeat at Aston Villa. Trautmann's own performance had been superb and his ability, by rights, should have given extra confidence to the rest of the team. The defence was as porous as a tea-bag and the forwards were missing easy chances. They came into the New Year with an FA Cup third-round tie against Derby County on 7 January 1950. Trautmann was Cup-tied, his last appearance for St Helens against Bangor City excluded him from the side, and he sat in the stand at Maine Road watching his colleagues winning 3–2 at half-time. City, of course, managed to lose 5–3. The following Saturday, 14 January, Bert played his first game in the capital. Jack Friar, who had done as much as he could to cocoon Bert from the racial taunts, was at his most astute in recognising that his first game in London would be the most critical and possibly most traumatic. The City followers, and most neutrals in the north, had been persuaded by Trautmann's ability and character into a whole acceptance, one Mancunian had told a bewildered Bert, 'Those bastard Norman Cockneys don't understand'. To a certain extent the Celtic and Anglo-Saxon northerners would have had trouble understanding as well, but the remark was succinct in many ways and Jack Friar endeavoured to explain Bert's possible predicament. The North-South rivalries were something new for Trautmann in his sociological concept of England. He had not really comprehended the 'plum in the mouth' officers from the south alienating the northern-based regimental forces at the PoW camps and was also unaware that the canny northerners in 1950 regarded London as the epitome of degradation.

'Vot is t' smoke, Jack?'

'The smoke is London, Bert, it's a term for London.'

'Vhy?'

'Because it is very foggy Bert, and seems to be full of smoke all the time.'

'So it's just like Manchester zen, you know.'

'Yes Bert, and no.'

'I don't understand Jack.'

Bert soon related Jack's explanations of the concept people had of London and the reality. On his journey to Berlin, the *Land Jahr* boys had been regarded as the country bumpkins, while at the same time the evils of pre-war Berlin were uppermost in the German provincial mind as the image of depravity. Similarly, the provincial English mind, at that time totally unsophisticated in terms of travel, regarded London as the scarlet lady of England. Post-war London was not discouraging its 'spiv' image and the northern and southern Press encouraged the rivalry.

On a more pragmatic level, Jack outlined to Bert the initial reaction of the Londoners to a German playing against one of their teams. Football was the game of the masses and the post-war crowds were eager to find heroes and villains in this sport. The Londoners had suffered more than most at the incredible bombardment by the *Luftwaffe,* and their city had been subjected to the most appalling damage. Jack said to Trautmann, 'You've not achieved anything yet, what you have to do now is get the whole of the national Press behind you down South, when you go to London you must play as you've never played before.' It was a tall order by anyone's standards.

London was a vast bombsite and Trautmann shrank his large frame of a body into his seat as the team bus made its way to Craven Cottage. His only previous visit to the area in May 1949 was a serendipitous opportunity presented by Tommy Lloyd from St Helens. All clubs affiliated to the Football Association received tickets for the Final and the Town had received four. Tommy, as president of the club, was in charge of the allocation and always managed to procure one in the lottery, which allocated the tickets to the supporters. On the eve of the match a recipient of the Cup Final ticket who worked at the gasworks had been called out to deal with some emergency and had to cry off from the excursion. Bert was awakened very early in the morning by Tommy Lloyd asking if he would like to travel down to Wembley with the St Helens' party. He dressed quickly and was on his way south. Trautmann had returned from Wembley with a taste for the big time and was impressed by the atmosphere of the English Cup Final. Now he was playing in London for the first time, at the homely little Craven Cottage ground.

Fulham were also struggling against relegation and were in the bottom five clubs as they took the field against City. The London crowd threw all the insults they could at him, in such a small stadium you could hear a pin drop in any moments of silence, and the 'Nazi' and 'Kraut' insults were relentless before the match. Jack Friar's words were in the back of Bert's mind as he started the game; he summoned his self-discipline to shut out the crowd and went on to give one of the most superlative displays ever seen in London. His team might well have played with six men as far as the defence were concerned, the white-shirted Fulham forwards poured through the gaps in the defence and bombarded the goal. City lost 1–0 but, were it not for Trautmann, the score could have been much worse. At the end of the game the crowd gave him a standing ovation and, unbelievably, the Fulham players formed a line to applaud him off. Bert Trautmann had really arrived, and the newspapers sang out his praises, but, nevertheless, there was no disputing City were a very poor side indeed. Despite this, the loyal supporters were still urging them on. Against Middlesbrough, in February, just under 60,000 had turned up at Maine Road to watch the home team lose 1–0, and the result was made more miserable for Trautmann because after a collision with Billy Linacre the forward was rushed to hospital with a broken leg.

Jock Thompson tried desperately to improve the side. City had gone 14 away games since September 1949 without scoring a goal, and the forwards were playing with the aggression of a Carmelite nun. Thompson brought two players, Bill Spurdle and Dennis Westcott, to try to improve the dreadful scoring record. If nothing else, Westcott certainly improved the atmosphere in the dressing room. He had an excellent goal-scoring record with Wolves and Blackburn Rovers before joining City, and he was a man of keen humour. The atmosphere at the club was becoming extremely tense and Westcott's character was a much-needed boost to the team. He scored his first goal for the club in a 1–0 home victory over Burnley before City were due to play the current League leaders, Sunderland, at Roker Park. In characteristic style, they upset all form and established a 2–0 lead before Sunderland replied with a penalty from Stelling. Shortly afterwards, the home side were awarded another penalty, which Trautmann saved comfortably. The referee judged him to have moved before the full-back had taken the kick and ordered a retake. Bert was furious, he grabbed the ball and, exploding with anger, booted it as far as possible into the crowd, who it turn hooted their ridicule and chants of 'Sieg Heil' started, doing little for Bert's application to Stelling's third penalty-kick. He saved it again, silencing the crowd, while Westcott sidled up to the referee to ask, nonchalantly, if he thought the second save was better than the first one. (Over his career, Trautmann went on to save six out of every 10 penalties.)

Regardless of Trautmann's efforts, City's grim struggle against relegation ended when Charlton Athletic beat Derby County, while they could only draw with West Bromwich Albion. They had finished with the third-worst goals against record in the division, 68, and had scored only 36, only five better than the bottom club, Birmingham City.

Trautmann's personal life was also eventful. His relationship with Margaret had become a torrid and passionate romance. Late in February 1950 Margaret had led Bert away from the house to tell him she was pregnant. Unlike his affair with Marion, Trautmann decided immediately he would marry Margaret, and they faced Jack and Clarice to tell them the news. For the second time Bert had deeply hurt Jack by his actions, and he was profoundly offended by this breach of trust and irresponsible attitude. Hurried arrangements were made and the couple were married at Ravenoak Church, St Helens, on Friday 30 March 1950. Rudi Hering, who had remained in England after marrying a local girl, was best man and Jack laid on a muted reception at the Co-op Hall in the town. That evening the happy couple left on their honeymoon for London, accompanied by the players and officials of Manchester City Football Club. They were playing Arsenal at Highbury the following day and allowed Bert's new bride to accompany the party. City lost by a resounding 4–0 margin and, with typical wedding party vulgarity, Trautmann was blamed for a poor, post-wedding night display. In truth, the entire team played as if they had been engaged in nuptial bliss.

At the end of that season City decided to fulfil their obligation to St Helens and sent a side to Hoghton Road. On Thursday 27 April 1950 they arrived in St Helens. The City board had not taken their commitment seriously and the Town club, who had been preparing for the match for weeks, were far from happy with the strength of the opposition. St Helens had invited a number of their footballers, now playing for football League sides, to make a reasonable contest and considerable publicity had been generated in the area for the match. The crowd and the officials felt utterly deflated when only Trautmann and Andy Black from the City first team appeared. Bert was particularly upset and said shortly afterwards, 'We managed to win 2–0 and I don't think anyone could have cared less except for me. I felt, under the circumstances, that City might have sent a more representative side and I know the Town club were as disappointed as I was.' Bert was to learn quickly that promises in football were not always binding, both from clubs and players.

The day after the match at St Helens Jock Thompson resigned as manager of Manchester City. Bob Smith had given him the choice of doing so, rather than the debacle of being sacked, and he announced his intention of returning to Scotland to run a hotel.

The City directors announced the same day that Les McDowall would succeed Jock. McDowall, a former City player, had been managing Wrexham in the Third Division without any distinction, but the board's decision would prove to be an excellent choice for the club over the next few seasons. Bert Trautmann was to spend the close season making plans for the future with his wife and the Friar family.

# INTRIGUE AND COLLUSION

*There was a man came up to me,*
*He said 'I know you well,*
*Within your face I'm sure I see*
*The tinkling of a bell'*

*I said to him 'I rather doubt*
*We've ever met before!*
*I cannot recollect your snout*
*Retire and say no more.*

MERVYN PEAKE

L ES McDOWALL had joined Manchester City from Sunderland in 1938. Despite an undistinguished career with the Roker Park club, City signed him for the substantial fee of £7,000. Born in India, the son of a church minister, he was a calm and thoughtful man. Shortly after he joined the pre-war relegation side, McDowall was made the captain by Wilf Wild. He proved to be an intelligent player and became renowned for his coolness under pressure, and he developed a great rapport and understanding with Frank Swift on the field.

Bob Smith had kept an eye on McDowall when he left the club to manage Wrexham, and he did not hesitate to pluck him from the obscurity of the Welsh club when Jock Thompson departed from Maine Road. McDowall told his board he needed to recruit new players for the promotion campaign. The first of the new arrivals was Ken Barnes from non-League Stafford Rangers, hardly a sensational event for the City supporters. The second proved to be an inspired choice, though the player concerned had a reputation as a tough individual and a man of difficult character. Roy Paul was a Welsh international playing for Swansea Town, and had just returned from an abortive trip to Bogotá. Along with Jack Hedley, he was hoping to join the other British footballers in Colombia at the start of the decade, but things had not worked out for them. On his return to Wales, Paul was immediately placed on the transfer list. McDowall and Walter Smith moved quickly, signing him in July, but negotiations for other players were less successful.

A number of prominent players expected illicit signing fees and certain clubs had a reputation for paying them. Indeed, rumours were circulating about Paul having refused to sign for City unless he received payment. Swansea were reputed to have paid him in order to receive their transfer revenue. (Paul always gave an enigmatic smile and a wink when asked but neither denied or admitted receiving any payment.)

Manchester City had the reputation of being a straight club, the shadow of the 1904–05 scandal had been carried by successive directors, and while they were certainly involved in skulduggery in their methods of signing players, the circum-stances surrounding Trautmann being an example, no illegal payments were made to players and in football circles they were known as 'tight-fisted bastards,' to quote one former player. Trautmann first experienced the meanness of the club during the Easter period of 1950. City were due to play a game on Easter Monday, and with the train services being disrupted because of the holiday he arranged to travel to Manchester from St Helens in a taxi with Johnny Hart and two Manchester United reserve players. When Trautmann and Hart tried to recoup the cost of the journey the club refused to pay their expenses.

As the players reported to Maine Road for pre-season training, McDowall had more or less the same squad of footballers inherited from Thompson. Unlike Thompson though he did not have any worry with his goalkeeping position. His goalkeeper was now living at 19 Woodford Road, Bramhall, in the prosperous suburbs of Cheshire. The tree-lined roads and avenues, with large attractive houses, were in sharp contrast to St Helens and the smoky grime of the Manchester area. The CWS workmen had converted the former shop into a fine family house covering three floors. Two rooms at the top of the house were to be used by Bert and Margaret as their bedroom and nursery for when the baby was born. The couple spent the summer organising furniture and decorations for their part of the new home.

Trautmann returned for the new season sublimely happy. Although McDowall had arrived with the reputation of a football tactician, no immediate differences were noticed by the players as they fell into the old routine of physical exercises. McDowall proved to be an aloof manager, very much in the mould of most others of that period, and most of the communication with his team would be through trainers Laurie Barnett or Jim McClelland, there were no new or radical methods introduced. The trainers certainly did not have any great tactical knowledge and, although both useful footballers in their time, their job was to ensure the team was fit. It was left to the players to analyse their opponent's weaknesses on the field, and Trautmann felt frustrated by the lack of tactical discussion. With time, however, his impatience was to be rewarded by a fusion of players whose tactical awareness proved to be unique.

For his own part, Bert was left to devise his own training routines. He would line twelve footballs on the edge of the area and ask players to hit the balls from the different angles in quick succession while he dived and plunged at every shot.

In the gymnasium, under the main stand, he threw or kicked balls against the wall trying to catch the ferocious rebounds coming back at him, while all the time he analysed the various movements of the ball through the air. Trautmann was toning his reflexes to the full and developing the concentration of a chess master.

The morale of the team was helped enormously by the arrival of the two new players. Barnes had no immediate first-team prospects, he was essentially a reserve-team player, but he was a cheerful character with a mischievous sense of humour. Roy Paul formed an immediate attachment to his Welsh international teammate Roy Clarke, naturally known as Nobby, and the atmosphere at the club was good. The English habit of calling people by a nickname appealed to Bert's developing British humour. Ken Barnes had a nose like a bald eagle and was immediately called Beaky, Paul was Pauly and Bert became Trauty, but behind his back in moments of tension he was unkindly known as Krauty.

City roared into the new season and were unbeaten in their first 10 games. Roy Paul was outstanding and his mixture of robust and cultured football had a gal-vanizing effect on the team and, together with Trautmann's superb ability, the club quickly found themselves at the top of the Second Division with only Birmingham City in hot pursuit. In the meantime, McDowall was not idle in his office, and he introduced new players into the first team as he discarded his inherited older players. Westcott and Westwood were dropped and he brought in Frank McCourt and Ken Branagan. The effect, at first, disrupted the momentum of the team, and by the late autumn City were faltering. Despite Trautmann's impressive form, a depressing run of only one win in six matches allowed the pursuing teams to catch up. The seemingly detached McDowall did not panic and in his pre-match team talks calmly reassured his players. The team responded well, but bad weather caused a number of postponements and they fell behind an emerging Preston North End team.

On a personal level, Bert was preoccupied by the birth of his son, John Michael, on 4 October 1950 and, at the same time, with his role within the household.

He now called Jack and Clarice mum and dad and they had completely replaced Carl and Frieda in his life. Jack was still nursing him through his infancy as a sports star and providing him invaluable advice. His father-in-law's own great humour helped him to understand more the subtleties of English humour, which helped him to understand the constant banter of professional footballers, particularly from Barnes and Paul. A television series at the time, *Forces for Victory*, was a history of the allied invasion of Europe. Paul would say casually to Barnes:

'Hey Beaky, did you see the TV last night?'

'Yes, we won again, did you see it Trauty?'

'No I bloody didn't you bastard.'

Like the supporters, however, the team were fiercely protective of Bert, and any opposition player who tried to bait him during a game would be subjected to a severe bruising from one of Paul's crunching tackles. Within himself he was still trying to fathom out the British. They seemed such a poor, downtrodden race, with an appalling class system, yet they had a tenacity about them and such a rich cultural heritage, which Jack would spend hours explaining.

His life at Bramhall was not harmonious all the time, particularly with Granny and, at times, with Margaret. Both women were tremendously proud of him, but Sarah and Bert used to bait each other in a peculiarly ambivalent way. He had developed a pre-match regime of powerful concentration and would try to shut everything out of his mind as he prepared mentally for the game ahead. Sarah would shuffle about in the background asking:

'Does he want a clean shirt?' or 'Shall I get him some tea?'

'Shut up old woman, I'm concentrating.'

'Bloody football.'

If the team had lost Sarah always knew by the crashing and banging when Bert returned home.

'They bloody lost, now we're for it.'

And they were, he brooded for hours, going through every move of the match, finding faults with his own game and inwardly cursing any mistakes.

It was difficult for Margaret. To an extent she was jealous of Bert's fame and felt shut out from his thoughts at weekends, with a certain amount of justification as there was no doubt Bert was difficult to communicate with around match days. Conversely, Margaret craved attention and was upset because her husband tended to ignore her needs at times.

Christmas, above everything else, was the highlight of Bert's family's year and the one of 1950 was made extra special because of John. Trautmann still thought back to the bitter cold and memories of his wartime Christmases. He fostered an almost manic passion for the festivities and was as excited as a child as the celebrations approached. The Friars always had large family gatherings. Jack's brother Dick and his family came over from St Helens and after lunch they played party games for hours, with sundry friends and neighbours dropping in during the evening. Dick Friar now came round to accepting Bert as one of the family. He had been bitterly opposed to Jack's and, later, Margaret's relationship with Trautmann because of his anti-German feelings. Christmas Day was a riot of fun before Bert retired to bed early. He had a match to play on Boxing Day and, with reverence to his professionalism, the family party wound down. Invariably, Les McDowall telephoned his players on the eve of a match to ensure they were in, and he made no exception now. Bert Trautmann and Manchester City went into the new year facing a difficult promotion fixture list and an FA Cup tie at Birmingham City.

St Andrew's had not been Manchester's favourite ground, the Brummies invariably won the games and in the last FA Cup game between the two, Birmingham had registered a resounding 5–0 victory. The depressing story continued with Bert unable to prevent two goals, while Gil Merrick kept a clean sheet at the opposite end. The League programme also started to falter again and by early March they had slipped to sixth position, although with a number of games in hand over the promotion pack. McDowall made another inspired signing in Jimmy Meadows, who immediately brought more pace to the side. Slowly but surely City regained their composure and form, finishing as runners-up to Preston. They were back in the First Division after one season.

Once more McDowall was to spend the summer trying to strengthen his side, while Trautmann could look back on 43 consecutive games in the League and Cup, with a further three friendly matches for good measure. He had also captured the attention of the German Press and regular reports on his performances appeared in the newspapers. The German League teams became interested and that interest would bring about the most bizarre set of circumstances over the next year. The 1950–51 season was completed with a fixture against Wacker Innsbruck in a Festival of Britain game. A relaxed Manchester City side won 2–1, while Bert did his public relations bit for City by acting as translator and tour guide at Maine Road. Needless to say, he received no financial reward for his help, and little thanks.

Bert was still working for Bill Proctor at the garage in Hulme within the terms of his contract with City and also under the conditions still imposed by the government. In relation to his professional colleagues, Trautmann was being paid less as a part-timer while at the same time having the obligation of completing his commitments to Proctor. While Proctor had been an accommodating employer for Bert, after two seasons in the major world League he was receiving only £5 a week for two jobs. He was now beginning to understand the arguments that his teammates had put forward regarding the poor conditions and salaries within the game. It became a subject that came to dominate his thoughts.

At the end of the first post-war season, the Players' Union had tried to obtain an agreement with the Football League to increase the maximum wage for the professional footballer. In terms of professional entertainers to the proportion of crowds they attracted, the pay was ludicrously low, especially for the more talented players. The Union and the League took the matter to a national arbitration board under Lord Terrington, who ruled in favour of the players. The maximum wage was increased to £12 per week during the season and £10 during the summer break, while the minimum wage became £7 and £5. Trautmann was receiving the minimum wage. Although the increases in pay were welcome, many players felt the award was still insufficient despite further benefits with percentages of transfer fees and appearance money. Throughout the 1950s illicit and illegal payments were still prominent throughout the game.

Trautmann opened the 1951–52 season by being offered substantially increased terms, for two reasons. Firstly, the City board and McDowall were aware of Trautmann's dissatisfaction with his remuneration and the knowledge that he was proving to be one of the great goalkeepers and star attractions in the League. The other reason was Trautmann's alien status restrictions on being a full-time professional were about to end and new legislation coming into effect in 1952 released him from his obligations to Bill Proctor. His contract at Manchester City now gave him £12 per week during the season and £10 during the summer, with bonuses of £2 for a win and £1 for a draw. If he played in the reserve team he would only receive £8 per week.

Manchester City returned to the First Division with diluted distinction, gaining only one point from the opening three games. McDowall had still to make the signings he needed and at the end of September went to the board for funds. He had in mind two men of marvellous talent, both of whom would command big transfer fees, and with Walter Smith in alliance McDowall received the go-ahead. The first move was for Ivor Broadis, who cost £25,000 from Sunderland. He was an excellent ballplayer with a whole repertoire of tricks, and the crowd took to him from the start. Two weeks after Broadis, McDowall brought Don Revie to Manchester, an association that was to prove as turbulent as it was successful. City paid £29,000 plus Ernie Phillips as part of the deal with Hull City. The football world was staggered by the transfer fees, while the fans had great expectations from the side. McDowall felt confident now that his team would start to make headway.

Broadis and Revie had an immediate impact with a number of outstanding displays, but they were individual performances rather than all-round team efforts. In Broadis's case, he was a naturally instinctive player and as such fairly unpredictable. On the other hand, Revie, a man of deep intelligence, was a tactician who analysed the game as thoroughly as Trautmann did, and the two of them formed an instinctive affinity.

City were knocked out of the FA Cup in the third round once again, losing 4–1 in a replay to Wolverhampton Wanderers. But, more alarmingly, from early January to mid-April they did not win a single game, and crowds at Maine Road plummeted to 14,000. McDowall and his players were under great pressure and, while the manager tried to convince the board that with patience the results would come, the dressing room atmosphere was tense. Trautmann's displays were, fortunately for City, as reliable as ever, but the team, considering the talent available, was not gelling. Broadis and Revie were not functioning together in the way McDowall had hoped, while the defence was falling apart at the seams.

After a game against West Bromwich Albion had been lost 2–1 at Maine Road, Trautmann sat alone in one of the baths in the dressing room, staring through the steam at the conduit of pipes, deeply depressed. He had given one of his great performances that day, frustrating the West Bromwich forwards time after time. They could well have reached double figures, but his own frustration with the club created doubts in his mind about where his future lay. He had heard from a number of the former Camp 50 players who had returned to Germany and some of them were now playing in the re-emerging German Leagues, and the first notions of a plan began to form.

'I don't know why the team did not reach the potential it should have done, to a certain extent we expected such a lot from Ivor and Don but things did not happen. I discussed this with Revie and he felt that their styles clashed, they both liked to play from deep positions and Don felt they were getting in each others way, a conclusion I had reached. Les McDowall seemed to think that it would just sort itself out, but it was apparent to me that it would not. Ivor was a fast player where Don, on his own admission, needed time and space to play his own game. He was very unhappy with things and told Les McDowall.' Roy Paul was convinced, along with McDowall, that Revie's best position was at wing-half, while Revie was convinced he played better at inside-forward.

'As far as myself was concerned I had started to think seriously about returning to Germany, despite my status as a player in England and the great empathy with the players and people in Manchester, I felt I could enjoy a better lifestyle and have a better financial future for my family if I returned home.' At the end of the season Bert began making moves to secure that future, which in the end were to cause a great deal of heartache and bad feeling.

Manchester City finally pulled themselves up to finish 15th in the division, but Manchester United had won the League Championship convincingly, which was particularly galling to the supporters and club directors. During that year, Ivor Broadis was selected for the England team and Revie, who had been suffering from a groin injury for some of the season, was bitterly disappointed. Revie decided he wanted to leave the club and asked for a transfer. Bert Trautmann decided he was also going to leave but did not tell anyone.

At the end of the season Bert went on his first overseas tour with City, when they played three matches in Spain. It proved an eventful trip for him, and he had to travel on his own because of visa difficulties. When he joined up with the City party they played the first match in the scorching heat of Seville and were slammed 5–1. After winning 3–1 against Real Zaragoza, they were beaten 5–1 again by the mighty Barcelona. He was hugely impressed by the technical skill of the Spaniards, and some of the moves had made City look pedestrian in terms of speed and invention. They were the sort of football skills that were so well known to the players in Germany, skills that were sorely lacking in England. During the trip Bert had his wallet stolen, upset the locals by walking out on a bullfight and on his return caught the wrong train home and finished up in Liverpool, not Manchester. He had a two-month break before the start of the season, and it was now that he started to put into action his plan for returning to Germany for good – getting himself involved in the most bizarre of situations.

Trautmann had received a letter from Karl Krause suggesting that his own club, Schalke 04, would be interested in signing him if he wanted to return to Germany. He immediately replied indicating he was very interested, but he would have to give good reasons to City for his release. Bert made it known that he was becoming increasingly worried about the health of his mother and that his family had fallen on distressed times, and so he would be going to visit them in Bremen before the season started. Margaret did not want to go along on the trip, she thought John was too young to be travelling, and so, at the beginning of June, Trautmann made arrangements to travel to Germany. Early in 1952 a letter had arrived at Maine Road from Peter Kularz, Bert's old army colleague in Russia who was now living in Bickendorf, Cologne. Kularz had invited his old friend to visit him if he was in the area, and in a burst of nostalgia and affection Bert decided to stop off in Cologne before meeting up with Krause. He arranged to fly to Düsseldorf where Peter was to meet him. Trautmann later recorded, 'When I arrived at the airport I walked through the reception hall but could not see Peter anywhere. I passed a small group of people and was looking around when I felt someone tap me on the shoulder. I turned and looked into the face of a man I had never seen before. He smiled at me and asked if I was unable to recognise him. I certainly did not and when he held out his hand I shook it half-heartedly. He told me he was Peter Kularz.'

This man looked nothing like Peter, and Bert thought even the most skilled surgeon could not have reconstructed his face to look like this. Intrigued, he allowed himself to be driven to Cologne in the man's car. Peter was strangely reticent to talk about the war, with Trautmann providing all the reminiscence, and by the time the car arrived at the house in Bickendorf he was deeply suspicious. These suspicions were further aroused when, within minutes of arriving, a newspaper reporter turned up to interview him. Other than Kularz, nobody knew he was in the area. The Pressman asked about his career in England and took a photograph, which appeared in the morning Press together with a report outlining his visit to Cologne, where he was visiting an old army friend named Peter Kularz. In another part of Cologne a disfigured ex-paratrooper read the report with disbelief and immediately telephoned the newspaper office to find out where in Cologne Trautmann was staying

That evening Kularz took Trautmann to a restaurant near to Cologne football stadium. Shortly afterwards a man joined them at their table and introduced himself as Herr Kramer. He was a director of Cologne Football Club. Kramer got straight to the point. He had heard rumours that Trautmann wanted to return to Germany. He wanted him to sign for Cologne. At last the penny dropped with Trautmann and he realised he had been set up. Regardless of that, he was interested in what Kramer had to say and, without committing himself, agreed to meet again the following evening. In truth, Trautmann was a little worried by his situation. This was an illegal tap by Cologne, and he was hardly able to agree to anything without formal approaches to his club. He returned to Kularz's home in an anxious state and still had not faced the fact that Kularz was not the man he knew from Russia. He was still going along with the game in his own naive way and decided to see what would happen. Events unfolded the following day.

The next morning Trautmann returned with Kularz from a visit to the city and found Mrs Kularz in an anxious state. She told Bert a man had been to the house hoping to see him and he was going to call back later. Bert asked who he was. 'His name was Peter Kularz,' she replied.

Trautmann sat down and refused to say anything other than, 'OK, let's wait to find out what's going on.'

The melodrama continued when a furious banging at the door was answered by Mrs Kularz.

Trautmann recalled, 'I heard a voice I easily recognised: "*Ich bin wielder da. Ich bin Peter Kularz* – I have returned. I am Peter Kularz." I called out "*Komm herein Peter*" and in walked the visitor. Badly disfigured as he was, I recognised my Peter Kularz immediately, the Peter Kularz from the Russian battlefield.'

Trautmann's real Kularz glared at him and asked in the Jack Friar and Burnley style, 'What the bloody hell is going on?' According to Trautmann, his host really was named, coincidentally, Peter Kularz and he had, through various means, contrived to act as an agent on his own initiative to entice Trautmann to join Cologne.

He had read in an article that Bert had expressed a wish to return to Germany when the conditions were right, an interview given two years previously. Acting as Trautmann's unofficial agent he had approached Krammer at Cologne and suggested he might be interested in signing Trautmann, while Kularz in turn received some *ex-gratia* payment for his efforts. The original Peter Kularz had managed to track Bert through the newspaper. Again, according to Trautmann, 'Peter had tried unsuccess-fully to get the address from the newspaper concerned. The photograph appeared again the following morning and Peter went along to see the editor to explain about his friendship with me and how he was convinced I had been duped by this other Kularz. But here at least was one editor who didn't recognise a good story when he heard one, and poor Peter was literally pushed out of the office.' Kularz had eventually traced him through the reporter who took the photograph.

Trautmann and his friend Kularz left the house and arrived at the next Kularz house, where Bert caught up with his friend and family.

Rumours of Trautmann signing for Cologne circulated around the city, and the newspapers, sensing a good story, descended on both Kularz homes, incidentally a couple of kilometres apart. The 'fake' Kularz made no comment while Trautmann and the 'real' Kularz were picked up by Karl Krause and driven through the late evening to Gelsenkirchen.

Trautmann had left himself wide open to speculation. If the first editor had not recognised a good story others were in pursuit, but, with Trautmann away from the scene, Kularz in Bickendorf incommunicado and Kramer at Cologne without comment, the answers to obvious questions were not given.

If Trautmann was convinced the Cologne (to use his own words) 'third man' was dubious, why didn't he walk away from the situation?

He had been spotted at the same time with Kramer, a prominent man in Cologne, with Kularz in attendance, and was not in a position to deny the meeting. Above all, his naivety, on his own admission his great fault, had put him up the creek without a paddle. As the trio headed north towards their destination, Trautmann was consumed with worry that the story would break in England. Fortunately it didn't, but whispers had reached Manchester on the grapevine that Trautmann might be leaving.

Again nothing was followed up and Bert was allowed to dig another huge hole that proved difficult to fill in. On arrival at Gelsenkirchen, Trautmann and Kularz were installed in a first-class hotel. Krause arranged to pick them up the following day and introduce Bert to Albert Wildfang, the president of Schalke 04. Bert and Peter had a couple of beers and retired to bed.

In Germany at that time the German Football Association were building slowly towards a unified league system, but the Leagues were still on a regional basis with the winners of them going on to the national championship finals at the end of the season. The players were all part-time and the majority worked for the directors' own companies or for friends of the directors, who were more than happy to release their employees for training and matches for the clubs – not unlike Trautmann, Proctor and Manchester City.

Karl Krause worked as a chauffeur to Wildfang, driving his boss between various social and business appointments, while the rest of his time was spent at the football club training and playing. Like England, the postwar German public were piling into the stadiums to watch their teams, and the standard of play was improved further as the league clubs developed their structures. These were, to a certain extent, based on the pre-war structure. As a yardstick the rest of the European clubs were formed from huge sports clubs, Barcelona and Real Madrid in Spain, or from large industrial concerns who had interests in Juventus in Italy or PSV Eindhoven in Holland. Germany kept to the pre-war system of large sports clubs with several teams from eight year olds to the senior sides, like the Tura club in Bremen. They also offered a diverse number of sports and as such they had large memberships.

One other consideration about post-war Germany was the introduction of George Marshall's plan of economic aid to Europe to restore the industrial fortunes of the continent. Germany had benefited more than most and responded eagerly and practically. Trautmann, who had heard of Germany's economic revival in letters from friends and family and from his regular perusal of available German newspapers, was now seeing, on his first visit for three years, the great developments Germany had made. The huge rebuilding programme was well under way and the shops had a far greater variety of goods and food available than in England, a country that in 1952 was still subject to rationing. He became proud of the way his country had responded to recovering from the war years.

Trautmann was immediately impressed by the terms Albert Wildfang had to offer, a player-coach position at £100 per month, plus a petrol station and garage that Bert would own and run as his own business. It was also pointed out to him that Sepp Herberger, the national coach, was building up a revolutionary coaching system and a useful-looking national team, who were to be admitted by FIFA into the 1954 World Cup Finals. Although Germany would not have much of a chance, Trautmann could become an important part of the squad and his contribution would be valuable to his country. Trautmann needed little persuading, as he said at the time, 'My future would be guaranteed and in every respect the offer was far too generous to ignore.'

It was now down to Wildfang to make an official approach to Manchester City, and he told Trautmann he would do this in the autumn. After a final evening with Peter Kularz, who returned to Cologne the following day by train, Karl Krause had Wildfang's car at his and Bert's disposal so they headed further north to Bremen where the Trautmann family had yet another muted reunion.

To a degree, Frieda was not in the best of health. Bert's mother, in her mid-50s, was unhappy and prone to fits of depression. She had given up hope of her Bernd returning for good, while Karl-Heinz, who had been unemployed for a while just before Bert's visit, had been making plans to marry his fiancée Craudi and would soon be fleeing the nest. Karl-Heinz was, to some extent, grudgingly aware of his brother's fame but was still an insular individual. On his visit Bert discovered that Karl-Heinz had escaped after the war by panyer, a wooden horse-drawn buggy, all the way from Hungary to his home, eluding both his own forces and the Allies, a formidable feat of skill and endurance. Bert looked at his younger brother in a new light of respect.

As the prodigal son, Bert Trautmann thought he would return home in a blaze of glory, fame and secure future. A few little details had to be attended to in Manchester first, like telling his wife and his employers he wanted to leave. If he stopped to think about it long enough, both very daunting prospects, and so it would prove.

# FURTHER CONTROVERSY, AN UNHAPPY TIME AND THE MAGICAL MAGYARS

*The 100,000 crowd rubbed its eyes in disbelief. Few, if any, had ever seen such astonishing football before. The Hungarians were as men from another planet.*

GEOFFREY GREEN

TRAUTMANN arrived back in Bramhall stimulated by his prospects in Germany and confident that any deal with Schalke would progress quickly and without any major problems, a naive assumption at the very least. He did not tell Jack or Margaret about his plans and quietly waited for events to unfold.

He started his pre-season training in a buoyant mood and Nobby Clarke, in particular, noticed his happy state. In private Bert discussed his wish to return to Germany and his divided loyalty to his country and England, but he kept the move he had negotiated to himself. He mentioned to McDowall his desire of one day returning to Germany to play and coach, but a transfer request was not mentioned.

The season opened with a depressing run of results for the team and murmurs of discontent from the players concerning the way McDowall was managing the club. He began with a number of changes to the established side, particularly at centre-forward where four different players were used without success. Unsuccessful positional changes did little for any consistency, and by October Manchester City, together with Manchester United, were bottom of the First Division. This coincided with the news that Trautmann might be leaving Maine Road.

He had now started to make comments to a number of reporters, notably to Eric Thornton and Eric Todd at the Manchester papers, and Press speculation of his departure from Maine Road began to grow.

Schalke had contacted him late in October and indicated their intention of sending over a deputation to England. Trautmann quickly warned them not to contact him directly, to keep away from his home and for them to open negotiations formally with the City board. Eventually a telegram arrived at the house in Bramhall from Karl Krause. Schalke representatives would be arriving in

England officially to watch the international against Belgium at Wembley on 25 November, before watching Manchester City play Derby County on the 28th.

Albert Wildfang, his son Dieter and the coach, Fritz Szepan, arrived secretly in Manchester on 26 November. Trautmann met with them at a clandestine rendez-vous in their hotel, where it was agreed Wildfang senior would approach City for guest tickets as part of their visit to study English football and to assess tactics. Bob Smith, Walter Smith and Les McDowall smelt a rat immediately. The newspaper reports on Trautmann's unrest and now this visit by the Germans fuelled their suspicions but, nevertheless, the directors offered, out of courtesy, the hospitality of Maine Road, and the three Germans were treated with a generous welcome. They were shown around the stadium, looked at the facilities and then joined the directors in the main stand for the match. It was noticeable that their eyes were on Trautmann's every move during the game.

Afterwards Trautmann made a brief appearance to be introduced to his fellow countrymen before the Wildfangs and Szepan were invited into the directors' lounge for drinks. Bert had arranged to meet them at their hotel later in the evening. The original plan, as far as Trautmann had been aware, was for Wildfang to thank City for their welcome, perhaps to suggest a friendly between the two teams and then suggest to City they might be interested in transferring their goalkeeper to his club and make a formal offer.

Such was the confidence of Trautmann and the Schalke delegation in assuming City would agree, they had done little to address the complications of the English transfer system, the binding contractual conditions, or given any consideration to a transfer fee. In the German Leagues players transferring between clubs were signed for fees relative to their wage structure. Thus, if a player was earning £15 a week a total of £750, the equivalent of one year's salary, was paid to secure his registration. Any notions of larger sums were completely alien to the system.

The lack of research by Schalke into the English transfer values meant that any hopes of an immediate move were quashed, and Trautmann's own naive belief that City would let him go easily was quickly dampened. Once ensconced with the City directors and without any formal build up, Wildfang immediately offered £1,000 for Trautmann's transfer to Schalke. The grizzled jowls of Bob Smith wobbled with indignation. 'He's worth twenty times that,' replied the chairman. Albert, Dieter and Fritz gulped on their drinks at the figure of around 200,000 marks at the 10.52 exchange rate. The negotiations came to an abrupt halt and the Germans, feeling savaged by City's valuation, returned to their hotel to lick their wounds. Trautmann joined them, expecting City to have agreed to a transfer, and was astonished to discover the size of the fee that had been mentioned.

While forwards and wing-halves regularly commanded fees of over £20,000, no goalkeeper had commanded such a large figure, the record at the time being around £7,000. Trautmann felt desperate, he had already told Eric Todd his move back to Germany was being negotiated, and in an exclusive that night the *Evening Chronicle* had reported, under a story from their own correspondent originating from Berlin, the presence of officials in England, who were having preliminary talks with Manchester City. Todd completed the article under a separate byline in which he outlined Trautmann's ambitions to return home, and Todd was sympathetic to those ambitions.

The following day the nationals had picked up the story and once again Trautmann caused all hell to break loose. The words of Jack Friar came back to haunt him again, 'Well you've made your own bed, now you'll have to lie in it.' The fact Bert had neglected to inform his wife and father-in-law of his plans to return to Germany caused Jack more despair, while Margaret was furious that he had not discussed it with her and was adamant she would not live in Germany. Bert explained for the first time to his family the offer from Schalke, telling Margaret of the progress his countrymen had made in rebuilding Germany and the exciting prospects available for them over there. Jack was impressed by the possibilities, and he urged Margaret to think again. She was at her most obstinate and refused to discuss the matter any further. Trautmann, in turn, was desperately unhappy about the turn of events, but his own stubborn nature made him determined to secure his transfer.

At Manchester City the directors and McDowall were all now certain that an illegal 'tap' had been made on their player, and the possibility of Trautmann's involvement in the affair became more obvious as articles appeared in the newspapers, which made both Smiths furious. They contained their anger and Bob Smith and Les McDowall made statements.

Smith stated: 'Prior to our interview with the German representatives, Trautmann's transfer had never been discussed by the City board and, anyway, how could any such sum be transferred from Germany to this country under present currency restrictions?'

In turn, McDowall issued a statement in which he commented, 'There are no negotiations at the present time. I don't wish to complicate matters further, but even if we did decide to transfer Trautmann to Schalke there must be a transfer fee. Manchester City, like any other League club, need some sort of protection, and although we ourselves did get him cheaply enough we have also tried to do our very best for him.'

In the meantime, Albert Wildfang, in an interview with *Die Welt*, was putting forward his version of the story, particularly regarding the size of the transfer fee. 'After the match we attended in Manchester we had talks with the Manchester officials and all our proposals were heard quietly. I explained to them the conditions of contracting a player in Germany and told them we could find a sum of £1,000. They replied, laughingly, under no circumstances would they part with him for that sum, Trautmann was worth much more, in fact twenty times more.'

The relationship between Trautmann and his employers were as strained as an injured ligament.

Bert was approached by the *Evening Chronicle* to give his side of the story and it was billed as yet another exclusive, headlined, 'Why I have to leave Manchester

City'. Trautmann gave his version of the events, which were an aggregate of the reasons concocted in Germany with Krause. He opened the story by stating he would be returning to Germany at the end of the season, regardless. He then went on to explain he had made a promise to his mother to return home, she had been in poor health for four years and that he had been deeply shocked by her physical condition. He went on to describe the awful conditions she and his brother, Karl-Heinz, were living in and his determination to provide for them. Bert also stated that his wife and her family would stand by him in his decision. He was digging himself a very large hole indeed.

With the *Evening Chronicle* and Eric Todd in support, they followed his article by publishing an emotive letter to the Manchester City board from Basil Easterbrook, a Kemsley Newspaper Group journalist writing for the nationals in London. Easterbrook wrote a long, rhetorical article about freedom and the philosophy of natural harmony and accord with others.

He concluded with, 'You are reported as having asked £20,000 from a German club for his transfer, this ex-PoW who cost you a £10 signing fee. You know as well as I do that no goalkeeper who ever breathed, not even Frank Swift at the peak of his career, has ever been worth that kind of money.'

Perhaps Easterbrook should have asked why a goalkeeper was not worth that kind of money, perhaps he should have suggested City might have bought Gil Merrick or Jack Kelsey, the English and Welsh internationals respectively, to replace Trautmann, they, after all, had not cost Arsenal and Birmingham City much when they were signed and perhaps their clubs would happily accept £1,000 offers. Unfortunately, Basil Easterbrook and a number of other journalists were not aware of the full facts, and Trautmann was fully aware that the furore had been caused by his inexcusable deceit. In his own mind a number of doubts had appeared about his move back to Germany. His more immediate reaction was to observe the various twists and turns as the circumstances developed.

McDowall became less diplomatic in his next statement. 'I was led to believe the Germans had come to England to study football methods, but it is possible their visit to Maine Road was a 'cover' for negotiations leading up to inquiries about Trautmann.' In reality, McDowall was saying Trautmann had been tapped, City knew it, Schalke knew it and so did the player – and so did the journalists by now. Trautmann did not give in and, needing to save face, he wrote to both Stanley Rous, the FA secretary, and to Fred Howarth, secretary of the Football League, in which he repeated the reasons stated in his newspaper article for his need to return to Germany. He then sent a similar letter to Bob Smith pleading for his release, but without mentioning his letters to Rous and Howarth. Bob Smith did not reply to his letter and developed, with McDowall, a new strategy in handling the problem. They would make no further comment and refused to discuss the matter further with the Press or with the player.

When details of Trautmann's letter to Rous were made known to Bob Smith he immediately sent one of his own giving City's version of the events and did not pull any punches. He accused Schalke of making an illegal approach to one of his players, a club whose own Football Association were members of FIFA and to whom Manchester City would make an official complaint through Rous if Schalke continued to make erroneous statements to the German and English newspapers.

Rous replied diplomatically that he regarded it as a situation to be handled between the club and player, while at the same time making the German FA aware of the problem. The message was passed on to Gelsenkirchen.

Trautmann was now a worried and troubled man. He was expecting some form of disciplinary action by his employers and an article by Archie Ledbrooke in the *Daily Despatch* brought out the real issues, which Smith had stated in his letter to Rous.

*'Footballers are notoriously out of touch with the rules and Trautmann can be excused for discussing his future with another club, but for Schalke there is no such get-out. In my opinion, Manchester City have a duty to other League clubs to draw the attention of the FA to what was undoubtedly an improper approach to a professional footballer – poaching is the non-technical word.*

*It was just as illegal as though it had been done by an English club because West Germany are in membership with FIFA, whose members acknowledge each other's contract.*

*Do the Continental clubs think they can have the benefit of international matches and all the other privileges of FIFA without sharing the responsibility? Arising out of this illegal approach Manchester City stand to suffer abuse from Football fans not fully cognisant of the rules or the background of these affairs.*

*If foreign clubs are allowed the law of the jungle – which means no law at all – players may well be given leave to go Bogotá or Eire as in the old days when there was a real threat that playing contracts would be valueless.'*

It is more than probable that Bob Smith had let the contents of this letter be known to Ledbrooke, who had been particularly vexed by the exodus of players to Colombia in 1950. More newspaper men took up the sentiments expressed by Ledbrooke. Schalke and Trautmann had blown it, and Bert now had to face an angry football club and public.

A torrent of letters was still pouring into the club and newspapers about the affair – it was as large a controversy as the time he first signed for the club. One supporter pointed out that Trautmann was supposed to be the best goalkeeper in the First Division and yet they were at the bottom, they could still be there if they had had the worst goalkeeper! He went on to suggest City sign Doug Daniels of Accrington Stanley, he was a local boy and, 'If he wanted to see his mother, he would only have to go to Salford.' Hardly helpful to Trautmann's cause.

By the middle of December the publicity and the subject was closed. Trautmann was not disciplined by his club, who did not wish to antagonise him further, while at home he convinced Margaret his actions stemmed only from his wish to improve their lifestyle. He also persuaded her to make a visit to Bremen with him the following summer. The storm slowly blew itself out and the season continued.

Les McDowall was still making disastrous tactical switches with his team and decided to move Roy Paul to centre-half, resulting in 12 goals against them in two matches. The blending of Broadis with Revie was still not working, and with the Trautmann affair still a cause for unspoken bitterness at the club they entered 1953 as firm favourites for relegation.

McDowall could not get his team formation right, and Trautmann was lifting his net to drag the ball out with dismaying regularity. For a team of thinking footballers this was a disheartening experience. Don Revie thought the team had a strong defence, but the goals were piling against them, and the attack was an impressive and talented forward line, but the goals were not going their way.

'We were a team of two units,' Revie said, 'but there was nothing to link us together properly.'

Another problem was the continuing aloofness of Les McDowall. Revie, together with Paul, Trautmann and Clarke, had regular discussions on team tactics, but McDowall was not receptive to any of their ideas, preferring to devise his own plans before passing them on to the trainers or briefing the team only in pre-match team talks. His reserved nature isolated him from the players and difficulties on the field continued.

In February the real crisis came. City were walloped 6–0 by Cardiff City, who had not scored a goal in the League for two and a half months, and by March, with six more games to play, they were in dire straits. They managed to collect three points from their next three games before they were on the receiving end of another thrashing, this time at the hands of Derby County, the bottom club already consigned to the Second Division. City were saved from relegation by meeting Blackpool a week before their opponents were to play in the 1953 Cup Final. City tore into the careful Blackpool team, winning 5–0, and escaped relegation by the skin of their teeth, finishing one point above Stoke City. The record of 87 goals against was the worst in the division and Trautmann felt cruelly hurt by this statistic.

Immediately the season finished, Trautmann needed to distance himself from his year of discontent and made plans for Margaret and John to accompany him to Germany.

Margaret met Bert's parents for the first time in early June. They were utterly charmed by their daughter-in-law, who was in fine form and relaxed on her first journey outside of England, and adored John. Bert did all he could to arouse Margaret's enthusiasm for Germany. He took her on shopping expeditions, showed her the countryside and parks, while all the time expounding the benefits in education, health care and housing.

The authorities and people of Bremen greeted Bert and his family with great affection, he was now one of their famous sons, and his visit generated immense interest from the Press and radio, to which he gave a number of interviews. Trautmann again stated his interest in returning as a player and coach.

In his own mind Bert was anxious for some international recognition and despaired at not being able to play for his national team. He had no thoughts of becoming a nationalised British subject, he was proud of his nationality and the credit he had brought to Germany, but by playing in England he would never be considered for the German team. Sepp Herberger was fully convinced of Trautmann's playing talents and strengths, but he needed Trautmann readily available as, at that time, the idea of footballers playing in foreign leagues and returning for international fixtures was fraught with political and travel difficulties.

Herberger had to consider, therefore, the problems of gaining regular release from Manchester City and at the same time introducing a 'foreign' player into his closely-knit and loyal squad, with its implications towards petty rivalry and jealousy. Trautmann met Herberger during his visit, and Sepp explained his reasons for Trautmann's exclusion from his plans, reasons Bert fully respected. He had a great admiration for the national coach and his methods and the exciting potential for the German players, and he also knew he could be included if he was playing in one of the German leagues.

Trautmann had a lot to consider as he prepared to return to England. His 30th birthday was approaching and he envisaged only three or four seasons before seriously considering retirement. While he was an immensely popular and successful player, the lack of success with the team continued to discourage him, and he was not instilled with any high hopes for 1953–54. The idea of a job as a player-coach became more appealing, but in Germany a coach had to be fully qualified before he took charge of a team. The German FA had started a coaching course at Cologne University, far more comprehensive than the English FA's coaching badge, which included many other aspects of sports management. Trautmann decided to apply for the two-year course. He hoped a German club would make a formal transfer bid to City and arrived for training in early August convinced it would be his last in the English League. His one most important problem to resolve now was Margaret. She had enjoyed her visit enormously but, unhappily for her husband, she was not convinced by his judgement they would have a happier life there. He would have to apply all his persuasive arguments over the next year.

Bert arrived at Maine Road in his new car, a Volkswagen Beetle, to the amusement of his teammates. He had been riding around on a motorcycle during his initial years at City or was usually picked up by Ken Barnes on training days. His financial resources having improved considerably since 1952, he naturally plumped with pride for his country's most famous car.

Rumours that City had received offers for Trautmann were circulating again at the start of the season, including one from Werder Bremen, however, McDowall gave no indication of the interest, while the goalkeeper waited impatiently for any developments.

Bob Smith and his manager were more determined than ever to keep Trautmann at Manchester City. They were coming under increasing criticism from supporters concerning the team's dreadful performances over the past seasons, and if Trautmann was allowed to leave they would have an even greater crisis on their hands. Bob Smith remained loyal to McDowall; he was, after all, his chosen man, while McDowall was hoping for more money from the board to strengthen his side.

During the close season they had invested in floodlighting and other stadium improvements, and as a result the manager faced the new season with instructions to make do with his current squad, buy cheaply if possible, but, above all, ensure Trautmann stayed. Len Shackleton's infamous blank page in his book that depicted the average director's knowledge of football struck a chord with McDowall. Regardless of the fact the directors were ignorant to a great extent, they were businessmen and Bob Smith knew better than anyone that Trautmann was a crowd-puller.

At this time Bert Trautmann was still blighted by intermittent interviews by British Military Intelligence, who were keeping former German soldiers remaining in the United Kingdom under surveillance. The insinuation that he was still possibly under suspicion of Nazism did nothing for his frame of mind, although the inter-views were conducted with the utmost cordiality, indeed the intelligence officers were often in awe of talking to this most famous of former prisoners and more often than not the conversation was overtaken by football. On one occasion at an interview at Belle Vue, where City would often be training in the pre-season, an officer who had been involved in the operation at Kleve told a fascinated Bert over 8,000 varying aircraft had passed over the town that day. He had often thought he might be exaggerating when his own estimation had been around 3,000. His nationality was still an issue though and his inner conflicts in respect to his country of allegiance nagged at his thoughts repeatedly. His fame and family life had been gained in England, a country – despite its inadequacies – he loved, while at the same time his fame could secure a better fortune in his own country, which he now missed. He was becoming exceedingly forlorn in his attempt to reconcile this conflict. As always, he turned to Jack Friar for solace and understanding.

Jack pointed out that as long as Bert's employers held his registration, Manchester City held all the cards and, until such time that the professional footballers could change the contractual structure, he would have to sit it out. But, practical as ever, Jack also pointed out the high expectations the German nation would have of him if he returned to play there. With this food for thought, Trautmann faced the 1953–54 season.

Bob Smith's assessment of Trautmann's crowd-pulling was confirmed by an invitation from Frankfurt FSV to play in a pre-season friendly in Frankfurt, and the German club offered £1,000 plus a guaranteed £500 if the goalkeeper played.

Manchester City travelled on the route well known to Trautmann, the Harwich ferry to the Hook of Holland. The party were to take the Rhine express on to Frankfurt, but once again Trautmann's visa arrangements were not satisfactory and the team went on without him. He was left behind to organise his own visa and waited for some hours to catch the next train to Frankfurt, together with an intrigued Miss Wood, the daughter of Sir Henry Wood who was the instigator and founder of the London Promenade concerts. She was captivated by his Lancastrian German, and they both enjoyed each other's company on the eastward journey. City had arrived in Frankfurt without their main attraction, much to the dismay of the waiting Press and public. Such was his charismatic appeal that hundreds were still awaiting his arrival, and he was besieged by reporters when he turned up five hours later. Bert was linked up to speak to Frieda in Bremen by the German Radio Service. He felt overwhelmed by his welcome.

The match itself was attended by 35,000 spectators and started spectacularly as the match-ball was dropped on to the field by a passing helicopter. Trautmann's adrenalin was flowing, he desperately wanted to do well in front of his fellow countrymen and felt a little annoyed by the *laissez-faire* attitude of his side, who regarded the game as just a warm-up for the season with nothing at stake. Trautmann had a lot to prove to his nation and to the watching German league club representatives. He urged his team to put on a good show. After an entertaining but goalless first half Trautmann and, to his surprise, McDowall urged the team to step up a gear. They did, established a 2–0 lead and, to Bert's further annoyance, sat back on their advantage. Don Revie contrived to handle a throughball in the penalty area to give away a penalty, which Bert spectacularly saved. The roar of approval was immense. The German football public had seen the famous Bert Trautmann play for the first time as a professional on his own soil and were completely overwhelmed by his talent and virtuosity. The resulting 2–2 draw was an acceptable result, and after a pleasant three-day visit the City organisation returned to Manchester to start the new First Division campaign.

Les McDowall arrived back from Germany very impressed by the innovations there and also by way the clubs were organised. He came back full of ideas but, as always, refused to share them with a collection of players yearning for new direction and receptive to any new ideas.

Unhappily, it was the same old story for City as the first matches were played, they were good in patches, atrocious in others and by October were once again in the lower reaches of the division. McDowall accepted by now that Broadis and Revie were not the ideal partnership and, after a great deal of thinking, he decided one would have to go. To the surprise of many he sold Broadis. He knew at the back of his mind Don Revie could be the foundation of an excellent team, but the solution to his problem was still to be found.

Around the time of Broadis's departure from Maine Road two friendlies against Fenerbahçe of Turkey and Admira Vienna were played. His side had performed well against technically superior teams, playing a typically controlled British side.

Les McDowall knew, somewhere within his enclosed thoughts, that a combination of control and technical superiority would give him a winning for-mula. This conclusion had already been reached by Trautmann, Revie, Roy Paul and Nobby Clarke, but how they could produce the kind of football they wanted to play within the capabilities of the players available became just as unsolvable to them as it was to McDowall.

On Wednesday 25 November 1953 the answer became obvious. Hungary defeated England by six goals to three at Wembley with a display of brilliant football. The main revelation was the unorthodox centre-forward play of Nandor Hidegkuti, a 30-year-old veteran whose game was played 'behind' his inside-forwards. His uncanny understanding with Ferenc Puskás and the half-back Jozsef Bozsik, the small but perfectly formed politician from Budapest, was phenomenal, and with the very agile Gyula Grosics in goal the Hungarians were formidable. In the Chorlton-cum-Hardy suburbs of Manchester, the City 'Mafia' of Revie, Paul, Clarke and Johnny Williamson, the City reserve forward, watched on television, mesmerised by the Magyars' ability. In leafy Bramhall, Bert Trautmann sat on the edge of his armchair with disbelief, this stunning display of football was exactly the same as his own idea of how the game should be played and developed.

On the following morning the Manchester City players reported for training in an excited huddle and discussed with a relentless passion the Hungarian display. The trainers and coaches arrived and dished out the usual stint of lapping the pitch and circuit training in the gymnasium. Les McDowall was not unmoved by the Hungarian display but regrettably moved in the wrong direction.

Over the following two months he made nearly 40 team changes as he struggled to create the right blend of players. The first team's dream of emulating the Hungarian display was obliterated by an array of obscure and disruptive team selection. McDowall's profligate decisions reduced the collective enthusiasm of the team into disarray and as December approached the mood at the club was, once again, one of unfilled ambition. If only McDowall could communicate with his players somehow the unanimity that was so desperately needed could be realised.

In Trautmann's case, things were not helped by a new bout of speculation in the Manchester papers relating to a new development in a possible transfer to Germany.

Eric Todd in another *Evening Chronicle* exclusive had revealed plans by a German football pools company to transfer him back for a fee of £25,000. Could this possibly be Bert's most hoped-for Christmas present?

# SPECULATION, PERSONAL TURMOIL AND THE BEGINNINGS OF A PLAN

*minds ignorant of stern miraculous*
*this every truth – beware of heartless them*
*(given the scalpel, they dissect a kiss;*
*or, sold the reason, they undream a dream)*

E.E.CUMMINGS

ON 10 DECEMBER 1953, Eric Todd, in his article in the *Manchester Evening Chronicle*, suggested a German football pools company were organising a bid to transfer Trautmann and quoted a fee of £25,000. Todd's information came from an unknown source, about an unnamed organisation who were willing to raise the equivalent of 250,000 marks, which would allow Trautmann to return to Germany. Curiously enough Schalke 04 of Gelsenkirchen were, according to Todd, to be the main beneficiaries of the scheme.

He outlined the concept of the arrangement thus: 'Each investor on the pools will be asked to increase his investment each week over a period of four weeks by ten pfennigs (around 5d) and the extra money will go to a Bert Trautmann fund. Inside four weeks it is estimated that 200,000 marks will be raised. This money would go to a transfer pool and the pools promoters would seek another 25,000 marks to make up the difference and this balance would be paid over by the club Bert wished to join.'

In effect the article was saying that the German public, irrespective of what club they owed their allegiance to, were willing to raise the money for another club to then play Trautmann against their own side. The successful German club would have complete control of his contract while the pools company clients would have the great satisfaction of bringing him home. Todd went on to say the German football public were anxious to have him back and implicated that their one and only desire was to enable him to be included in Sepp Herberger's World Cup plans.

Trautmann was completely mystified by this turn of events and he had no prior indication of the plan. Neither had he discussed the possibility with Todd before the article appeared. He was, however, stimulated by the revolutionary nature of the proposal and excited by the possibilities.

Jack Friar quickly advised him not to make any rash statements until the fuller details were available, and certainly not until the Manchester City board had time to consider the offer. In an expedient response to the speculation he commented, 'It is a splendid gesture and one that I appreciate tremendously. Of course I should like to go back to Germany and play and coach for my own country; but everything depends on the attitude of Manchester City.'

The attitude of Manchester City was slightly baffled, no formal proposals had been received and it was as much a surprise to them as it was to Trautmann. The chairman of Manchester City was asked for his statement on the subject by Eric Todd, and he naturally asked the instigator of the reports for more details. Todd could not provide them, and Bob Smith became more utterly despairing with the renewed speculation about Trautmann. Nevertheless, he issued a cautious statement. 'It is certainly something to think about, it is of course by far the biggest fee ever offered for a goalkeeper and any such offer, whoever the player, must obviously be given serious thought. I cannot give any answer without consulting my colleagues on the board and we should be very sorry to lose Trautmann, but as I say it is a big offer and will require serious thought. Until we get that offer, however, I think it would be wiser to say no more.'

In private, Bob Smith was absolutely furious with Todd and also considered Trautmann had again been illegally approached. Smith decided if the offer did arrive he would not put up any great objection, but his board would screw the Germans for whatever they could get. Presumably he and McDowall would then be able to afford a bid for Doug Daniels of Accrington Stanley.

McDowall, himself under increasing pressure as the performances of his team were degenerating each week, issued a separate statement to the general Press. 'We are not interested. We are not in need of money but of top class players – Traut-mann is certainly one. He was naturally eager to return home when the last approach was made but now seems very happy and as far as we are concerned, he stays at Maine Road.'

Three contrasting statements had now been made, and the chairman, the manager and the player all seemed to be contradicting one another.

In reality, the two contrasting statements by the chairman and manager were a collusion. Manchester City had not received any offer and they viewed Todd's journalistic enterprise with a deep suspicion. This suspicion was further developed when Todd did not follow up his story with any further details. Bob Smith declared the story was a total canard to his fellow directors and with good reason. He was fully conversant with the rivalry between the two Manchester papers, and he was on more personal terms with Eric Thornton of the *Evening News* than with Todd, who in turn had developed a good professional relationship with Trautmann. Bert himself was beginning to learn the politics of football and journalism.

This author, after comprehensive research, could find no foundation for the pools story. The German Football Association had no information in their own records, while the archives of the German newspaper had all quoted their sources of the story from the *Manchester Evening Chronicle*.

Bert Trautmann himself could not throw any light on the mysterious origin of the reports and it could well be Eric Todd, a much-respected journalist, was the victim of an elaborate hoax.

It is possible the foundation of the story came from dissatisfaction with the lack of funding by English pools companies, a subject of much debate over the years.

In other parts of Europe, most notably in Scandinavia, large amounts of pools profits were contributed to national sports projects. There was certainly a great lobby in England among sports journalists and footballers for a proportion of the vast pools revenues to be allocated back into football. Just after the war the pools companies had made some offers to the Football League, which had been rejected, while each season some new speculation was put forward. The subject was certainly close to Trautmann's heart, and Todd could have picked up his thread of thought as the basis of the article. Trautmann approached Christmas a confused man, while the niggling doubts about returning to Germany came back.

These doubts were based on the immediate success his countrymen would expect from him, he was a great believer in Sepp Herberger's philosophy that the foundation for any successful team lay in long-term planning and the development of a sound youth policy. An immediate example of this was just across the city of Manchester where Matt Busby was building up a fine youth squad, many of whom were now breaking into the first team.

One of Trautmann's great weaknesses was criticism, he could not face any form of stricture and was deeply hurt by any disparaging remarks about his play, and he knew if things did not go right for him then the Germans would be merciless. The difference in the professionalism of his City teammates and the playing attitude of the Germans also became an important issue. At Maine Road any mistakes were acknowledged, the players accepted they could happen and they backed each other up whereas the continentals seemed to bicker and criticise each other during a game and in the Press. Regardless of City's terrible recent performances, the morale and rapport between the players was first class, even if collectively they were a little melancholy about their failures. Trautmann became further confused when Margaret indicated she was having second thoughts and considering the possibilities of living in Germany. Jack's wise counsel was again sought and he urged Bert to remain patient and await the outcome.

At Maine Road, Les McDowall was busy trying to revive the fortunes of the club and had been active in the transfer market during the last month of the year, busily spending some of the money received from the sale of Ivor Broadis. At the behest of Bob Smith he had signed another goalkeeper as cover for Trautmann, not as urgent reserve cover because Trautmann's exceptional fitness had caused him to miss only one game since his debut at Bolton Wanderers. Smith's reasoning was more insidious, he wanted an experienced goalkeeper available if Trautmann did leave.

John Savage, a huge, 1.92 metre-tall man, was bought from Halifax Town and had a good record and reputation in the lower divisions. He was to provide cover in case of injury or the transfer of Trautmann, until a great goalkeeping prospect signed earlier in the year would be ready for the first team.

Steve Fleet, a 17-year-old, had been plucked from the clutches of Manchester United. Fleet was a member of the same Salford side as his best friend, Eddie Colman, and both had been wooed by the offers from United scouts. Colman was delighted to sign for the club they both supported but Fleet had far more aesthetic considerations. Although a United supporter, he had often travelled to Maine Road to watch only one player, Bert Trautmann. His reasons for signing were to be able to work with and be taught by his great hero. Meanwhile, he would soon have to complete his National Service in the RAF, in three or four years though he was convinced he would be taking Bert's place when he retired. His future was assured.

Les McDowall also bought Bill Leivers from Chesterfield around the same time as Savage in November 1953, and at Christmas he secured the signatures of two other players, Bill McAdams from Distillery in Northern Ireland and Paddy Fagan from Hull City, all well within the brief from Bob Smith to buy cheaply.

City entered the new year with yet another early exit from the FA Cup, this time losing to Tottenham Hotspur 1–0. After defeating Bradford City 5–2 away in the previous round, the supporters were anticipating a decent run in the Cup to compensate for the disappointments in the League. City let them down again. The match against Tottenham at Maine Road was a desperate game of long ball play and, unfortunately for Trautmann, the winning goal was an utter farce. When Bennett, the Spurs forward, received the ball he was in an offside position, and his half-hearted shot rolled towards the goal while the City defence did little but await the referee's whistle. Bert, meaning to tap the ball back to Roy Paul for the free-kick, missed it completely and it trickled into the net. The referee signalled a goal and Trautmann had to be restrained by his equally incensed colleagues from chasing the official.

Granny Winstanley and the rest of the family kept a very low profile indeed as the front door was slammed with earth-shattering force when Bert returned home that evening.

The season once again crumpled beneath them and they finished inauspiciously in 17th place, while in contrast the City reserve team had gone for 26 consecutive games without losing, their style being based totally on the play of the Hungarian team, who had devastated England at Wembley and inflicted further humiliation with a 7–1 win in Budapest.

John Williamson, Don Revie's great friend, had been the instigator of the revived fortunes of the reserves. Without the pressure being experienced by the first team, he had decided to put into practise the tactics the City players had discussed incessantly since November. With Ken Barnes as an enthusiastic collaborator and, more importantly, a rapidly emerging talent, the success of Williamson, assuming the Hidegkuti role with Barnes, as gifted as Bozsik, was phenomenal. By the end of the season Revie, Trautmann, Clark and Paul were all completely swayed by the deep-lying, centre-forward plan. It was a conviction that was also shared by McDowall and his trainers, who unfortunately did not immediately share their conclusions with the senior players.

The German interest in Trautmann's career was further emphasised by a close-season tour of Germany, which their Football Association were influential in organising. City were to play a series of five matches over a ten-day period starting against Bayern Munich on 9 May 1954. It would provide the German clubs, and in particular their international players, with good experience before the World Cup Finals in Switzerland later that summer. Trautmann arranged for Margaret to join him during the tour, after which they were to enjoy a long holiday there.

Once again Bert urged his team to play to the full against the German teams, he wanted a thoroughly professional attitude adopted. The rest of the City party wanted to relax after another long and difficult season while at the same time appreciating his keenness to entertain the crowds with a high standard of football. With a little compromise to their hedonistic approach to the tour they decided to implement subtle changes to the English League style. Revie, still playing as a conventional inside-forward, had gained his first international cap for England that March, but he was still unhappy with his role in the Manchester team.

In the match against Bayern, with no great restrictions from McDowall, he started to adopt the role played by Johnny Williamson. After an entertaining 3–3 draw the party moved on to play Fürth SV, whom they defeated 2–0, and then drew 2–2 against Stuttgart Kickers, who lived up to their name by inflicting a number of off-the-ball hacks at the City players. Following a 1–0 win over FSV Frankfurt, they travelled to play a Wuppertal Combined XI in the Ruhr. Bert's sensibilities were once again upset by the attitude of the City club. Their performances on the field had been good, without any great effort they were so far undefeated, but had drawn the line concerning a number of invitations from their various hosts. They had declined a number of excursions, for example to tour the Mercedes-Benz factory or visits to pottery kilns, preferring, for some strange reason, the various bars and clubs of the German cities.

While Roy Paul organised these unofficial distractions, Trautmann was left to accompany the rest of the City party of directors and wives to most of the official functions and receptions. His public relations role became more pronounced on this tour and he gave numerous interviews while all the time fuming to himself as the directors gave him little of their time or any credit. Here were a club receiving £500 a match guaranteed if he played, he was acting as guide and interpreter, all while on summer wages, plus a few shillings a day expenses. He was beginning to envy Paul and his reprobate waywardness.

The final match against the Wuppertal team had attracted a capacity crowd, included among them large numbers of British Forces stationed in the area, and the atmosphere was exceptional for a friendly game. Behind the scenes, the commercial importance of playing Trautmann was further underlined. He had picked up an injury in a previous match and this developed into blood poisoning of his right leg. The pre-match publicity for this last game of the tour had been considerable, and the German officials were particularly anxious for him to appear, while City faced depositing in their bank £500 less than they anticipated.

An injection from a local doctor enabled him to be sent out on to the field in acute discomfort. His humour was not improved by the gamesmanship of the opponents, particularly when Bill McAdams was sent off the field after a dubious incident and the match finished with the players and the crowd in an ugly mood. A number of clashes developed between the Germans and the British while the police escorted the players off the field. Les McDowall moved to the players' tunnel to pacify his team when he was approached by an over-zealous policeman who assumed he was about to attack one of the players. In the ensuing *mêlée* he was sent sprawling down the steps (Roy Paul and Beaky Barnes were particularly amused by the incident) and the tour ended on a completely sour note.

Trautmann was in a foul mood after the match and had not calmed down when attending the after-match banquet. A discourteous German official made a comment about the behaviour of his colleagues and Bert stormed out, reportedly saying, 'I don't care if I ever play in Germany again.' The bad feeling eventually subsided, and, with apologies and explanations of the misunderstandings all round, City returned to England the following day with McDowall instructing Trautmann to get the best possible care for his leg injury.

Bert and Margaret, who had left John in the care of Sarah and Clarice, journeyed to visit Karl Krause, who had moved to the small town of Tus Meerbesk on the lower Rhine near the Dutch Border. Bert organised a course of treatment for his leg costing him 200 marks and then spent a further 10 days of his holiday receiving treatment from the medical staff of a local colliery, which Krause managed to arrange.

Once the problem had cleared they moved on to Bremen to visit Carl and Frieda. During the visit a number of offers had come his way to play for German teams, but having learned his lesson he asked the interested parties to contact his club. But it was also becoming more apparent to Trautmann the German attitudes to players and coaches were merciless in any critical review. The incident at Wuppertal had upset him deeply, and he had received some bad Press concerning remarks made after the game. To a degree, his enthusiasm was becoming a little dampened but he was still willing to consider an agreeable offer.

The couple left Germany at the end of July on the Hamburg to Hull ferry and were reunited with John and the Friars before the start of the 1954–55 season. When he turned up at City's new training ground at Shaw View in Urmston there was no indication from Les McDowall of any offer from Germany.

While in Germany he had of course watched on with colossal pride as Sepp Herberger's team, against all the odds, had won the World Cup in a wonderfully refreshing style of football. Bert's beam of pride was aimed primarily at Beaky and Pauly who both kept well out of his way, but who privately were impressed by the achievement of the Germans. It was a bittersweet start to the season for Bert with his national team as World Champions and a recuperative holiday behind him, but he was in fine fettle for the new season, whatever might happen. The immediate response of his employers on his return was to refuse to pay the bill for the treatment to his leg injury. When Beaky and Pauly heard the news they kept an even lower profile when Trautmann was around. He was despairing at the pettiness of the City management. Roy Paul was convinced Bert would finish up in a state of explosive self-combustion, 'He looked like he was going to go off like a fucking V2. City were treating him like shit at the time, well all of us really, but Bert was far more sensitive than the rest of us cynical sods. We had realised on the tour how much he was becoming an international celebrity on the continent, not just in Germany, and on a more personal note I was approaching the end of my career without much success, either on the field or materially. It was going to be a make or break season for everyone but at the same time we all felt incredibly sorry for Trauty.'

Pauly and Beaky, with the rest of the players, also kept apart from Bert for other reasons. It was with astonishment that the City players found a complete change of attitude in Les McDowall. During the tour of Germany the party had stayed at a coaching camp before the first match, set in beautiful woodlands just outside Munich. In the wonderful Bavarian surroundings, McDowall had been deeply motivated by the coaching methods and the set-up.

Now he was brimming with *bonhomie* towards his players and with enthusiasm for the new season, and he had reached the conclusion that Manchester City would have to embrace some of the continental methods. Furthermore, he persuaded the directors, who in turn immediately made money available for him to achieve his ideals. Cannily, McDowall decided to persevere with his current squad, he was aware of their ability, now he had to achieve that increasingly elusive blend.

The players could hardly believe this turn of events, suddenly the formerly detached manager was oozing with conviviality towards them. One of his first actions was to call Don Revie to one side. Don knew something was in the air because the day for the pre-season training had been brought forward. 'We reported for training two weeks earlier than usual. This was the first surprise.' Revie was being diplomatic, he had been furious about the new dates. His wife Elsie was a schoolteacher and they had always exploited the extended time off their jobs allowed to give them maximum time together.

Revie went on, 'The second surprise was that from the word go we really got down to the job – mornings and afternoons – in what I can only describe as top pressure training under Laurie Barnett. Surprise number three was the fact we were told we could have as much ball practice as we wanted. If a player wanted a ball out he could have it. If he thought he was seeing too much of the ball then he could lay off.'

When the players were told of the new methods they spent the first few minutes tripping over each others chins as they thudded to the ground in disbelief, but as Revie recalled, 'There was a sense of urgency about our camp, more keenness, more interest.'

Les McDowall had addressed the whole City professional staff, yet another innovation for an English manager, gathering them together in a large group. 'We are going to play football this season. By football I mean football. We are going to keep the ball down, no big kicking and no wild clearances from defence.' He glared at his stylish but at times animalistic captain when he said this. Paul, with typical grace, replied, 'If you get Laurie to organise the bastards properly boss, I'll fucking deliver.'

McDowall, Tilson and Barnett worked the City players long and hard at passing and intricate touches while the trio of Trautmann, Savage and Fleet went through their own routines in isolation from the rest.

# THE REVIE PLAN AND THE 1955 CUP FINAL

*There are various theories on how it was brought about – all of them perfectly sound – but in the final summing up, individual praise is out of place. The road to Wembley and to an exalted position in the League table was paved with confidence fostered by team spirit, on and off the field.*

ERIC TODD

MANCHESTER City were the subject of intense Press coverage as speculation and hearsay about their new style of play began to circulate. The football world, deeply suspicious of any new style or technique, treated the news with cynicism, while the City supporters, hopeful for any sign of an improvement to their team, looked forward to the season start with great expectancy. Eric Thornton of the *Manchester Evening News* claimed to have christened the new system as the Revie Plan, while the *Daily Mirror* and the *Daily Express* made similar claims, either way Don Revie's name became synonymous with The Plan.

It is perhaps indicative of the closed mind of English football that, despite the emergence of other football nations and continental club sides, only one club out of the 92 League teams had tried to learn something from abroad and, more importantly, were prepared to give it a try.

The Revie Plan was basically a copy of the Hungarian system that had marvelled the soccer world the previous year. Revie played as the deep-lying centre-forward inside his own half, linking up with his wing-half and inside-forwards in a triangular formation. Revie used both wings for space while the wingers found space inside. Revie realised, however, that the success of the plan depended heavily on a goalkeeper who could read the game well and whose distribution from the penalty area was unfailingly accurate. Trautmann was dragged from his isolation on the training ground and became an essential link for the plan to work. Revie and the rest of the team conceptualised that keeping possession was the basis of good football and that started with the goalkeeper. The normal method of play with goalkeepers was to hastily kick the ball up field after making a save, often without any direction or accuracy. The Hungarian, Grosics, had shown how constructive the goalkeeper could be with a display of careful and thoughtful throws to his teammates.

Bernd in 1928 (left) and Bernd in 1938, 10 years later (right).

Frieda, Carl, Karl-Heinz and Bernd in Bremen in 1929 (left). Bernd, aged seven and unhappy in a sailor suit at Burger Park, Bremen.

Frieda and Karl-Heinz.

Trautmann with members of the bomb disposal squad at Huyton in 1948.

St Helens Town, February 1949. Bill Twist is third from the left on the back row, George Fryer is on the extreme right and Bert Trautmann is on the front row, extreme right.

Trautmann in action for St Helens Town against Bangor City, just before he joined Manchester City.

Bert Trautmann being welcomed to Maine Road by his new teammates in 1949.

From left to right: Roy Paul, Bert Trautmann and Don Revie before the start of the 1954–55 season and the introduction of the 'Revie Plan'.

The Manchester City team line-up, with Bert Trautmann third from the right on the back row.

From left to right: Trautmann, Branagan, Whitfield, Paul and Hart.

Obstacle training for Bert in the gym.

Bert with Carl and Frieda in 1955. Behind them is Jack Friar.

On tour with Manchester City in Germany in 1955. Les McDowall and Roy Paul look on as Bert Trautmann and Don Revie talk to a German official.

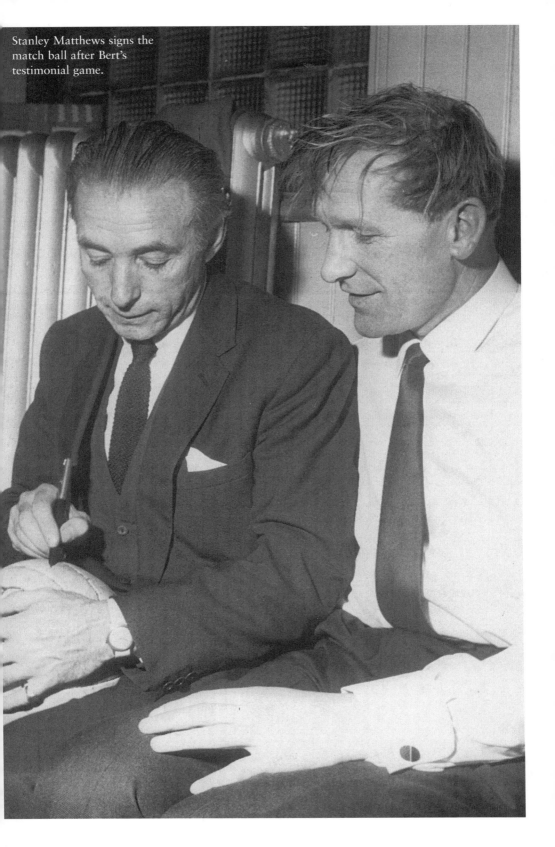

Stanley Matthews signs the match ball after Bert's testimonial game.

Trautmann pours the champagne after his testimonial game. To his left are Denis Law and Derek Kevan

Taking pride of place in the centre of his awards is the Football Writers' Association Footballer of the Year trophy.

Bert Trautmann enters football folklore, diving
at the feet of Peter Murphy and sustaining a
broken neck in a Wembley Cup Final.

Wembley 1955, and the first German to appear in an FA Cup Final is introduced to the Duke of Edinburgh.

Opposite: Dave Ewing and Bill Leivers help Trauntmann on a City lap of honour.

Bert and Margaret with Klaus in Germany in 1956.

Bert and Klaus at Bramhall in 1956.

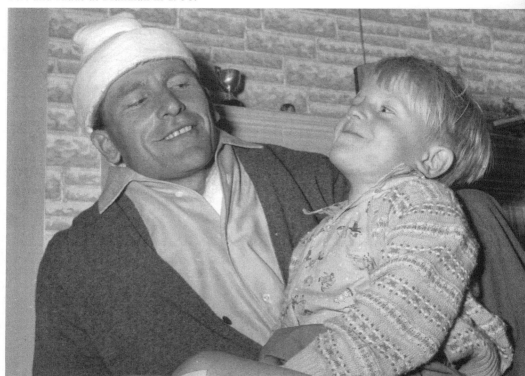

With Adolf (Adi) Dassler, the founder of Adidas.

THE FOOTBALLER
OF THE YEAR
PRESENTED TO
BERT TRAUTMANN,
MANCHESTER CITY F.C.
BY THE
FOOTBALL WRITERS' ASSOCIATION
MAY 1956

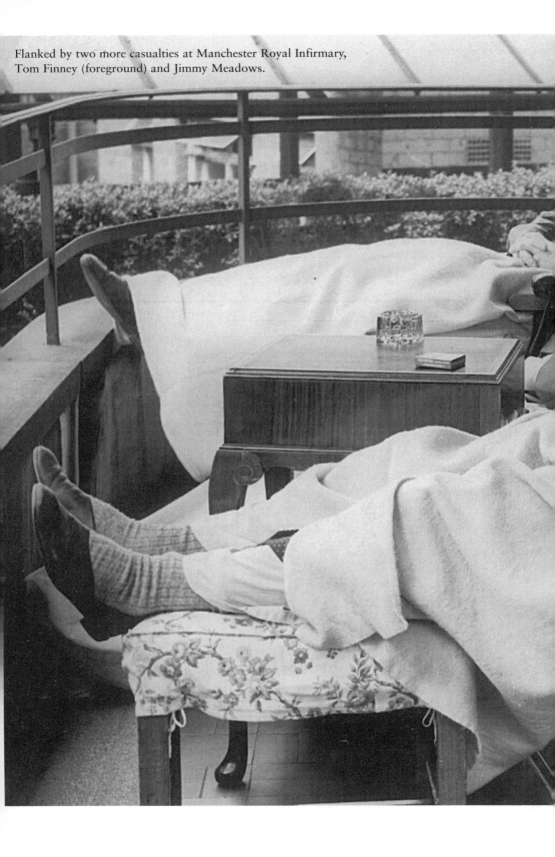

Flanked by two more casualties at Manchester Royal Infirmary,
Tom Finney (foreground) and Jimmy Meadows.

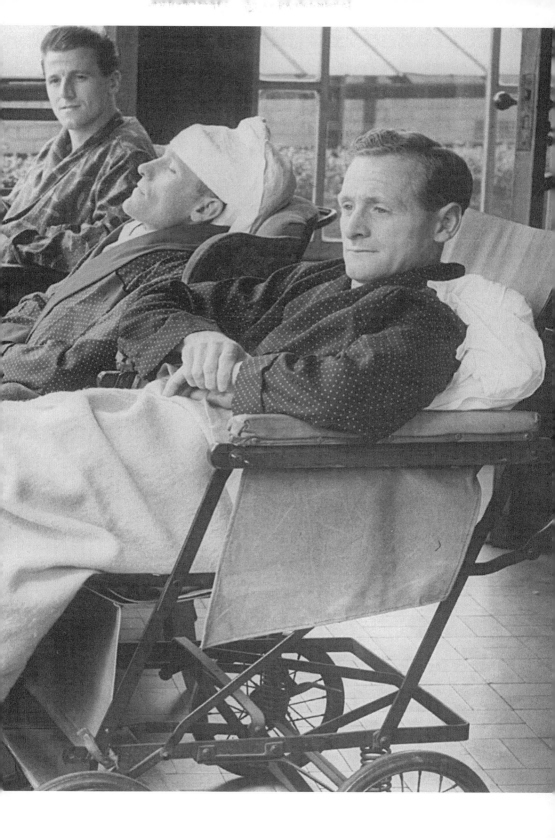

Being discharged with a fond farewell from Manchester Royal Infirmary.

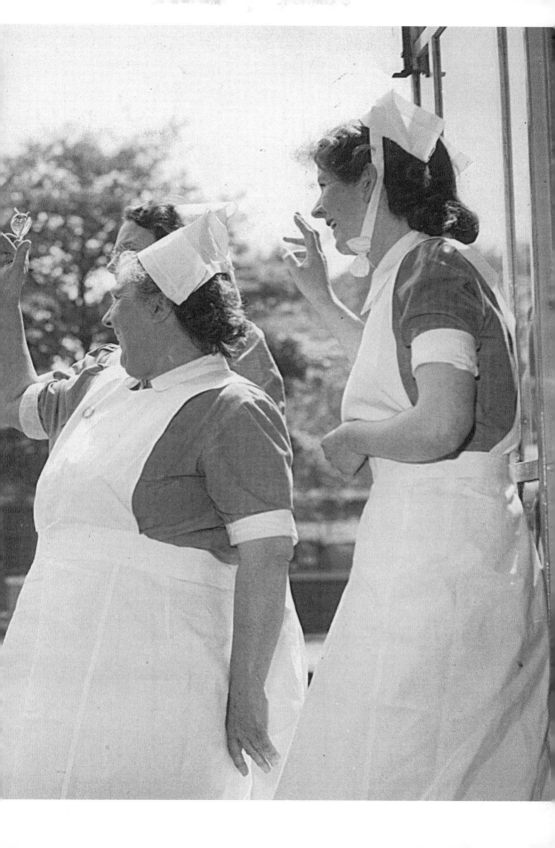

Manchester City about to set sail on the RMS *Mauretania* in May 1958.

Bert Trautmann meets another Manchester City legend, goalkeeper Frank Swift, nicknamed 'Frying Pans' because of his enormous hands. Swift was one of the casualties killed in the Munich air crash when working as a journalist.

A rare moment of relaxation aboard RMS *Mauretania*.

Bert Trautmann as
general manager of
Stockport County,
sorting tickets before
an FA Cup tie against
Liverpool in February
1965.

Sons Mark and Stephen in 1965.

Bert Trautmann is third from right, with the Burmese national squad.

Trautmann training with the West German team before the 1966 World Cup Finals in England.

Trautmann pictured with Preußen Münster in 1967.

With West German manager Helmut Schön in 1966, and, right, with Franz Schain at Aachen in 1967.

Meeting the Queen.

Trautmann being awarded the Bundes-Verdienst-Kreuz, Homeministr, in Germany.

Bernhard Carl Trautmann OBE.

Trautmann's exceptional skill at throwing the ball was immediately recognised as the foundation of the side's mobility. Not only could he throw the ball with unerring accuracy and power, but he could also actually put back spin on the football. His style was also unique – he did not employ the usual overarm method favoured by other goalkeepers, but he used a technique of 'pushing' the ball through the air almost like a shot putter.

Revie recalled, 'In training I would run towards Bert when he had made a save. He held the ball until I was in the clear with my own wing-half in close attendance. Bert would throw the ball out to me, but as soon as he shaped up to do so the wing-half ran forward to take a short pass from me. At that stage I usually had a yard or two to work in. The opposing left-half had almost certainly been bolstering up his own forwards, if he came towards me I turned the ball to my wing-half and then ran on until I was once again in open space. He in turn would hold on until I was in position then pushed a 10 or 15-yard pass down the touchline. I was beyond the opposing half-back with the opposing full-back some distance away. I could either run forward or hold the ball to chip a long through pass for our wingers and strikers bursting through. The great skill in football is in not standing still, but depends on men not in possession getting into position. The key factor in this strategy is using short accurate passing at first in building up an attack, until one man is in the clear. Unlimited possibilities stemmed from this move started by Bert.'

Many variations of the move were developed as the players became used to the system, with Trautmann the catalyst for each attack from deep. While the new methods worked perfectly in training matches, they now had to be proved in a competitive game.

The plan was first put into action at Deepdale on Saturday 21 August 1954, when City played their opening League game against Preston North End. Most of the major football correspondents took their places among the capacity crowd awaiting the dramatic unveiling of the new style. The newspapers had built up the story for days and the 'City players felt under considerable pressure as they took to the field'. All teams started a season with high hopes and here the setting was a perfect arena for the City players: a pitch of newly laid turf, a clear sunny day and a large crowd.

They blew it, and the Revie Plan was an unmitigated disaster from the start. Bill Leivers had been brought into the team at right full-back with John McTavish playing as link man to Revie at right-half. McTavish was injured early in the game and Leivers also received a knock. Preston, with their two talented attacking wing-halves Tommy Docherty and Willie Forbes surging through midfield, broke down every move. Revie was left chasing shadows, while Tom Finney, exploiting City's weakness on the right, cut the defence to ribbons. At the end of the game the City players trooped off the field with their heads down while Preston North End celebrated their resounding 5–0 victory.

Journalist Eric Thornton said afterwards, 'The team coach on the way back was like a funeral coach, many of the players gladly accepting lifts home in supporters' cars, eager to dodge the depressing atmosphere. Everybody was wondering if it was going to be another of those seasons and they didn't like the thought!'

The newspapermen rushed to file their copy and the Sunday papers poured ridicule on the plan and the team, while poor McDowall had to face the anger of Walter Smith (who had succeeded Bob Smith as chairman that summer) and his directors.

Trautmann was utterly depressed as he looked at his newspapers in Bramhall the following day. He, more than anyone, had such high hopes for the plan, and his dream of an integrated continental and English style was shattered. He went through each part of the game time and time again while his toes curled with embarrassment as he analysed the team's inept performance. Normally, after a defeat, he would have regained his assurance by Sunday but this time Margaret and the Friars could not help him shake off his melancholic mood. He arrived at Maine Road for training on Monday 23 August to meet his similarly unhappy colleagues. Les McDowall faced his players with a defiant stance: 'We are going to play this system for a month. No matter what the public, Press or anyone else says, one match is not a sufficient test.'

Trautmann and particularly Revie were still not sure that they could do it. They were concerned that the way Preston had played, with attacking half-backs, quickly exploited the weakness of the plan, what the team needed was an attacking wing-half to link with Revie, not a defensive player like McTavish. On Wednesday 25 August City were to play their first home match of the season, against Sheffield United. McDowall decided to make three changes to his team, bringing in Jimmy Meadows and Roy Little as full-backs and Ken Barnes, who had been in and out of the side for so long, at right-half.

Sheffield United were beaten 5–2, the plan had worked to perfection and Barnes was an absolute revelation. It had been a bone of contention for some time between the manager, trainers and players of how good a player Barnes was. It had been reasoned that a half-back played three-quarters of his game as a defender with the remaining time spent going forward. The strong tacklers always retained the first-team places because their main role was to supply balls to the forwards in a no-nonsense manner. For the City plan to work they needed, in Revie's words, 'an attacking wing-half who was not only clever in possession but who also had plenty of stamina and an ability to bring the ball up and use it intelligently'. Barnes filled these criteria and more. While not a well-built player, his stamina was outstanding and his running ability over a mile made him close to the top athletes of the time, but above all else he developed an uncanny understanding with Trautmann. Don Revie said, 'As soon as Ken came into the team it was obvious where we had gone wrong at Deepdale. It was imperative to have an attacking wing-half to combine with the deep centre-forward and at the same time we had to have mobility in defence to cover up for Ken, that was the answer, mobility in defence as well as attack.'

Beaky Barnes and Bert's good relationship off the field was also a major factor; they were close colleagues despite Beaky's ceaseless leg-pulling about the Germans.

Barnes would often call Trautmann away from his goalkeeping clique with Fleet and Savage for a game of head tennis in the gym. He would deliberately mis-head the ball and watch as Trautmann scrambled around to retrieve it. 'Come on you big, useless German twat, I thought the master race could do anything.' The big, useless German twat, wild with rage, would chase Barnes all over Maine Road while the others collapsed in laughter as Bert's angry face and Barnes's giggling figure disappeared into the distance.

Barnes, together with Roy Paul, was in charge of the social arrangements on away trips and would frequently arrange visits to the cinema, especially when the team had a chance to see the latest release in London. City stayed at Bailey's Hotel on Gloucester Road, the players would pile into one room while Beaky scanned the entertainments page for a suitable film. It was invariably a war film. 'Hey Trauty, you coming out tonight to watch us stuff you again?' Bert's reply was always related to sex and travel.

Barnes was always profoundly impressed by Trautmann's professionalism and talent. 'He really gave the rest of us so much confidence, it got to the point, when Trauty made a save, we just turned and ran, we knew the ball would arrive at our feet within seconds, he read the game so well and we had an almost telepathic understanding. It got to a point where I would show off, knocking the ball over the heads of the opposing forwards to him and then I'd sprint away for his throw without looking back.'

Nobby Clarke was also a great benefactor of Bert's throwing ability but was not always grateful. 'If the others had been closed down, Bert would switch the ball easily from wing to wing, he could throw past the halfway line without great effort. He had a knack of swerving a ball around opponents, something I have not seen before or since, but for me it sometimes created a few difficulties. Throwing to his right he would swerve the ball with a little flick into the path of Barnes or Paddy Fagan, with me on the left the ball used to swerve away from me creating a lot of fifty-fifty situations. I used to call them Red Cross balls because my opposing full-back and I used to get some knocks. I used to glare at Bert sometimes while he would smile and give me a knowing wink, the bastard.'

In mid-September 1954 Manchester City were at the top of the First Division and the rest of the soccer world was sitting up and taking notice, the spectators were flocking to Maine Road again while they were attracting huge crowds to their away matches. The team and the players individually were becoming the centre of attention everywhere they went.

Bert Trautmann was achieving sublime self-assurance and was besieged by admirers at matches and socially, while invitations to functions and dinners were being received all the while. Although his personal popularity soared, the awareness of an anti-German feeling towards him was still apparent, and, while he had learned to handle the taunts from the terraces and the good natured teasing of his teammates, he became greatly distressed at any form of criticism of his countrymen in newspaper articles or any adverse comments he heard made. He became resolute in his determination to prove the

Germans were a worthwhile, considerate people. Spurning the bright lights of the Manchester club circuits, he embarked on a one-man crusade in building up Anglo-German relations. The public relations skills he had developed on the German tour were put to good use. He gave his time free of charge to promoting and escorting German trade delegations or acting as a guide on tours around Maine Road for any visitors.

Of all the Manchester footballers of the time, he was the most prominent in forging links with local football clubs, mainly the youth side and in particular the Jewish lads clubs. A number of local Jews still harboured bitterness towards Trautmann and City, even after five years of playing at the club, and it was through Bert's efforts that a number of them realised his valuable contributions to the local sports clubs was both genuine and generous.

Outside of football and his sports contacts, Bert preferred to be with his family in Bramhall, and his closest friends at the time were an unpretentious and fun-loving couple whom Bert and Margaret met when they first moved into the area.

Audrey Wilson worked in her brother-in-law's confectionary shop in the village where Margaret and the Friars were regular customers. The two young women had the same sparkling sense of humour, and Margaret invited Audrey and her husband Stan to visit the Friar house for a drink and to watch a football match on television. Like the two wives, Bert and Stan hit it off from the start and the two couples started their close friendship. Stan Wilson cared little for Trautmann's celebrity saying, 'Your only a bloody footballer,' while Bert found it easy to relax in Stan's company away from the pressures of his fame.

'I think Bert liked the way we just accepted him as a normal human being. He was also wary of hangers-on and the shallowness of other people. I was just an ordinary working bloke and in my eyes so was Bert. He just had to accept Audrey and me for what we were.'

Shortly after they met, the Wilsons moved to a new council flat in the village. For the first years of their marriage they had lived with Stan's father. The Trautmanns helped them move their possessions and Stan recalled a number of surprised people as they watched the famous goalkeeper pushing furniture along the street.

Margaret found two people who shared her mischievous sense of humour and accepted her eccentricities. Shortly after the move, Stan and Audrey held a Lancashire hot-pot supper as a house-warming party. One of the fellow guests was a particularly strait-laced and correct man, the sort, as Audrey put it, 'who polished his garage door and ironed his underpants'.

Margaret decided to drop a prophylactic into the man's food while Trautmann looked on in horror. As they sat around the table, with Margaret's face gleaming with anticipation, the man picked up the condom in a fork full of red cabbage and the thin rubber stretched out below it, swinging like a pendulum. Bert rushed out into the garden where his laughter could be heard echoing over the fields.

'I always thought Margaret was pixilated,' Stan Wilson said. 'The more we got to know her she did more bizarre things. She had a very Bohemian approach to life; I think she could easily have become a beatnik as we called them then, or a hippy later. She was developing an interest in art and poetry; in fact, she was quite good. She always carried a huge bag with her everywhere, as if she had come for the night and it was crammed with so many things she could never find anything she needed.'

Stan was active in the local sport scene, a good cricketer and involved in running a local boys side. Margaret's total disinterest in football meant her complimentary season ticket was unused. Bert gave the seat to his friend. It was Stan Wilson who, in the early days, urged Trautmann to use his throwing ability more and, other than Jack Friar, was the only other person from whom Bert would allow criticism. Stan also told Trautmann that his use of goal-kicks tended to be a little aimless at that time, they needed more power and direction, a fact Bert accepted and something he improved.

'He was such a perfectionist and thoroughly professional and he moped if things went wrong, or if he had allowed in a goal. He used to sit on his haunches sulking and picking at daisies,' Wilson recollected. 'I used to tell him not to be such a daft sod and get on with things.'

As the autumn of 1954 progressed things started to go wrong with the City team. The Revie Plan had worked perfectly on the dry, harder pitches, but the heavier conditions slowed down the speed of the attacks and a number of defeats had been experienced when City faced Charlton Athletic at Maine Road on 27 November. This inconsistency that haunted the Manchester City teams resulted in a 5–1 defeat, and a few incidents during the match brought out Trautmann's hot headedness. A number of decisions had gone against the home team, and with Charlton winning 4–1 they were awarded a penalty in a hotly disputed decision that enraged Bert. He harangued G.W. Pullin until the referee had no choice but to book him, Trautmann stupidly giving his name as Stanley Matthews. After the penalty, which Trautmann made no attempt to save, Pullin blew for time. As the players made their way down the tunnel a boot, suspiciously similar to Roy Paul's, tripped the referee, who fell on to Trautmann. Trautmann pushed him away and slapped Pullin's face with his cap. Trautmann faced an FA disciplinary enquiry that resulted in a two-game suspension and a fine of two weeks' wages. He missed two games at the end of the year and came back in time for a vast improvement in the team performance and second half to the season that brought them to the verge of a Cup and League double.

The third round of the FA Cup took City to Derby County, the scene of Trautmann's worst performance in the City goal. He came away with great satisfaction after a superb personal performance had helped his team to a 3–1 win. The draw for the fourth round was against their biggest rivals, Manchester United, and 75,000 packed into Maine Road to see Joe Hayes and Don Revie score the two goals that saw them through to the fifth round against Second Division Luton Town. The match was played in a raging blizzard, the atrocious conditions reminding Trautmann of his time in Russia, but two goals from Nobby Clarke saw them enter the draw for the quarter-finals. They drew the Second Division leaders, Birmingham City.

On 12 March 58,000 watched a hugely exciting match in which Trautmann made two stupendous saves to keep City in the game, a solitary goal from Johnny Hart seeing them through to a semi-final against Sunderland at Villa Park on 26 March. The team were on course for achieving the incredible, the First Division Championship and the FA Cup.

The two weeks between the Birmingham game and the semi-final proved very eventful indeed. McDowall, to everyone's amazement, paid a reported £25,000 to Hibernian for inside-forward Bobby Johnstone, a player of delightful and intricate skill, but with the team doing so well it was a mystery to all where McDowall intended to play him. In truth, McDowall's idea was for Johnstone to take over Don Revie's role in the team. McDowall and Revie did not have a good relationship and he found his player opinionated and strong willed. Trautmann and the rest of the players worried that Johnstone's arrival would upset the balance of the side, while at the same time understanding the need to strengthen the side as they progressed towards their goal.

The strength of character of both Revie and Paul worried the normally imperturbable manager, and stories of a bribe scandal involving them both before had made him wary. Both players had taken cash to under perform in matches, both had also involved opponents in match fixing and sums of £1,000 were involved. Two years before his death, Paul admitted on television that he and others had regularly thrown matches for cash. After Don Revie's death, several stories came out of his involvement in alleged bribery during his managerial career, while his reputation was further tarnished when he resigned from the England manager's job to take up a lucrative deal in the Middle East.

When Johnny Hart broke his leg on 19 March the problem of playing Johnstone and Revie was merely academic. Both were in against Sunderland.

The match at Villa Park was a classic, played on an energy-sapping, glue-pot pitch, with Johnstone and Revie displaying exquisite ball skills. City scored with a glorious diving header from Nobby Clarke, who was carried off injured towards the end. Bert Trautmann was about to become the first German to play in a Cup Final at Wembley Stadium. Now they could concentrate on the Championship.

Unfortunately, the Final began to dominate all their thoughts. The Football Association Challenge Cup in the minds of all players and football supporters was the competition, above all else, that held the glamour and romance of the national game. Despite the League Championship being the test of consistency, the Cup Final elevated players to the centre stage of Wembley while live television gave an audience of millions, as a result not one player at the time would have given up the chance to appear in the Final in return for a Championship medal.

As the Manchester City players approached the run in for the Championship their minds were already preoccupied with the visit to Wembley. A souvenir brochure was produced with the proceeds to be divided between the team, while the pressure on the players to provide tickets was immense. Trautmann was involved with the rest of the squad in obtaining as many tickets as possible, they would make more on selling on their ticket allocation than playing in the match itself.

The tickets aside, he attempted to close the Final from his mind and concentrate on the immediate professional task. Six teams were in the running for the League title and City had an excellent chance provided they could maintain their concentration – they didn't.

After defeating Sunderland at Maine Road they gained only one point out of the next three games, which effectively ended their hopes. When they defeated Wolves 3–0 the other teams began to falter slightly and a glimmer of hope appeared. This faint new hope was crushed like a dry leaf when Blackpool came to Maine Road and inflicted a 6–1 defeat, a reversal of 1953 just before Blackpool's Cup Final and a reflection on how important the Wembley appearance affected players. In the last game of the season they lost to Aston Villa and Nobby Clarke suffered a devastating injury that ruled him out of the Final.

Trautmann was bitterly disappointed. He was convinced if the players had applied themselves more the Championship was there for the taking. The preoccupation with Wembley, fame and financial dealings reduced the concentration of key players and the side finished seventh, only six points behind champions Chelsea.

Despite letting themselves and the supporters down, they faced the match against Newcastle United with supreme optimism. Although the Tyneside club had the experience of appearing in the 1951 and 1952 Cup Finals, many neutrals expected City to win and interest in the club and players was enormous. Don Revie had been voted Footballer of the Year by the Football Writers' Association, but he was the first to admit he owed this great honour to his teammates who basked in the vicarious pleasure of the award. The team spirit was superb and as Roy Paul remarked, 'We really fancied our chances against Newcastle.'

City travelled to Eastbourne a week before the Final leaving a disconsolate Roy Clarke in Manchester to have an operation on his knee, with Johnny Hart, of course, also missing from the party. After checking in at the Queens Hotel the team did some warm-up routines on the Saffrons, where they would be training all week, before returning to the hotel under the strict supervision of McDowall and Barnett. Pauly and Beaky were to be denied even a half of bitter. The Press converged on the hotel where Trautmann was in constant demand for interviews concerning his own historic appearance at Wembley.

The *Manchester Evening Chronicle* had arranged to fly Carl and Frieda over from Bremen for the game and they were due to arrive in London on Friday to meet Margaret. Bert was a little concerned for his mother because she was terrified at the thought of flying, but he was looking forward to seeing them on Saturday and helping them enjoy their first visit to England.

As the week progressed a number of injuries dogged the preparations, Dave Ewing twisted an ankle, which was heavily bandaged for two days, Meadows and Fagan both developed heavy colds, while Trautmann was suffering from myalgia, a form of muscular rheumatism. He aggravated the complaint while diving for a ball at the Saffrons, and he was in considerable discomfort before the party left Eastbourne to travel to the Oatlands Park Hotel in Weybridge on Friday morning. Treatment from a blind physiotherapist was arranged for him before travelling up to Surrey.

The mood of the players had also been disrupted at Eastbourne when Elsie Revie telephoned Don to complain about the seats allocated for the wives at Wembley. In an angry confrontation with McDowall, Revie and Paul threatened to withdraw from a television programme in London on Cup Final eve. McDowall quickly reallocated new seats for the women. Trautmann's nerves were building up, and, although giving the impression to the others that he was imperturbable, he could feel knots of tension in his stomach.

The tension was relieved by an appearance on the McDonald Hobley show that evening. Newcastle had declined the invitation and Millwall took their place. The teams were invited to ask scripted sporting questions, which 'Memory Man' Leslie Welsh would answer. In the rehearsal before the live transmission, Hobley had trouble identifying the players and confused the effervescent Joe Hayes for Revie. 'I'm not bloody Revie, I'm 'Ayes from Bolton.' Hayes, the youngest player at 20, had nerves of iron and was completely unruffled by the media interest. When a journalist was interviewing Trautmann and Hayes he asked Joe if he was nervous. The journalist, with his pen hovering over his notebook to record the profound, innermost thoughts of the inside-forward, gaped as Hayes replied 'Am I fuck' before he sauntered away, hands in pockets, whistling *The Ballad of Davy Crockett*.

The wives and girlfriends had been invited to the studios, and they all had a brief reunion before the team boarded the coach back to Weybridge. As they waved goodbye to their loved ones the plaintiff voice of Roy Paul broke through, 'No chance of a leg-over I suppose boss?' Even McDowall laughed loudly.

Despite his nerves, Trautmann managed to sleep well, and on the morning of Saturday 7 May 1955 he strolled around the gardens of the hotel preparing mentally for the match. His neck and shoulders felt better, treatment from the physiotherapist in Eastbourne had done wonders and after an early lunch they boarded the team coach to take them to Wembley. The magnitude of the occasion hit them, the butterflies returned and Trautmann closed his eyes and tried to relax as they moved slowly towards the Empire Stadium.

In *Steppes to Wembley* Trautmann recorded his reactions. 'We had to fight our way to the dressing-room past people we knew, past people we had never seen before and whom we probably would never see again and past people who, even at this late hour, had loitered in a strategic position hoping one of the players might have a spare ticket! We relaxed as best we could in the dressing room – some of us making an effort at singing, others reading telegrams and letters of good wishes, some of them from players and supporters of the clubs we knocked out of the Cup.'

In describing his feelings as he waited to go out on to the pitch he said, 'For the life of me I cannot describe it. I suppose people get such a feeling when they are about to be interviewed for an important job, or when they are in a dentist's waiting room. But I doubt whether their feelings resemble even remotely those of a footballer as he changes for a Cup Final. "Try and hide your feelings." "Try and keep calm." "Try and look on it as an ordinary League game," advise the non-participants. Maybe we did try and carry out these instructions, but I must admit we didn't see a great deal of each other during those last few minutes before we left the dressing room. We were too busy dashing to and from the toilets.' The players were evacuating their bowels with startling dashes to the stalls and Ken Barnes remarked, 'It was like we were releasing flocks of starlings from our over active stomachs.'

The players were used to their own, large stadium at Maine Road, but the spatial elegance of Wembley was overwhelming. The huge concrete tunnel and the seemingly vast distance from the dressing room to the pitch were daunting. The dressing rooms themselves were enormous, hugely spacious with high and expansive windows.

During the pre-match preparations, Wembley officials were constantly darting in and out with last minute reminders of the etiquette required when presented to the Duke of Edinburgh, how to address the Queen during the medal presentation, while all the time the team were trying to adjust their minds to the game.

The Finalist's shirts were provided by Humphreys Brothers, under the brand name Umbro, who were based in Wilmslow just outside Manchester. The super-stitious among the players took it as a portent that they were a local firm, almost on Maine Road's doorstep. Umbro had also provided them with tracksuits and McDowall, who was influenced by the continental style, decided that his players should wear them.

When the Manchester City and Newcastle United players lined up in the cavernous tunnel, City would be the first team to wear tracksuits in a Final as they took to the field. The pressure on City was further increased when the bookmakers had made them 7/4 favourites to win.

Trautmann found himself lined up with the superb Jackie Milburn, fourth in line behind the respective captains, Paul and Jimmy Scoular. Trautmann was shivering and asked Milburn if he felt cold. Milburn replied, 'I've been here before Bert, you will be fine once we get going.'

Trautmann's sudden realisation that the Newcastle players had such a vast experience of Wembley gave him further shudders. The noise as they entered the field was staggering.

The *Daily Express* provided the supporters with song sheets, while on a rostrum, dressed in his white suit, Arthur Caiger conducted the band of the Coldstream Guards in the pre-match entertainment of awful community singing. The Newcastle supporters had deafened the stadium with *Blaydon Races* before the Mancunians were allowed to sing *Lassie from Lancashire*. The tear-inducing *Abide with Me* was sung prior to the teams walking into view. The emotive sentiments of the hymn moved Trautmann to say, 'There was a sudden hush, the working people of

England were on common ground with royalty. What does it matter if they were off key or not sure of the words [many couldn't read the song sheet]? No Cup Final then was complete without it.' At the end of the spine-tingling emotion of the song, the teams entered the huge bowl of a stadium.

Roy Paul introduced Trautmann as the first German player to appear in a Cup Final as Bert bowed to receive the royal handshake, '*Sehr gut?*' acknowledged the Duke.

Within a minute of the game starting, Trautmann's net bulged as Jackie Milburn headed in from a Len White corner. Roy Little covering on the line tried to head it out, his back arching like a dolphin doing a flip. Trautmann was rooted to the spot and Newcastle supporters and players celebrated their early lead.

With the impetus of that early goal, Newcastle were relentless in their pressure but Trautmann's agility prevented them from increasing the lead. The team tactics of attacking from the moment that referee Reg Leafe blew his whistle were decimated by Newcastle's early goal and the City players, unable to play their normal game as Wembley nerves affected each and every one of them, even the internationals among them, including Paul, Revie, Meadows, Johnstone and Fagan, most of whom had played at Wembley before, could not get going.

Utter and complete disaster struck the Manchester side after 20 minutes when Jimmy Meadows, near to the left corner-flag, went down clutching his right knee while trying to catch Newcastle winger Bobby Mitchell. Meadows had ripped his ligaments to shreds and, unable to take part in the game, he was carried off the field by Laurie Barnett and City physiotherapist John Beeston. The injury to Meadows seemed to spur the rest of the team into action, and in the last period of the first half they displayed a wonderful flow of controlled football, with both Revie and Johnstone to the fore. At the back Bert Trautmann was giving an assured and confident display, and, unbelievably, Johnstone equalised with a magnificent diving header just before half-time. They returned to the dressing room in good heart and, although depressed by the injury to Meadows, they felt they could overcome the odds. Les McDowall agreed, they were beginning to open up the Newcastle defence, playing their own attacking game, and rather than pull back on defence he urged them to keep on as they had been at the end of the first half. Jimmy Meadows changed into his slacks and blazer to join the City bench, a victim of what was to be known in the fifties as the 'Wembley Hoodoo'. This had started in 1952 when Wally Barnes was severely injured, and in 1953 Eric Bell, despite scoring a goal, hobbled throughout most of the match on the left wing. Now Meadows had been stricken and the Press and public were convinced that a jinx was evident.

Trautmann was far more realistic in assessing the situation. After the heavy and rutted pitches of the English League grounds the lush Wembley turf was a stark contrast and the speed of play made judgement and timing inaccurate. The 'jinx' would claim a number of victims over the next few years, including Trautmann.

Don Revie later commented, 'The plain truth is that I believe it is impossible to win a Cup Final at Wembley with ten men – it is hopeless to compare a League match with a Cup Final. Quite often in the League, ten men can beat eleven – but that's only because there is not so much at stake and the eleven men haven't known how to take full advantage of their superiority in numbers – Wembley has lovely turf but it takes a lot out of the leg muscles, extremely tiring when you have to do all the chasing.'

Across the corridor Duggie Livingstone, the Newcastle manager, was telling his side to keep possession, make City do all the chasing.

Manchester City played well for the first few minutes, but the inevitability of tiredness began to manifest itself. Mistakes became commonplace and they lost possession time after time. Trautmann was involved in a number of goalmouth scrambles and his distribution of the ball suffered, the Newcastle team marked tightly and Bert was reduced to hoofing the ball up field in the hope of a forward player latching on to it. In the 57th minute Mitchell, exposing the weakness on City's right flank, cut inside the penalty area. Trautmann judged that Mitchell would cross into the middle and moved to his left to cut out the expected centre. Mitchell outwitted the goalkeeper and drilled in a low shot from an acute angle. Trautmann was furious with himself at being psyched out. Stan and Audrey Wilson watched Bert from the stand with Barbara Friar, who had travelled down with them. Stan knew that Bert would have his work cut out now.

After 66 minutes Mitchell found himself in the same situation, and Bert judged correctly that he would attempt to cross the ball. He could only parry it out and George Hannah caught it with the outside of his boot to squeeze it in through a mass of players into the opposite corner. Again Bert was upset at the goal, he felt he should have held the cross, and as the last period of the game continued the City players knew there was no way back.

Reg Leafe blew for time and Newcastle United had won the Cup for the third time in five years. The City team followed the victors up to receive their medals with Trautmann still anxious about the way the second half goals had been conceded. He also realised that the experienced Newcastle side might well have defeated City with eleven fit men and he was determined to savour what remained of the centre stage. He ushered the hobbling Jimmy Meadows to precede him up to the Royal Box to receive his medal. Trautmann again bowed to the grace of royalty when receiving his own medal from Queen Elizabeth, he could not remember fully any conversation other than 'Well done' from the Queen, he had been briefly distracted by the sight of Dr Pecco Bauwens, the President of the German Football Association, waving to him. Trautmann then committed a *faux pas,* which Beaky Barnes witnessed with roguish delight. The Duke of Edinburgh, to the Queen's right, stood in his customary poise with his right hand inside his coat. The Duke withdrew his hand as Trautmann passed and Bert, thinking Phillip wanted to shake his hand again, moved back and held out his hand. Beaky teased Bert mercilessly for weeks.

The scene in the dressing room afterwards was chaotic, even though they had lost, the attention of the Press did not allow the team to brood on their defeat. Trautmann had to complete a live broadcast for German Radio, while the after-game responsibilities would fill his time until late into the night. Roy Paul related his feelings about the defeat. 'Several critics pointed out that I had lost us the Cup by not pulling everybody back on defence. The truth is, we lost because we were a man short and we were slightly over the hill when the match was played. We had passed our peak in late March some five weeks previously. Don Revie was just a wraith of the player who had been awarded the Footballer of the Year trophy. You could say that about a lot of us. But don't let anybody say we didn't fight, that we didn't give our best.'

After the final Press quotes and the match inquests Trautmann and his colleagues were coached back to Baileys Hotel to be reunited with their families before attending an official banquet at the Café Royal in Regent Street.

Trautmann had a happy reunion with Margaret, Carl and Frieda at Baileys Hotel. Stan, Audrey and Bert's greatest fan, Barbara, met them briefly for a quick drink and excited chat before Bert, his wife and parents were taken to the official reception.

The team was remarkably buoyant, helped by the booze and the occasion. They dined on soup and salmon, *poulet de printempts roti au lard* (chicken and bacon) soufflé and *petits fours*. They drank Cordon Rouge 1947 vintage champagne, fine burgundy and cognac. However, at the end of the evening, very drunk, the depression set in. Toasts to the Queen proposed by Walter Smith, toasts to the Football Association and to Manchester City followed. Roy Paul staggered to his feet, the great competitor had no use for a losers' medal and was in no mood for formalities. The iron man from Rhondda said, with feeling, 'We'll be back again next year to win it.'

The players knew he meant it and within himself Trautmann felt they could do it. Twelve months from now could he be in the Café Royal as a victor?

# FOOTBALLER OF THE YEAR AND THE 1956 FA CUP FINAL

*We must learn the lesson of the ever important question of human balance. It is courage that counts.*

PETER REDGROVE

ON SUNDAY Trautmann arranged to meet his old PoW friend Rudi Hering, who was now living in Surbiton, just outside London. Rudi joined the Friar and Trautmann families and later took Bert's parents on a visit to Windsor Castle while Bert and Margaret tried to find some time together. The following day the families travelled with the official party back to Manchester, where they received a huge and rapturous reception from their supporters. For a team that had lost in the Final, the huge crowds were an indication of how much the team meant to the City, and Pauly's resolve to win the trophy for them next year was stiffened.

The whole group were driven through the streets, the players on an open-top bus, and arrived at the Town Hall in Albert Square for a civic reception. Carl and Frieda were staggered by the warmth and feeling towards their son. Frieda dabbed at her eyes with a handkerchief, reminding Bert of the times he used to tell her stories about soppy love films. Carl was just immensely proud and beamed munificently as people pumped his hand, the fact he could hardly understand a word didn't matter. The old standby of thumbs-up was sufficient. When Carl and Frieda returned to Bramhall Granny Winstanley made a fuss over them, while they in turn did the same to their grandson, John. With space at the house a premium, it was arranged for them to be accommodated in the Wilson's flat in nearby Lumb Lane. Stan, who had been stationed in Germany with the Army, had some elementary knowledge of the German language, although at times communication did become a problem, particularly for Audrey.

On a visit to the butchers Carl took a fancy to some ham, which Audrey tried to explain was uncooked but Carl insisted he wanted it for his supper. In Bremen all hams were cured or smoked and Carl assumed the same applied in England. He pulled a face like a gurning champion when he later chewed on his piece of meat.

The *Evening Chronicle* laid on a reception for Carl and Frieda, who were to be guests of honour at a party in a Manchester hotel. During the evening Frieda was presented with a fur coat by a Jewish friend of Bert's. She was delighted and swooned like a young girl and, back at the flat, she paraded around in it for Stan and Audrey.

'*Ist Gut Stan, Ja?*'

'*Ja, ist Sehr Gut Frieda,*' smiled Stan.

It was busy time for Trautmann. He was due to leave on another tour of Germany on Friday, while his parents were due to fly back on Saturday. He was grateful to the Wilsons for looking after his parents so well, although feeling a little guilty that he could spend so little time with them.

Manchester City played the first match of their tour and lost to Racing Club Strasbourg. They lost again to amateur club Mainz, and Trautmann was left fuming at the attitude of his team. Interest was not just in Trautmann on this tour, the reputation of City's bold approach to football caused great interest in Germany and the club sides had something to prove against a team that was now one of England's top football clubs. Spurred into action by Trautmann's tongue lashing, they defeated Eintracht Trier 5–1, drew 4–4 against Saarbrücken, then lost against Karl Krause's local team, Alemania Aachen.

It was on this tour that Trautmann met two men who were to become good friends, one of whom was to have a great influence on his later life.

Wilfried Gerhardt had studied at Cologne University and was a confirmed anglophile. He had visited England for holidays during his student days, touring the country and staying at YMCA hostels. He was a passionate football fan and a great admirer of the English style of play. He had just joined the German Football Association as their Press Officer. While studying for his degree, Gerhardt was working as a freelance journalist specialising in English football. Wilfried Gerhardt recalled, '... I was keeping in close touch with the (English) football and Bernd of course was then a unique person for us – a German playing in England, in the English League, that must have been in the late forties, early fifties and I read every newspaper I could get my hands on, on English football. I was of course familiar, to a degree, with Bernd's story – for me he was an idol from the very early days and I was all the more pleased and proud later on when I met him and worked with him.'

Their first meeting at a German Press dinner forged a close and lasting friendship for the rest of their respective careers.

Trautmann also met and befriended Adolf Dassler and his family. Known as Adi, he had founded the family sportswear company Adidas. Bert was given pairs of the remarkable low cut, soft leather boots Dassler had designed and Trautmann was to become the first player to wear them in England. Bert found the lightweight boot incredibly comfortable compared to the traditional, heavy, high-sided boots and had often winced at the thought of the pain while breaking them in. Many English players used to urinate in their boots in order to soften the hard leather, and Stan

Wilson recalled, on one visit to Maine Road, rows of boots in the urinals! Dassler also offered Trautmann the chance to become the agent for importing the shoe to the North of England and Bert left Germany for England to think it over.

In June the Friars and the Trautmann's travelled on their family holidays to the Welsh island of Anglesey, linked to the mainland by a vast bridge over the Menai Straits. The Friars had been visiting the island for years, and Bert fell in love with the place from his first visit, so much so he purchased a small caravan, to Margaret's delight. She adored the place and would wander along the beaches and sand dunes in her solitary world. The Wilsons joined them for part of the holiday and Bert left the families there while he came back to Manchester to get ready for the forthcoming season.

The players had left each other after the German tour still a close and happy group of players. They had every reason to expect more success in 1955–56 and Trautmann was in an excellent frame of mind when he reported for training. Beaky and Pauly greeted Bert with huge grins, making comments about his suntan.

'Heh Trauty, you been bleaching your hair? It looks blonder,' asked Barnes.

'Your bluddy nose looks longer,' replied a beaming Trautmann thwacking Barnes in the middle of the back with a huge hand. The happy return to work also brought them a little puzzlement – Don Revie had not turned up. Roy Paul knew why, he was having an extended holiday with Elsie. According to Trautmann, 'Pauly told me Don thought City still owed him two weeks holiday from last year, after the long season and tour he felt he deserved a longer rest. When he asked McDowall, the manager refused. Don said, 'Sod it, I'm taking it anyway,' and he did.

McDowall and the board were incensed by what they perceived as Revie's extreme arrogance. He was suspended for 14 days without pay and Walter Smith quickly made the facts known to the newspapers. Trautmann, knowing how stubborn Don could be, like himself in many ways, was concerned about how the excellent team spirit would be affected. In his own mind he fully sympathised with Revie, but as a professional sportsman he had contractual obligations to fulfil for his employers and at the same time a commitment and loyalty to the team. McDowall intended to replace the Revie Plan with the Johnstone Plan. The Press were on his side and the club supporters were making their own feelings known, they accused Revie of having a swollen head by thinking he was more important than the team, and letters agreeing with the board's stance poured in.

It was hardly the best preparation and City struggled in the opening games, while Revie, on his eventual return, was played in the reserve team. The 1955 Footballer of the Year was playing with the 'stiffs'.

Jack Dyson, who was also a professional cricketer, being the opening batsman for Lancashire, was introduced to the side and started to develop a good partnership with Joe Hayes, playing as the spearheads of the attack. The team played brilliantly on some days, banal as could be the next and so maintained with startling consistency the tradition of inconsistency. It was rumoured in later years that the producers of valium did their drug trials among the Maine Road supporters.

Bert Trautmann, for the first time, was also displaying signs of lapses in concentration, which further contributed to the mountain of chewed fingernails at the end of each home match.

Each year Bert received letters from cranks who blamed him for the excesses of the Nazis, and he had learned to live with them, even those that threatened his life and the life of his family. Towards Christmas, for some inexplicable reason, the hate mail had built up. Bert destroyed most of the letters and did not discuss the problem, not even with Jack Friar. His assumption was that they came from extreme Jewish groups or ex-soldiers, but he remained greatly disturbed by the content.

The team performances improved somewhat towards the end of the year and Manchester City had been drawn against Blackpool at Maine Road in the third round of the FA Cup on 7 January 1956. The confidence within the team of achieving a second appearance in succession had slowly eroded as the ongoing Revie saga and individual loss of form continued. Trautmann threw himself into the Christmas celebrations with his usual enthusiasm, a relief from the problems he was going through. Christmas with the Friars was its customary mixture of fun, noise and rows. Granny Winstanley argued with Margaret, who rowed with her younger sister Barbara, whom Bert defended, who was then picked on by Margaret before Jack smoothed things over. Bert made Margaret laugh, joined by Granny and Barbara, and things became jolly again. As Bert's stardom increased, Margaret had become more eccentric and demanding of him while he in turn often baited her into moods. The ambivalence of their relationship drove Jack to further despair. 'It will end in tears,' he commented more than once.

Barbara Friar noticed that Margaret left John's upbringing more and more with Granny, Jack and Clarice, who were more than happy to assume the responsibility. Margaret in turn was demanding more attention from Bert, who could not always provide it and again her jealousy of his celebrity status consumed her. At the same time her own need for attention caused her bravado to increase. It was like 'Beddlington' when they were around Granny Winstanley. Stan Wilson had no doubts that the couple loved each other, but at the same time had some destructive force in their relationship, which was always bubbling at the surface, while both had developed an almost maniacal sense of humour. Wilson felt Bert's antics were typically German, loud and physical but always in control. Margaret took hers to the limits, which to many people in the early 50s was shocking and daring. Stan remembered Margaret at a dinner they once attended, slipping her hand under the table and unzipping a man's fly. He was a complete stranger to her. Another time she arrived at the Wilson's flat and found Stan in bed. She and Audrey whipped back the covers and chased Stan, who was completely naked, into the garden. Stan recalled, 'She was theatrical in her way; she liked a sense of drama and would goad Bert into situations. Christmas and Guy Fawkes night were always his favourite times, they used to arrive at our place and put a rip rap (Chinese crackerjack) or a penny banger through the letter box, while we were frightened to death they would walk in laughing and joking. He did this once and then went into the garden to set up the fireworks, my dog pissed on his leg and he was as amused as a eunuch being given a cricket box. Each Christmas we would visit them at the Friars or, if he had a match on Boxing Day, they would come to us in the evening. Bert was such a professional he wouldn't touch a drop of alcohol over Christmas, but he would want to let his hair down after the Christmas match. We used to play all sorts of games and then would do a 'turn'. I'd sing, Margaret would dress up and recite something, but Bert would not do anything despite our pleading. In desperation I said, 'Show us your dick' and he bloody well did. Margaret was convulsed with laughter but I never asked him to do anything again.'

Trautmann's fame and popularity were becoming the destructive influence on the marriage and Margaret refused to become involved with his sporting life or any ancillary activities. Stan and Audrey would often accompany Bert to charity functions to which he was in constant demand, and Trautmann was becoming increasingly disappointed in Margaret's lack of interest.

As 1956 progressed the fame and adulation were to propel the Trautmanns even more into the public glare.

While City's progress in the League was as inconsistent as ever, they embarked on their assault of the FA Cup and became involved in a number of controversial ties. The match against Blackpool was remarkable because of the fact that Bert conceded a goal after 10 seconds, certainly one of the quickest against any goalkeeper, before fog descended on Maine Road like a grey shroud. City equalised just before the match was abandoned with the replay arranged for Wednesday 11 January. Trautmann was worried after the Saturday match. Blackpool, and Ernie Taylor in particular, had picked their way through City's defence with ease and Bert was not confident of City winning the second game. Luck was on their side as they scraped a 2–1 win to then face Southend United at their brand new Roots Hall stadium in the fourth round.

Eric Thornton of the *Manchester Evening News* telephoned Southend to find out some facts about the club and was amazed to hear that the match might be postponed. Thornton travelled down to Southend, arriving in torrential rain that had been pouring over Essex for days and in his words, 'I booked a taxi for the ground and gazed upon a fantastic scene. Workmen were digging up the pitch. The chairman, a farmer, was watching the operation and he explained that the ordinary drains were not taking sufficient water. A zig-zag trench was being cut across the pitch. The pipes were being opened. And tons of cockle shells were being tossed into them before the soil was shovelled back all over again.'

When Thornton's story appeared in the *Evening News*, the nationals picked it up and the Southend tie became the story of the fourth round.

The City team arrived in Southend on Friday 27 January, the day before the match, and were more than a little worried about the pitch. The Press, with predictable headlines, had screamed about the pitch being a great leveller and they were looking for a shock win by the Third Division side. The Manchester players' trepidation was confirmed when they saw the playing area for the first time and the 'Sand and Cockleshell Heroes' headlines began to loom before them.

Roy Paul wrote afterwards: 'The pitch was dreadful to play on and most of the lads came off with skinned knees caused by sand and shells. One man got us through that match – Bert Trautmann.'

Many people considered Trautmann's display that day to be the finest exhibition of goalkeeping they had ever witnessed. The 25,000-crowd were in awe of his breathtaking reflexes, as the Southend players were used to playing on a quagmire and City could not master the conditions. Shots flew at Trautmann from every angle, he was diving headlong at the opposing forwards with heart-stopping bravado and he caught, punched or tipped away everything the United forwards threw at him. Joe Hayes broke away to score the only goal and Manchester were through to face Liverpool in the fifth round. As the players were trudging wearily off the pitch, Paul commiserated with one of the Southend players, particularly about a penalty decision in which the referee had denied them.

'Don't worry Roy, Bert would have fucking saved it anyway!' On 18 February over 70,000 watched a goalless draw against Liverpool at Maine Road before the daunting prospect of a replay at Anfield on 22 February. The Liverpool club were pushing hard for promotion from the Second Division and their passionate crowd were capable of lifting them to stirring performances, with their idol Billy Liddell at the peak of his form.

Liverpool scored the opening goal, Hayes and Dyson gave City the lead, while Trautmann frustrated Liverpool and the Kop with some exceptional agility. The referee blew his whistle just as Liverpool were mounting a last furious attack. Trautmann, most of the players and certainly the crowd, did not hear it. Liddell pushed the ball past Trautmann and turned in triumph. Bert, in despair, was about to retrieve the ball from the netting when Roy Paul ushered his players to leave the field. Somewhat mystified, Bert rushed off with his team while the Liverpool players surrounded Mervyn Griffiths, the referee, when they discovered, to their absolute horror, the goal did not count. Bert was delighted with Pauly's presence of mind in dragging his players off the pitch quickly. They speedily departed for home leaving the Anfield club to seethe away at the considered injustice.

Trautmann knew that after that game they had every chance of reaching Wembley again, luck, which every team needed in the Cup, was on their side and in the League they were playing smooth, fluent football again. The Southend match had fully restored his own confidence, which in turn surged to the other players.

The sixth round brought Everton from Merseyside to Manchester on 3 March, the two teams attracting over 76,000 to Maine Road. Hayes and Johnstone contributed goals to the 2–1 win, and after the semi-final draw they were to play a struggling Tottenham Hotspur at Villa Park on 17 March.

The game did not turn out to be a classic, Bobby Johnstone scoring from a Nobby Clarke cross and City defending desperately to hold on to the lead. A few minutes before the final whistle George Robb bore down on Trautmann. In the ensuing scramble Bert grabbed Robb's leg to prevent him scoring and pandemonium broke out when the referee did not award a penalty to Tottenham. City won the game 1–0, while Trautmann was once again the centre of controversy. The incident was captured on the *Pathe and Movietone* news cameras, while most of the newspaper photographers also recorded with conspicuous clarity Trautmann holding Robb's Leg.

Trautmann issued vehement statements refuting allegations that he had deliberately fouled the Spurs player, who in turn tried to play the incident down. In truth, Trautmann had committed a professional foul, before the term became fashionable, and he had got away with it. In later years he explained. 'In a way I was desperate to prevent George scoring. I hoped to get the ball but as I dived into the ruck of players I knew he would get the ball before me. It was more instinctive than premeditated; I just grabbed his leg and held on. I had a better chance of saving a penalty than preventing a certain goal, so I went for it.'

There were no recriminations in the dressing room, the euphoria of a second Wembley appearance in succession did not allow Bert, McDowall or any of the players to dwell on the incident, City were the team of the moment and would face Birmingham City in the 1956 Cup Final. The hate mail, mainly with North London postmarks, started on Monday morning.

In essence, they summed up the aggregate of feeling against Trautmann. Eleven years after the war he was a cheating German bastard, not a cheating goalkeeper or professional footballer, he was a Nazi, a symbol of the hate against the Germans, and he became, once again, the focus of prejudice. In a quirk of perverse fate, Manchester City were to face Spurs in a League match at White Hart Lane the following Saturday. The abuse that greeted Trautmann as he took the field was the worst he had experienced since his debut season. To his great credit he concentrated on his task and, while City lost the game, his personal performance under con-siderable stress was superb.

Trautmann confided to Eric Todd about the letters and he immediately wrote a story about the poison-pen mail, which became a front-page feature in the *Manchester Evening Chronicle*. The nationals picked up on the story and by the middle of the following week a deluge of mail descended on Trautmann.

'In the next few days I received well over 500 letters from various parts of the country – including Tottenham – telling me not to take any notice of the poison-pen letters, but to realise that all genuine sports-lovers and sportsmen sympathised with me and held nothing against me. I was deeply moved and the clouds lifted still more when, at the end of March, I learned I had been voted 'Player of the Year' by readers of the *Evening Chronicle*.'

His sense of guilt over the Robb incident was further dispersed by the encouragement of the team, who realised the circumstances from a professional point of view had meant the difference between a Cup Final and nothing. As Roy Paul said, 'If you hadn't have done it Trauty, I'd have kicked your bloody arse.'

Shortly after receiving his 'Player of the Year' trophy from the *Evening Chronicle*, it was announced by the Football Writers' Association that, for the second successive year, a Manchester City player had become the 'Footballer of the Year'. It was Bert Trautmann.

He became the first goalkeeper and the first foreign player to win the award and his fellow professionals were genuinely delighted for him.

Manchester City finished their League programme in fourth position, their best since the Championship year of 1937, but 14 points behind the runaway champions and rivals, Manchester United. The question now was could City make Manchester the premier football city by winning the FA Cup?

City once again travelled down to Eastbourne the week before the match and set up their training headquarters at the Queens Hotel and the Saffrons. Don Revie was included in the party, but few gave him any chance of playing, Johnstone had assumed his mantle and few people doubted Don would be leaving the club within months. Les McDowall had a number of injury problems and was in no position to choose his line-up for 5 May. Bill Leivers was nursing a twisted ankle, but the most worrying problem was Bobby Johnstone's calf muscle.

On Thursday 3 May Trautmann travelled up to London with McDowall and Walter Smith to receive his 'Footballer of the Year' award at the Criterion restaurant. Archie Ledbrooke, the author the article that wisely summed up Trautmann's proposed move to Schalke four years previously, was the chairman of the Football Writers' Association and presented Bert with the award.

What Trautmann did not know was the furious debate that had preceded the decision. A few writers were concerned the trophy should be given to a player who had an exemplary record and Trautmann's had been marred by his suspension after the Charlton game and also by the furore after the Robb incident. Despite a fairly heated debate, Trautmann's detractors lost the argument, and he finally received three times the number of votes of any other nominee. At the age of 32 he had received England's greatest accolade. The trio left for Weybridge and the Oatlands Park Hotel the following morning to meet the rest of the party who had arrived from Eastbourne. Bert was met by a group of smiling players who were eager to look at the statuette awarded by the FWA, and Don Revie gave him a knowing wink and shook his hand with warmth and sincerity.

McDowall was met by Laurie Barnett with the news that right winger Bill Spurdle had developed a serious outbreak of boils and was doubtful for the match. McDowall decided to await the doctor's verdict and give late fitness tests to Leivers and Johnstone before announcing his team. Trautmann was in a superb state of fitness and mental preparation and his main concern was the fate of Don Revie. The centre-forward had played a superb last game of the season in City's 4–2 win at Portsmouth, a game which also saw the return of Johnny Hart in his first game for 12 months. Trautmann, Paul and Barnes all wanted Revie to play in the Final, not instead of but with Bobby Johnstone. Considerable speculation about the merits of both players developed into a frenzy of words in the newspapers and among the Manchester supporters, but by the morning of the match McDowall had still not decided on his team. His mind was made up for him when the doctor ruled Spurdle out. He decided to play Revie and replace Spurdle with Johnstone, who would play with a bandaged calf. They took the same route to Wembley, optimistic and confident, but this year they knew what to expect, while surprisingly Birmingham City were the favourites to win.

Trautmann felt his pre-match nerves starting as they approached the stadium and he could feel the tension mounting in the rest of the players.

The scenes in the huge dressing rooms were the same, officious stadium personnel fussing around, toilets flushing, pre-match rituals. Roy Paul fussed over the younger players trying to sooth anxieties; Don Revie, superstitious as ever, was playing around with two pieces of wood given to him by an old gypsy woman; Beaky and Roy Little tried to amuse each other with *Goon Show* impressions, while Trautmann tried to understand this bizarre English humour.

Paul led his team into the tunnel and they lined up with the Birmingham players. He put the fear of God into everyone, including the terrified opponents, by suddenly stopping, holding up his fist and shouting, 'If we don't fucking win, you'll get some of this.'

From the dark tunnel the teams entered the blinding light of the stadium, City wearing a new maroon and thin, white-striped strip, the design of which was based on the continental style, another first for an English side. Trautmann could sense the Birmingham players were feeling the tension more than his own team, what Manchester needed was an early lead and they managed it.

The Revie Plan worked to perfection. Revie picked up a short pass, swept the ball out to Clarke on the left and ran 50 yards for a return pass on the left side of the area, with a flick inside his legs the ball fell for Joe Hayes to rifle a low shot past Gil Merrick. They were one goal ahead after only three minutes. The pressure on Birmingham was intense for the first 20 minutes and Trautmann watched the proceedings from his goal almost with an air of detachment.

Birmingham slowly clawed back into the match and a fierce long shot brought Trautmann into the action when he flung himself at the ball to tip it away for a corner. Manchester were now being pushed more and more into defensive play when, after 30 minutes, Noël Kinsey struck home a fierce shot that beat Trautmann and cannoned into the net off a post.

At half-time Paul and McDowall urged the team to open up the play again, make the other side chase and above all keep possession. In the second half City's football was a positive delight, with Don Revie giving, even by his standards, a superlative display, while Trautmann could feel the confidence flowing back into the side. After 57 minutes Johnstone and Dyson combined skilfully for Dyson to run on to a through ball and score. Ten minutes later, after a Birmingham attack had broken down, Trautmann gathered the ball safely and was looking for a throw to Revie. He suddenly noticed Dyson and Johnstone up field and kicked high over the Birmingham players rushing back to defend. Dyson flicked the ball into the path of Johnstone and Manchester scored again. The team relaxed a little, Birmingham came back into the game and Peter Murphy, the Birmingham centre-forward, was starting to outpace Dave Ewing. Trautmann could sense the danger and he became alert to Murphy's increasing threat.

Seventeen minutes from the end Murphy chased on to a ball headed into his path, reached the ball before Ewing and looked certain to score, but Trautmann surged out of his goal, dived head first at Murphy and stole the ball away. Murphy's momentum caused a sickening collision. His right knee caught Trautmann's neck and the goalkeeper, still holding the ball, was knocked unconscious. Dave Ewing and referee Alf Bond realised immediately the impact was serious. Bond stopped the game immediately, allowing Laurie Barnett to race to his player's aid. Trautmann came round to a wave of pain cascading down his neck and shoulder, the intensity of which made him want to scream. Barnett thought he had aggravated a nerve or somehow triggered off the myalgia problem of last year. Whatever the problem, it was serious. Barnett rubbed away at the side of Bert's neck and waved smelling salts under his nose, slowly he seemed to recover and then just as suddenly relapsed. The injury sent ripples of anxiety through the players and the supporters. High in the stand Margaret looked on in fear, while Barbara Friar vomited unsparingly over one of the dignitaries sitting in front of her.

Nobby Clarke, Trautmann's great debating partner, looked on thoughtfully. 'It was difficult to gauge how bad it was, he was such a big, brave fellow and always seemed to recover from knocks quickly. In football then, without any substitutes, we would commiserate with an injured player and gee him up, get him to try and run it off, but with Trauty's injury my reaction was, oh no we're going to lose him'

Roy Paul was shocked at Trautmann's condition, 'He was reeling around the goalmouth like a drunk,' and immediately considered putting Roy Little into the goal. Trautmann insisted he would play on. The game restarted with a tense Laurie Barnett standing behind the goal with the Press cameramen, who were taking pictures of the goalkeeper's wretched position.

With renewed heart, the Birmingham players surged forward to take advantage of the situation. They broke away on the left, and as Eddie Brown raced in towards goal Trautmann suddenly rushed out and, totally from instinct, dived at the forward's feet and took the ball. He cleared the ball and then resumed his tottering stance on his goal-line. Paul closed his defence around Trautmann, with Bill Leivers and Dave Ewing forming a solid formation of muscle and gritty determination. Ewing, often described in the language of the day as a 'craggy, raw-boned Scot', played his heart out. Pauly told him: 'If the ball comes anywhere near just fucking hoof it away.' Ewing nearly hit the stand roof with one clearance.

Shortly after, a high ball came in from the right and Trautmann rushed at incred-ible speed to catch the ball and deny Murphy again. Ewing, trying to protect Trautmann, collided with him once again and Barnett rushed on to the field to revive this man showing such valiant courage.

Manchester City survived the barrage, Alf Bond blew for full-time and they had done it, they had won the Cup with style, and in Trautmann's case truly amazing bravery. 'Trouble was,' said Ken Barnes, 'he could remember sod all about it.'

Through the haze and noise Bert did remember snatches of the triumph, particularly the pats on the back, which sent searing torrents of pain through his body. Bill Leivers, who was Trautmann's roommate on away trips, supported his friend as they made their way to receive the Cup and medals. The climb up to the Royal Box was tortuous, with delighted supporters slapping him on the back as he ascended the steps. He remembered wiping his sweaty and dirty hands along the velvet-covered rails before shaking hands with Queen Elizabeth. While presenting his medal she asked if he had recovered.

'I'll be fine Ma'am, thank you.'

The Duke of Edinburgh smiled and congratulated him, no *faux pas* this time, and in a blur he descended the steps back on to the field with Bill Leivers supporting him on the lap of honour. In the greatest moment of his sporting career Bert Trautmann just wanted to crawl into a corner and die.

The FA Cup ranneth over with champagne, a huge swig from the trophy mixing with the adrenalin of victory bringing a sense of the ridiculous to Trautmann's mind. Players were screaming and laughing in the showers and baths, some still in their playing kit, Roy Little was screaming 'I've lost my fucking medal,' with Pauly and Beaky helping the distressed full-back's frantic search while giggling like maniacs. In his corner Trautmann wanted desperately for the pain to stop.

The mayhem slowly subsided; Trautmann was helped into his clothing after an uncomfortable shower and then boarded the team coach, which was to take them to the Café Royal for the celebration dinner. For the life of him he could not understand why the pain was getting worse.

'You'll be alright big fella, tomorrow you'll be as right as rain, you'll see,' grinned a jubilant Beaky Barnes.

# FROM A TRIUMPH TO A TRAGEDY

*When our relatives are at home, we have to think of all their good points or it would be impossible to endure them. But when they are away, we console ourselves for the absence by dwelling on their vices.*

GEORGE BERNARD SHAW

THE TEAM arrived at the Café Royal to be greeted by their wives and a group of reporters who made a beeline for Trautmann to ask about the injury. The German Press and radio correspondents were also anxious for his comments to relay back to Germany. Margaret was shocked by her husband's condition, his neck was tilted at a grotesque angle and he was cross-eyed like he had suddenly developed an astigmatism. Incredibly, no one had suggested that he should be taken to a hospital. Eventually the club physician, Dr Bailey, took a look at him and arranged for Trautmann to visit St George's Hospital the following morning.

The Trautmanns joined the others for dinner. During the meal his memory came back a little and he was able to recall incidents from the game. As the wine and spirits flowed it helped to anaesthetise the pain a little, but he was noticeably with-drawn and detached. A number of players' wives expressed their concern over his state, but in the general euphoria of victory the atmosphere was sparkling with too much conviviality for any great concern.

'We thought he would be OK,' said Beaky, 'just a recurrence of his muscle problem, but most of us were too pissed to concentrate fully on his predicament, but he was big tough Trauty, nothing would hurt him for long. If we had known then what the problem was we would have been mortified.'

Bert and Margaret sat through the speeches and the dancing before a car arrived to take them to Baileys Hotel, but on the way to Gloucester Road the movement of the car sent surges of pain along his body. He undressed with great difficulty before collapsing gratefully on the bed and, although sleep proved impossible, he swallowed aspirin after aspirin to deaden the excruciating ache and was grateful to see the dawn.

Trautmann and Laurie Barnett took a taxi to St George's Hospital where his neck was immediately X-rayed. The doctor on duty examined the areas of pain, each touch making Bert grimace. His head movements were now so limited he could not look to his left or right, but the doctor was convinced it was just a muscle problem, even more so when the X-rays failed to reveal any damage.

Trautmann knew something was wrong. 'I had no confidence in the doctor and wanted to see a specialist. They tried to reassure me but I just knew, deep down, it was a bad injury.'

His assumption was based on his superb fitness, nothing had restricted him so much before, his experience of pain and injury during the war was nothing compared to this. Barnes and Paul were right, he was tough and resilient, and his remarkable record of appearances was a testimony to his strength. He travelled back from Kensington to Baileys Hotel an unhappy man and Margaret tried to reassure him the doctor's prognosis was probably right.

On Monday morning the couple struggled to the lobby with their bags and met the rest of the group, most of them bleary eyed from the celebrations. Roy Paul squinted at Bert and knew the injury was far worse than he imagined. 'I was feeling lousy, I had a mouth like a badgers arse, but my heart sank when I saw Trauty. He looked like he'd gone 15 rounds with Marciano and his eyes were like owl pellets.'

On the train journey up to Manchester, McDowall and Barnett were now increasingly concerned about their player. The club were due to leave on a tour of Germany on Tuesday 8 May and it was increasingly apparent Trautmann would not be fit enough to play, or even travel with them. They had studied the doctor's report and Laurie Barnett decided an osteopath he knew would be able to provide the remedial treatment Bert needed. He would make an appointment as soon as possible. The team arrived at London Road Station to another rapturous reception from the citizens of Manchester. The team boarded the open-top bus for the journey to Manchester Town Hall with Paul holding the Cup aloft for the people to see. The city had cause to celebrate, with both the League Championship and the FA Cup won by their two clubs, the rest of the country could eat their hearts out. The reception at the Town Hall was crowded and noisy, but again the pain was searing through Bert as Margaret and the Friars tried to comfort him.

Through the throng stepped Frank Swift, then writing for the *News of the World,* and he slapped Trautmann's back in hearty congratulation. Trautmann staggered, the pain seemed to explode inside his head, while Les McDowall, who had just led him from the Town Hall balcony, looked on anxiously. Barbara Friar was moved to tears. 'There was my Bert suffering so much, when Swift slapped his back he let out such a cry of agony, his face went as grey as anything, it was grey, like the colour they paint ships. Poor Frank Swift was horrified and apologised like hell, but we still couldn't work out what was wrong, especially as the doctor in London had said he would be fine eventually.' Once the reception was over the family returned to Bramhall where Trautmann retired straight to bed. The following day, 8 May, he saw the team off on their tour from Ringway Airport before keeping his appointment with the osteopath in St Annes Square.

The medical world was still sceptical of the osteopathic practices in 1956, and the majority of people had not heard of the term osteopathy. It was a treatment fashionable with the Royal Family, the aristocracy and the elite of society. Within the sports world a growing number of people were convinced of the benefits for sports injuries. On his arrival at the surgery Trautmann stripped to the waist and sat on the table while the practitioner carefully felt around his neck and shoulders. His diagnosis was that five vertebrae were out of place, but with manipulation he would be able to remedy the problem. He twisted and turned Trautmann's body as the pain screamed through him. Eventually, after a few minutes, he was assured that four of the vertebrae were back in position, but the fifth would need another approach. Bert's head was grasped firmly and forced back and then he was hit squarely on the forehead with the palm of a hand. The pain exploded like a grenade, he could feel it from his toes to his fingertips and he cried for the man to stop.

'Don't worry old chap, everything is fine. Now I want you to travel up to my practice in Chester on Thursday and we'll have another look at you.' Trautmann resolved never to see this man again.

He returned to Bramhall in an even worse state and was now desperate for some relief from the pain. Shortly after his return, Harold Young, a friend of Jack's and a CWS official, called at the house. He had just returned from some treatment at the Manchester Royal Infirmary and the staff had been asking after Bert. Trautmann had made several trips there to visit patients and was on friendly terms with the doctors and nurses.

'I told Harold that I needed cheering up and decided to go over, I phoned them and told them to have the tea and biscuits ready, I would be there in half an hour.'

Young drove him to the Infirmary where they made their way to the medical staff's rest room. The staff were alarmed at Trautmann's appearance. One of the doctors asked Bert about the X-ray in London, he was not convinced the St George's people had been thorough enough.

Trautmann was taken to the X-ray department for further investigation, after which he returned to the staff-room. Half an hour later Professor David Lloyd Griffiths, an orthopaedic surgeon who had once treated John Trautmann's broken collarbone, appeared. Griffiths offered his hand, but looked grave. 'I'm sorry to tell you Bert, but I'm afraid your neck is broken.' The others in the room gasped in horror and Trautmann felt a surge of fear. Griffiths put an arm gently around his shoulder and led him to a chair.

Trautmann told Griffiths about his visit to the osteopath and the diagnosis. The professor exploded, 'What, the man's a bloody lunatic, its a wonder he didn't kill you, in fact considering what you've been through this last few days you should be dead.'

He was to be admitted to the hospital straight away. Harold Young was despatched back to Bramhall to collect some belongings and break the news to the family, while Griffiths prepared to carry out a complicated operation. The X-rays revealed the second vertebrae had been cracked in two by the collision while the third had wedged against the second, holding the pieces together and certainly saving his life. Griffiths had to carry out a complicated operation restoring the damage while constructing an elaborate structure of traction, which would mean Trautmann's head and most of his back would be encased in plaster and metal, to hold this firmly he would need to drill into the skull. Griffiths was to perform the operation the next day, meanwhile Trautmann was confined to his hospital bed with a temporary brace under strict supervision to prevent any movement or excitement.

Within hours the hospital switchboard was jammed with calls while reporters descended on the Royal Infirmary in droves. Bert Trautmann was front-page news again. The following morning Griffiths bored two holes at the back of Trautmann's cranium and bolted into place calipers that could support the neck and spine. The cervical vertebrae had been successfully repositioned, the frame now had to be encased in plaster. There was one big problem: the holes Griffiths had drilled were not sufficient to take the weight of the support structure. Trautmann was once again put under anaesthetic and two more deeper holes were drilled into the bone.

He came round from the operation totally rigid, he could not move a muscle and thought he must be paralysed, lying flat on his back with just the ceiling to stare at.

'I told myself that's it Trautmann, your career is over. It was a scary feeling but I suddenly realised the severe pain was no longer there. On the other hand I had no feeling at all and being unable to move a muscle in my top half I was a little bit frightened.'

Barbara Friar recalled with amusement the family's first visit to see him after the operation. 'Professor Griffiths made no secret about the serious nature of the injury and told us it would probably take a year for Bert to recover. When we went into his room Margaret and I just burst out laughing, he looked so ridiculous, like he was wearing a huge white space helmet. I remember him saying, 'Vot are you bluddy laughing at?' which made us laugh even more.

As far as the Press were concerned, the main story was whether or not Trautmann would be able to play again. No other player in professional football had suffered such an injury before, but the main consensus of opinion was that Trautmann would not play again. This was also preoccupying Bert's mind. When he asked Griffiths about his prospects, the doctor replied, 'I don't know Bert, I just don't know.'

Letters poured into the hospital, but one of the main problems for Trautmann was being able to read them. His bed was a basic wooden structure without a mattress or pillows and the medical staff had to rig up a system of pulleys so he could be lifted, but his movements were so restricted that for the first few days he could hardly move. Somebody gave him a homemade periscope to enable him to read a paper balanced on his knee, causing further mirth among his visitors. 'It's like being on a bluddy U-boat,' he complained. After four days he was allowed to move around, slowly at first to get used to the immense weight he was carrying. He was top heavy and had to readjust his sense of balance, but eventually he was allowed to wander around the wards. Two other footballers were having treatment in the hospital at the same time, the great Tom Finney in for a varicose vein operation and Bert's teammate Jimmy Meadows still undergoing surgery to the knee he had injured in the 1955 Cup Final. He discussed with them his concerns about his career being over, the same applying to Meadows of course, and Finney urged them both to be patient. Trautmann had more sympathy for Meadows than himself at the time because he knew if Jimmy's last operation was unsuccessful he would not be able to play top-class football again (Meadows subsequently had to retire from playing). Trautmann was discharged from Manchester Royal Infirmary two weeks after being admitted.

Just after the semi-final win against Tottenham, Margaret told Trautmann she wanted to move out of the Friar's home and find a place of their own. With other things on his mind, he agreed in principle as long as his wife took the responsibility of looking for a suitable property. In Marsham Road, Hazel Grove, the *Daily Mail* had built a showhouse as part of their Ideal Home Exhibition. Bert returned home to find he and Margaret were to be the owners. An immediate move was out of the question because of his condition, but he also wanted to accept an invitation from Wilfried Gerhardt and the German FA to travel to Berlin as guest of honour for the Germany v England international. He loathed being restricted to the house so he decided to go ahead with the trip to Berlin.

His body restrictions were causing a great deal of amusement to the family. Granny Winstanley thought he looked like 'Franklinstein', while Margaret and Barbara were having to perform a number of unsavoury tasks. The plaster cast encased his head completely, the circumference of his neck, and came over his chin to his bottom lip. When he ate food, particles kept falling into the plaster and each day Margaret had to scrape them out. (This was eventually overcome when the plaster was cut back to alleviate the problem). The plastered area of his back was already causing intense itching and Barbara's job in the evening was to force her school ruler into the gaps and scratch his back for him while he groaned in relief.

Margaret was furious with him for wanting to go to Berlin, even though she had been included in the invitation. She wanted to concentrate on the new home and spend some time at the caravan in Anglesey. The ensuing argument and the stubborn nature of them both created yet another schism in their stormy relationship when he decided to travel to Germany on his own.

Jack Friar kept out of the argument, he had his own problems because Clarice had been admitted to hospital with a severe back problem and was in the orthopaedic ward at Buxton Hospital, but he knew Margaret couldn't go and leave John in the sole responsibility of Sarah. He also felt Trautmann had been neglecting his family responsibilities of late and was hoping now, after the injury, he would have more time for them.

Trautmann left Manchester on 24 May, staying overnight in London before travelling to Düsseldorf the next morning to catch an internal flight to Berlin. He left Bramhall with a hug and kiss from John and a blast of Arctic cold indifference from his wife.

In the evening Margaret Trautmann left the house, leaving John in the care of Jack and Granny Winstanley and turned up at the Wilson's flat in Lumb Lane. Audrey answered the door. 'Margaret arrived carrying a portmanteau which had now replaced her large bag. She marched in and said she was going to stay for a while. Stan, who was by then working as a representative for Hoover, told her she couldn't, I think he had a lot of paperwork to clear up and she stormed off telling us if we couldn't be bothered about her she would go and see the Hillgroves, mutual friends of ours who lived near by.'

Margaret arrived at the Hillgroves' house in Woodford Road and was allowed to stay the night. The following morning, 25 May, she returned home to the Friar household and was met by an outraged Jack. He accused Margaret of neglecting her responsibilities as a mother and he was also annoyed she had not been to visit Clarice in Buxton. Father and daughter had a furious row, resulting in Margaret storming out of the house with John and returning to the Hillgroves. Stan Wilson, feeling a little guilty about Margaret, was driving past the house when he saw her standing outside with John. He pulled up and got out of the car to speak to her.

On the opposite side of the road a 'Tip Top' van, a kind of mobile bread and confectionary shop, had also stopped and was touting for business. This was the sole object of John's attention.

The boy was asking Margaret for some money to buy sweets and Stan reached into his pocket and handed him some pennies. Stan and Margaret watched as he carefully crossed the road to make his purchase.

John chose his sweets but was a penny or so short of the amount. He told the man he would go and get some more from his mummy across the road, then just turned and ran. The man leant forward to try to grab him just as a green blur appeared from the side.

Trautmann arrived in Düsseldorf to be greeted by Wilfried Gerhardt and a swarm of German Press, radio and television reporters. After a short Press conference he was taken to a Düsseldorf hotel to rest before travelling to Berlin later in the evening. The manager of the hotel escorted him to his room and asked if he needed anything. Trautmann suddenly had a great desire for strawberries and cream, which was immediately ordered for him. The hotel manager stayed to chat for a while and when the telephone rang the manager was annoyed because he had left instructions for his guest not to be disturbed. He grabbed the telephone to bark his displeasure when, in Trautmann's words, 'he went white, I literally watched the colour drain out of his face'.

'I'm afraid it's about your son Herr Trautmann, he has been involved in a serious traffic accident.'

# DIFFICULT YEARS AND THE STRUGGLE BACK

*The beauty of each season drenched with a colour scheme. They are beautiful until the day the whole damn lot turns black. Suddenly you are wide awake and no longer have your dream. You find that no one is a friend as you trudge a weary track.*

MARGARET TRAUTMANN

THE YOUNG man steering his green Standard Vanguard along Woodford Road was proudly showing off his driving skills to his younger sister two weeks after passing his driving test. He still displayed the careful habits of a newly qualified driver, checking his mirrors constantly with his eyes carefully surveying the road ahead. He saw the parked 'Tip Top' van, signalled as he pulled towards the centre of the road to pass it and kept his speed at a steady 30 miles an hour. The little blond boy suddenly dashed out from behind the van, the Vanguard driver hit the brakes down to the floor, but the heavy car hit the child, who soared into the air and landed with a nauseating thud some distance away. The driver, shaking with shock, jumped out of the vehicle as the penetrating screams of the boy's mother pierced his ears.

Stan Wilson and others rushed to John's unconscious body, within minutes Dr Fraser, the family GP who lived nearby, was on the scene. He immediately placed John on the back seat of his car with Margaret and drove to Stockport Infirmary.

Wilson remembered the squeal of brakes and the thud: 'It was the most horrible sight, when I got to John I knew in my heart he was gone. I felt sick to my stomach and was overwhelmed with guilt about giving him the money.'

Dr Fraser carried John into the casualty area where other doctors rushed over to try and treat his injuries. It was a futile task, and within minutes of his arrival the boy was pronounced dead. Jack Friar was in the house with Barbara and Granny when the call came through, and he broke the news to his daughter and mother-in-law through a veil of tears.

Barbara's recollection of her father's reaction was vivid: 'I had never seen such anguish in his face before, he was normally so calm and assured, but he just seemed to disintegrate mentally. He immediately tried to contact Bert, telling whomever he spoke to to try and get him home straight away but not to tell him John was dead. After that he got into the car and drove to Buxton to tell my mother, although afterwards he could not recall driving there or the journey back. Shortly after dad left, Margaret arrived back with, I think, Dr Fraser.'

In Germany frantic efforts were being made to get Trautmann home, the German FA and the British Consulate managed to divert a British European Airways plane, en route to London from Zurich, into Düsseldorf Airport to take him back.

All that Trautmann knew was that John had serious injuries. 'On the plane I couldn't understand how it had happened. Even at five we had instilled into John the dangers of the road and the importance of kerb-drill. I played little games in my mind as I stared out of the plane windows, I would see an opening in the clouds and thought, if I see another opening in the next thirty seconds, John would be alright.'

In London a Manchester-bound aircraft had been delayed for him to board, 40 minutes later he touched down at Ringway Airport. He was met by a family friend who escorted him through scores of waiting reporters. He knew then John was dead, a fact confirmed by his friend when they reached the waiting car.

In Bramhall Granny Winstanley let them into the house where Jack and Margaret were standing in the hallway, they held on to each other sobbing uncontrollably.

Within minutes of his arrival home the Press were clamouring outside the house for statements and pictures, the telephone was ringing incessantly.

Inside the house the family were trying desperately to console each other, as an increasing number of telegrams or messages of condolence were arriving by the hour.

The following day Margaret and Bert left to stay with friends who had a small farm a few kilometres away. They needed time to think and escape from the overwhelming attentions of the Press.

Stan and Audrey Wilson visited them at the farm where Margaret, in her grief, had started to hack away her hair with a large pair of scissors. Audrey said, 'She looked a sight, as she cut her hair she threw the locks out of a window.

Our friends, who lived on the farm with their elderly father, found the old man looking at his bean frames with a puzzled expression on his face. The poor old sod was convinced he was growing hairy runner beans. Even in her grief Margaret had created some bizarre humour.'

At the inquest the 19-year-old driver was cleared of any blame, a verdict of accidental death was recorded.

The Trautmanns later received a letter from the youth's mother offering her family's deepest sympathy. She was German.

The funeral cortège left the Friar's home for the service at St Georges Church, Stockport, before John was buried at St Nicholas Churchyard in St Helens.

Trautmann asked for donations to be made to the National Playing Fields Association in John's memory instead of flowers. Bill Leivers and three other Manchester City players carried the small coffin. Bert Trautmann, in three short weeks, had gone from triumph to personal tragedy that had left him exhausted and mentally shattered. Within the family John's death had triggered a collective guilt, which was now apportioning blame.

Margaret was cruelly insistent it was Bert's fault, if he had not gone to Germany the tragedy would not have happened.

Jack blamed Margaret, whose wayward and selfish attitude had caused the argument that resulted in her taking John from the house. The gap in their lives was absolute, while the strain on the Trautmanns' relationship was to cause an undercurrent lasting the rest of their married life.

Shortly after the funeral the German FA invited Bert and Margaret to Germany as guests of honour for the German championship playoffs in Berlin. Wilfried Gerhardt arranged for the couple to spend some time as his association's guests in Bavaria for a long holiday afterwards. They also received an invitation from the Dassler family to visit them.

In early June the Trautmanns flew to Berlin to escape the stifling atmosphere of grief and recrimination. The welcome escape to Berlin helped them enormously to recover from their trauma. The kindness of their German hosts was magnificent, the constant invitations and hospitality kept them fully occupied. Politically, Eastern Europe and West Berlin were being subjected to the intense atmosphere of the developing Cold War, waged between the Soviet Union and the West. Events in Hungary were unfolding while Berlin itself felt increasingly isolated from the rest of Germany. The sociological problems of the West Berliners were becoming extremely acute, and the East Germans were restricting any movement outside of the city to uncompromising limits. As a consequence, any way of escaping the claustrophobic incarceration within West Berlin was being pursued every which way. Many parents hit on the idea of temporary adoption of their children by Western European families as a means for their offspring to escape the ever-present threat of the Eastern Bloc. This resulted in a number of children being offered for adoption to prominent German families.

Into the midst of the anxious and beleaguered West Berlin adoption agencies, the high profile Trautmanns appeared.

Klaus was almost identical to John, and the uncanny resemblance was startling for Bert and Margaret, who were attracted to the child immediately. They discussed at length the possibility of adoption and retired to Bavaria to consider the situation further, while importantly they secured Klaus's mother's agreement to take him back to England for a holiday.

While in Bavaria, Bert and Margaret met up with the Dassler family, whose warmth and encouragement made them resolve to adopt Klaus. In the meantime Adi Dassler entertained the couple with lavish attention and further encouraged Trautmann to take up his offer of an agency in north-west England. Trautmann was completely honest with Dassler, he felt the events of the last few weeks had reduced his ambition, and he would not be able to represent Dassler with any great enthusiasm or interest. In a magnanimous gesture he nominated his great friend

Nobby Clarke, who had just opened a sports shop business in Manchester, to be the first Adidas stockist in the area.

Towards the end of their visit, Bert and Margaret collected Klaus from his mother in Berlin amid a barrage of Press and television publicity. They had in their own minds no firm plans to adopt the child immediately, only to introduce him to English life, with the intention of returning him to his mother in the autumn. If things worked out they would then go ahead with formal adoption procedures.

Prior to their return to Manchester, Trautmann was amused to find himself at the centre of attention by the German medical profession. David Lloyd Griffiths's treatment of his injury had received a great deal of interest in the medical world and the ever-vigilant German doctors had developed a keen interest in Trautmann's recovery. A number of prominent German orthopaedic doctors had discussed his case and were eager to examine the remarkable traction for themselves.

Trautmann, Margaret and Klaus left for England to face the family again.

Jack, Clarice, Sarah and Barbara were overwhelmed by Klaus's uncanny resemblance to John. Barbara remembered her father's immediate reaction as one of shock, followed by his total refusal to accept the boy.

'He had absolutely adored John, when they returned with this clone of his grandson he could not accept that they had replaced John immediately with a carbon copy. After two or three days he came round to accepting him as an innocent victim of circumstances and came to treat him with a great deal of affection.'

Bert and Margaret moved into their new home in Hazel Grove with every intention of rebuilding their lives and rekindling their relationship.

Klaus proved to be a delightful child. He was spoiled with endless gifts from the Trautmanns' family and friends in an effort to help Klaus replace John in all of their lives.

Jack taught him English nursery rhymes with the same verve and sense of fun that he had taught his grandson.

The Wilsons took him to Belle Vue amusement park and zoo and introduced him into their own family, while Granny and Clarice fussed over him with genuine affection. Everyone was now used to the idea of Klaus becoming one of the family on a permanent basis. Bert wanted to proceed with the adoption, but Margaret could not.

She had decided no other child could replace her own and she slowly cooled towards Klaus. Matters were not helped by a request for money from the boy's mother, who had also made some awkward statements to the German newspapers about the possible adoption.

In early October Klaus returned to Germany. He was never heard from again.

When the Trautmanns moved into the house in Marsham Road, Bert was extremely limited in what he could do around the home, while at the same time he was beginning to feel a little sorry for himself and was moping around. He started to drive to Maine Road each day to be around the other players.

Barbara Friar was amazed at his ingenuity. 'He couldn't turn his head at all, so he rigged up a series of mirrors all over the car which worked out every possible angle. I always thought he would be arrested but the only times the police stopped him was to ask him how he was.'

Most of the City team had been in contact with him, mainly to pull his leg about his encasement – they were as merciless as ever in the dressing room. In order to turn his body he had to shuffle his feet like a penguin with his arms stiff to his sides. Beaky Barnes and Pauly would wait for him to be facing away from them and shout, 'Hey, Trauty.' By the time Bert had manoeuvred his body towards the shout they had disappeared.

'You bluddy bastards.'

The team had returned from their tour of Germany undefeated, including a 4–1 win over Werder Bremen.

'See how we did without you Trauty, I don't think the boss is going to take you on the next tour.'

While in Bremen the team had been guests of honour at the Town Hall where Trautmann was to have been honoured. Reports in the Press had indicated he was to be made a Freeman of the Port by the Minister of Sports and Recreation. Les McDowall had received a scroll on his behalf, which he presented to Trautmann at Maine Road. When he read the document Bert was disappointed to find he had not been made a Freeman at all, the scroll merely conferred on him the right to dwell in his home port. There was no doubt the players were shocked by the extent of the injury and privately one or two of them had expressed doubts about him being able to fully recover. McDowall knew it would have to be a slow, patient recovery time and he treated Bert with great care and understanding. If it proved to be the end of his career the directors had insisted he would have a job, of sorts, for life with the club.

The plaster was to be removed in November, but the doctors at the Royal Infirmary could still not guarantee he would be able to play top-class football again and this nagging doubt was continually in his mind. Despite all the success of the last two years he was not a well-off man, in the 1956 Cup ties alone City had played in front of half a million people but his reward in helping to win the FA Cup was a take-home pay of around £14 and a £2 win bonus. The board asked the Football Association if the players could be presented with gold watches to commemorate the victory but were refused permission.

Trautmann's sources of income were limited, he devoted his entire life during the season to football, to his own disadvantage. A number of business ventures had been proposed to him, beside the one by Adi Dassler, but Trautmann turned them all down to concentrate on his football. He had received payment for some advertising work, mainly through Jack Friar and the CWS. At Maine Road a large advertising board was placed on the main stand with a picture of Trautmann endorsing JC cigarettes, the Co-op's own brand. He also had a number of photographs taken, which appeared in magazines advertising the same product, but the most he received from the CWS was a cheque for £50.

Most professional footballers had to take full-time summer jobs to supplement their close-season incomes or take advantage of any perks. Jack Friar used to offer two pound bags of sugar or other CWS products for every goal the team scored, and when the forwards turned away after scoring, many supporters misunderstood the two-fingered gestures towards the stand where Friar sat grinning.

Manchester City made an awful start to the season, while the players suffered severe morale problems caused by injuries and the ongoing dispute between Don Revie and Les McDowall. In November the board received a bid of £24,000 from Sunderland and they had no hesitation in accepting it. Revie showed no indecision in signing.

A number of players were now past their peak, with both Roy Paul and Nobby Clarke struggling to find form. The supporters and the players were expecting McDowall to go into the transfer market in a big way to strengthen the team, but he didn't and sold Bill Spurdle to Port Vale instead.

Shortly after Revie's transfer, Bert Trautmann returned to Manchester Royal Infirmary to have the calipers and plaster removed. A circular saw was used to cut away the great volume of greying plaster. The calipers were then unbolted from his skull and removed. Trautmann was sitting on a high casualty bed with his legs dangling freely, while his hands clutched the edge, his knuckles white with tension as the high pitched whining of the saw echoed inside his head. When it was finished he touched his hair, feeling the matted grease with disgust.

Trautmann felt further repugnance when he saw the fatty substance clogging the calipers and he immediately asked a nurse if he could wash his hair. She agreed to shampoo it for him and in his eagerness to cleanse his head he swung his body off the bed and, 'I fell flat on my bluddy arse'.

It took some time to readjust his sense of balance after carrying the weight of the traction for so long. When his hair had been washed, Trautmann felt his scalp gingerly, intrigued by the holes in his skull which he examined in the mirrors. 'The top of my head looked like the number four on a dice.'

Trautmann's head and shoulders were alarmingly stiff and did not give him a great deal of movement, but the relief of having the plaster removed gave him such a surge of freedom.

David Lloyd Griffiths was more than happy with the way the injury had healed, but he was cautious in his prediction of a quick return to football. It was an unexampled injury in terms of an athlete, predicting any return to professional football, therefore, would not be easy, while the uniqueness had brought requests for copies of the case notes from all over the world. Griffiths had his doubts about Trautmann being able to play again at the highest level. He advised Trautmann to take things easy, suggesting a light training programme that concentrated on regaining his muscle strength. Surprisingly, the doctor did not recommend any physiotherapy. Trautmann was fitted with a leather surgical collar, which he was told to wear for at least two months.

Les McDowall agreed with Griffiths. McDowall, however, was under pressure from the demands of the directors and the supporters, all of whom wanted to know when he would be able to play Trautmann again. One director had actually told him, 'Even a half fit Trautmann is better than most other bloody goalkeepers.' Alan Douglas, who had taken over from Walter Smith as chairman during the summer of 1956, was also anxious to see Trautmann back in the team. He thought the side would benefit from his comeback in terms of confidence, but on a more mercenary level the club needed a boost to the dwindling attendance figures at the stadium. Manchester City were losing the considerable number of neutral football supporters in the North West to the emergence of the Manchester United 'Busby Babes', who even by November looked likely to repeat their Championship success of the previous season, so Trautmann's comeback was essential in attracting back the spectators. From Trautmann's point of view, he was a little impatient to play again after his months of dormancy, and he was resolute and determined to play again. Since his debut he had played a number of matches when not fully fit. In the Cup tie against Everton the previous year, McDowall had asked him to play while he was suffering from a bad bronchial problem. In other games he had carried groin and muscle strains, bruised ribs and twisted knees, all for the benefit of Manchester City. On one ridiculous Saturday he had been badly concussed in a match at Burnley, but the manager and Laurie Barnett kept him on the field. He arrived home in the evening and went straight to bed. In the morning an anxious Margaret and Jack asked him how he felt and he was utterly baffled by their concern. Jack explained that the club doctor had treated him for concussion and given him some medication. Trautmann could not remember a thing about the incident, thinking Margaret was working on an elaborate joke against him. It was only after reading the match report in the papers he was stunned to find out he really had been injured.

Steve Fleet remembered his mentor returning to training. 'City had signed George Thompson from Preston as extra goalkeeping cover so we had four of us in for training. I could see straight away he was a little saturnine, he was not as sharp or as confident, while his usual agility was naturally limited. At the time I was having a frustrating time myself. John Savage had taken Bert's place in the first team while I was alternating with George Thompson in the Reserves or A team. I felt I was ready for the first team and envious of my mate Eddie Colman at United, Busby had given so many young players their chance, but, at City, McDowall wasn't interested. He was a good tactical manager but almost antediluvian in his attitude to blooding young players. Bert's return made me a lot happier, without disrespect to Savage or Thompson, his very character seemed to give me a lift. When I made my debut while on leave from the RAF, Bert had been very constructive in his comments and had given me great encouragement. I remember trying hard to boost his own confidence then, we stayed on after training devising special exercises to build up his muscle strength. I spoke to him about the neck injury and of course sympathised about John's death, his main concern was to shut it all away and get back to fitness.'

Only two weeks after returning to training, completely ignoring the advice of David Lloyd Griffiths, Bert Trautmann asked Les McDowall to play him in a reserve game against Preston North End on 1 December.

'McDowall wasn't keen, but I was desperate to prove myself. I was also a little philosophical about things, to a degree I accepted I might not be capable of ever reaching my top form again, perhaps in hindsight it was foolhardy, but I wasn't going to bloody well give up without trying.'

Many people expressed their grave concern about his quite remarkable comeback, while David Lloyd Griffiths was unhappy at the news.

Eight thousand spectators and scores of reporters turned up to watch the reserve game. Trautmann, looking a little apprehensive, took to the field to a rapturous reception.

His slowness and almost rigid stature were noticeable straight away, the precise positioning he used to display was ragged and he was hesitant with crosses. The City Reserve side opened the scoring to the biggest roar they had heard at a Central League game; normally you could hear the spectators slurping their Bovril.

Soon after the City goal, a cross from the left came towards Trautmann and he was bustled over the line for the equaliser. The crowd gasped in horror as Trautmann lay on the ground for a few seconds before rising slowly.

'I was more winded than anything else, but I should have held the ball and taken the collision easily. I was so concerned about the forward coming in I let myself be diverted. It was something I had never worried about before.'

The crowd, relieved he seemed unscathed by the incident, shouted their encouragement but Stan Wilson in the main stand looked at Bert squatting on his haunches.

'Jesus, he's started to pick at daisies again.'

Spectators and journalists left Maine Road sadly reflecting on the pale imitation of the superb goalkeeper they once knew. Trautmann played in the Reserves the following week in a 3–1 defeat at Liverpool without any noticeable improvement in his performance. Astonishingly, McDowall chose him to play against Wolverhampton Wanderers the following week – he was to make his return to First Division football. McDowall's reasoning may well have been influenced by the need to instil into his goalkeeper a feeling of confidence, while at the same time feeling Trautmann would be responsive to the big match atmosphere and the empathy on the field with the first-team players.

On the morning of Saturday 15 December Trautmann arose early and drove to St Helens to visit John's grave. This was an extreme departure from his usual pre-match preparation. His normal procedure before a home match was to have a light breakfast, arrive at the stadium around midday, well before the other players, and sip tea with the groundsmen in their hut. He would then join the arriving players in the dressing rooms for a pre-match warm up routine where the others were encouraged to throw balls at him to catch.

Trautmann arrived at Maine Road some time after the other players had assembled. The visit to St Helens had depressed him, and his teammates were startled by his unstructured pre-match preparation. His state of melancholia did little for their confidence, and despite a burst of ribaldry and disgusting jokes from

Barnes and Dave Ewing he arrived on to the pitch with a face set in grim impassiveness.

A crowd several thousand above the season's average turned up to greet his arrival back, Alan Douglas had been shrewdly perceptive. Trautmann perked up as the crowd roared their approval, while a trace of a smile appeared during the warm-up.

Wolves were pressing to catch Manchester United at the top of the League and were a good footballing side. Displaying the sentiment of a lion shaking a zebra, they put pressure on Trautmann from the start.

Trautmann fumbled and mistimed his dives, his positioning sense was poor and, above all, his bravery and willingness to come out at forwards left much to be desired.

Wolverhampton won 3–2, Trautmann's colleagues played well, but they knew in their hearts they could have won.

Trautmann departed Maine Road in a sullen mood while the reporters in the press box were already writing their criticisms of City bringing him back too quickly, with the supporters aiming their anger at the board for cruelly exposing Trautmann's lack of fitness and confidence.

In Hazel Grove the tension between Bert and Margaret was unbearable, while Trautmann brooded about his game she brooded over John. Margaret Trautmann had not removed any culpability from her husband regarding the accident, and his home life was collapsing, like his professional status, all around him.

Ten days after the Wolverhampton match, Manchester City played two games against Bolton Wanderers over the Christmas holiday. On Christmas Day they lost 3–1 at Maine Road, on Boxing Day 1–0 at Burnden Park and he gave inept displays in each. The time of year he most enjoyed became a period of despair and frustration. The defence of the FA Cup was to start on 5 January and the draw gave City a tough away match against their old adversaries, Newcastle United. Trautmann performed well to help earn a replay after a 1–1 draw.

The return match on 9 January turned out to be one of the most remarkable Cup games ever played.

City established a 3–0 half-time lead, playing some exquisite football, and more encouragingly Trautmann seemed to be recovering his form. Being Manchester City, of course, they lost 5–4 after extra-time. Gloom and despondency settled on the players.

Things were made worse for him by a sudden turn around by some of the Press and supporters, many suggesting he should give up his career and retire. A false report appeared in one paper concerning a coaching offer from Germany. The club? Schalke 04. Trautmann decided he would retire and asked for an interview with Les McDowall. If the supporters were turning against him he saw no point in continuing. McDowall urged him to carry on, telling Trautmann not to dwell on his recent games but to think about the countless times he had saved the side from defeat. In the end McDowall persuaded him to reconsider.

An article by the *Manchester Evening Chronicle* sports columnist, Arthur Walmsley, urging the supporters to give Trautmann more time, became a statement of how many people felt. 'I do not place Bert beyond criticism any more than I do his teammates (this referred to adverse comments made about Trautmann by unnamed players to other journalists) but the present tendency is not to judge him on what he is doing today as what he did in the past.

It was inevitable that after a long lay off Trautmann would take time to reach peak form if, indeed, he is ever going to reach it again.

It was doubly unfortunate that he should come back at a time when John Savage was playing so well in the first team, but with all sympathy to Savage, I believe the club was right not to keep Trautmann kicking his heels for too long in the reserve team. A fit Trautmann at his best is the finest goalkeeper in the country. It was vital that he found out as soon as possible whether he could regain that form following the catastrophe of a broken neck. And the only way that could be done was for him to play in the first team over a protracted period.'

Trautmann and City struggled along dismally for the rest of the season and only in the last few matches did they secure enough points to pull away from the relegation zone.

The last few matches were encouraging in more ways than one, and Trautmann had begun to show signs of his old confidence and agility returning. 'I knew he was getting back to normal when we played Birmingham,' smirked Beaky Barnes. 'One of their wingers called him a German bastard when they came up for a corner. Murphy was also playing for them by the way, he had this fucking great mark on his knee from the accident with Trauty. When the winger called him, Trauty chased the bugger to the halfway line, if he had caught him he would have thrown him on to the stand roof. Fortunately, Pauly or Bill Leivers stopped him and as he trotted past me on his way back to his goal he winked and said, Bluddy English bastard, he had got his old fire back.'

# 1958–1961 – TIMES OF CHANGE

*This, this is he; softly awhile, Let us not break it upon him, O change beyond report, thought or belief.*

JOHN MILTON

HE OLD fire was back, but the reflexes, agility and the superb fitness were not. Trautmann knew in his heart his natural talent had been considerably diminished by his injury and now had to readjust his attitude to playing, while at the same time come to uncomfortable terms with his increasingly difficult home life.

Manchester City embarked on their third successive German tour at the end of May 1957. While the great strength of the team over the last three years had been the exceptional spirit among the players, this tour would mark the beginning of the end of many of them.

The old war horse and inspirational Roy Paul decided to take up an offer to become player-manager of Worcester City in the Southern League and age and injury were creeping up on Nobby Clarke. Clarke played against Borussia Dortmund on the 1957 tour while still nursing a knee injury. His pace had gone and McDowall cruelly remarked within earshot of the other players that he would be making Clarke available for transfer in the near future.

At the start of the 1957–58 season, only five of the Cup Final side remained in contention for first-team places, Jack Dyson broke a leg in a pre-season practice game and on his return later in the year he broke it again, which effectively ended his career.

Les McDowall began to rebuild his side with Bert Trautmann still firmly established as his first-choice goalkeeper. The season started with moderate success, with the new influx of players blending reasonably well. McDowall decided to introduce a new tactical plan, this time revolving around Keith Marsden, a workmanlike but ungifted insideforward. Marsden dropped into the half-back line alongside Dave Ewing to form dual centre-half roles, the first time a back-four formation was used in Britain. The system was immediately dubbed the 'M' plan by the Press, who were as sceptical about it as they had been about the Revie Plan.

Trautmann was still learning to adjust his own game as it became apparent his neck injury had permanently reduced his mobility. 'I had to become more wily in dealing with forwards, it was apparent to me I could not perform with the same agility, not just from the neck problem but because age was creeping up on me. I learned to develop my anticipation more and worked hard on my positional stance. I gave forwards less to aim at and tried to force them into errors.'

Trautmann was as bemused by the Marsden Plan as the players trying to operate it were. 'I could see McDowall's idea, but in all honesty we did not have players with enough skill or intellect to make it work, Beaky and I urged the manager to buy more talented players but he always said the board would not provide the money.' The board were planning to invest in a huge new stand to cover the massive Kippax Street terracing, and McDowall was again urged to buy cheaply.

In the event the season proved to be a curious one, even for a club renowned for bizarre eccentricity. The goals came fast and furiously, but while the forwards were performing well, an equal number were flying past Trautmann with startling regularity. The defence played like buffoons, they became the laughing stock of the supporters as they tried desperately to stem the flow of goals. John McTavish, the left-half, contrived to score three own-goals in three weeks past the hapless Trautmann, and in September the team were annihilated 9–2 by West Bromwich Albion when John Savage was deputising. The team had a number of high scoring away wins, 5–2 at both Everton and Blackpool and 5–4 at Sheffield Wednesday. They also defeated Everton 6–2 at Maine Road in a match where Beaky Barnes scored three penalties, a feat he reminded everyone about for weeks. They called him Three Pen Ken for a while.

The topsy-turvy season continued with unabated unpredictability and, remarkably, at the turn of the year Manchester City were up with the leaders of the First Division. McDowall made a number of backroom changes to his staff, bringing in George Poyser, a former professional player and ex-manager of Notts County, as his assistant with responsibility for scouting, Jimmy Meadows was appointed trainer and Laurie Barnett, to the older players' sadness, was moved to the physiotherapist's room. Trautmann and Barnes were still concerned about the strength of the team as 1958 began. In the FA Cup the team travelled for the third-round tie to the scene of their humiliation in September, West Bromwich, where a 5–1 defeat was fairly moderate in relation to the League game.

Many players felt that Trautmann was now back at his best, but with the defence as leaky as a sieve he had more than ample opportunity to sharpen his reflexes. If nothing else, McDowall had created an entertaining side, certainly for supporters who were particularly fond of Ben Travers's plays.

Trautmann often looked with envy at the way Manchester United were being run across the City. He desperately wanted more success, the consistency and flamboyance of the Old Trafford club, with a manager and board who were close and caring towards their players, was a source of deep frustration for him. United looked set to win the Championship again and were also learning from their excursions into European Cup football. In contrast the City board and management were a conservative group of men, the directors were anachronistic in attitude to the players and supporters, while McDowall, for all his ideas, still presented a solitary countenance to the team.

On a grey, cold evening on 6 February 1958 Trautmann was listening to the radio in fascinated horror. While returning from a European Cup match in Belgrade, the United team plane had crashed in Munich with few survivors.

Manchester was plunged into a state of depression as slowly the horrific details emerged and the names of the dead became known. Frank Swift, covering the game for his newspaper, was one of the first deaths to be announced. Trautmann was deeply saddened by this news, while another name among the dead made his thoughts turn to one of his own colleagues.

The gloom over Manchester was absolute when Trautmann drove to Maine Road the following morning, and he immediately sought out Steve Fleet on his arrival. The young goalkeeper was beside himself with the death of his best friend, Eddie Colman. 'Bert Trautmann understood more than anyone how I felt about losing Eddie, he taught me how to handle grief and come to terms with it, it was not easy but Trautmann had such humility and a caring attitude he helped me tremendously to overcome one of the worst periods of my life. I understood he offered his help to Old Trafford in any way he could, presumably translation and contacts, but really there was very little he, or any of us at City, could do but offer our sympathy and pay our respects at the funerals.'

The season continued for Manchester City and two weeks after the disaster they travelled to a match at Leicester City. On the team coach the players were discussing the number of goals that they had conceded during the season, as the discussion became generalised Trautmann made the comment that the most goals he had scored against him was seven. City lost the match 8–4! In April they faced their final match against Aston Villa with every chance of finishing in third place in the First Division. City lost 2–1 and Villa's two goals meant that Manchester City became the first team in history to score and concede 100 League goals in a season. Trautmann had played in 34 of the matches and, despite his own fine personal performances, another unwanted statistic was added to his career record.

His personal life was also going through yet another difficult period. Margaret had been neglecting herself for some time and experiencing deep depressions. She had lost weight, while her behaviour was becoming increasingly idiosyncratic. She would frequently awaken the household after midnight by vacuuming or putting on the washing machine, more often than not with no washing in it. She would then retreat into John's bedroom for days at a time, sketching or painting in the half-light, or writing poetry dedicated to John. She would rally for a few days before retreating back into her enclosed thoughts.

The family were becoming increasingly anxious about this activity. Her mental state had always been a cause of concern, and Granny Winstanley's 'she's never been right in't head since' was always an uncomfortable family joke. Now her bizarre behaviour and mood swings were worse than ever. It was during this time she conceived again. Slowly but surely, her health began to improve, and she took pride in her personal appearance and hygiene again. Her mental state and attitude towards her husband was still as unpredictable as ever, but more worryingly she still blamed him for John's death. 'She was up and down as ever with Bert, some days she would not want him to be around and on others she was desperate for him to be with her,' said Barbara Friar. 'It got to the point we had to ask him what mood she was in.' At the time she needed him the most, without any discussion, Trautmann announced he would be going on a tour of the United States and Canada at the end of the season. This crass and thoughtless news left Margaret reeling. She confided to Barbara, 'He's going to abandon me again.' Jack asked Bert to reconsider, but he insisted the club would not let him stay behind.

Trautmann left Southampton for the Atlantic crossing to New York in early May and would be away for nearly six weeks. When he left Marsham Road for the trip Margaret refused to see him off.

The tour went extremely well for the club, they scored 36 goals in five exhibition matches and Trautmann was in great demand among the German-American community, who knew of his celebrity and reputation in Europe. He wrote back to Margaret long letters of interest about his tour and mentioned a number of people who had invited them both back to spend a holiday. As the players collected their own mail each day, unsurprisingly, letters from Margaret were conspicuous by their absence. It was not until the end of the tour he received any news from home when two letters arrived at the Royal York Hotel in Toronto.

His wife had written two long, chatty letters. It was as if their marital problems did not exist.

He arrived back from tour with a determination to improve the relationship and prepare the house for the new baby. He also had to consider the extra expenses of the house and family and needed to supplement his earnings.

Eric Thornton had arranged with his newspaper, the *Manchester Evening News*, for Trautmann to write a regular weekly football column during the season. Bert made his views known to Thornton on the current issues within the game, which Thornton then ghosted and the money from the newspaper almost equalled his weekly wages from Manchester City. Trautmann decided to take a part-time job and, through the influence of a friend, he drove around the Manchester area selling Johnson's Paints to hardware shops. The difficulties within the marriage started to erode as Margaret, now blooming with health, prepared for the birth of her child in December.

Trautmann signed his new contract for the 1958–59 season and training started in early August with the club in an optimistic mood. If they could plug up the defence they had a good chance of the Championship. Les McDowall wanted the League title above all else, it was his burning ambition and he thought long and hard about his tactical revelations. The Marsden Plan had been abandoned and he was now looking at different permutations for his players, but unfortunately as the season began he was still undecided in his mind. The team struggled from the start and only Trautmann's brilliant performances allowed them to steal the points in games they should have lost.

In September Bert's great friend Nobby Clarke was sold to Stockport County. He had been reprieved from McDowall's axe by the injury to Jack Dyson, but now the old campaigner was gone. McDowall brought George Hannah, who had scored the third goal against Trautmann in the 1955 Cup Final, from Lincoln in an effort to blend together his experience with the younger players he had brought into the team. Despite Hannah's clever ball play, his legs were past their best and the other exceptional ball player, Bobby Johnstone, was not achieving any consistent form. Johnstone was not helped by a long-standing dispute with McDowall and Jimmy Meadows. He was kept out of the team for long periods and his match fitness was always open to question, many felt his contribution to a game lasted only 20 minutes but for others that 20 minutes was always a touch of class. Johnstone was eventually allowed to return to Hibernian.

At Marsham Road the improving relationship between Bert and Margaret was shattered by the arrival of a solicitor's letter acting for Marion Greenall (now Pennington) requesting an increase in the maintenance payment for Freda, from 10 to 30 shillings a week. Marion, now living in Golbourne, had not been discussed by Margaret and Bert for years and this re-emergence of his past indiscretion triggered in Margaret a sudden burst of spite and vitriol that left Bert reeling. She told Bert not to pay, which resulted in an unpleasant court order case on 28 November in which details of his earnings were hotly disputed between his solicitor Bob Fishwick and the court. Trautmann finished up paying the extra payment and court costs.

Three weeks later, only one week before Christmas, Margaret gave birth to another boy. Stephen, named after Steve Fleet, was born on 18 December 1958 to the utter delight of his parents, the Friars and friends.

'It was a wonderful Christmas for us all,' Barbara remembered. 'We all felt that Margaret could face life again now she had Stephen and that she and Bert could build up their lives again because without doubt they were having a rocky time. Bert was in marvellous spirits, I remember the Wilsons came over and we started playing silly games. Bert disappeared and then came into the room wearing a pair of tights with a loofah stuck down the front. We all jumped on him and threw him outside in the snow.' Steve Fleet recalled Trautmann's mood of elation at Stephen's birth. 'I was of course very proud he had named his son after me while at the same time realising Bert was back at his very best, particularly frustrating for me because it seemed he would be playing for ever. Bert did not stop encouraging me, I was still only 22 at the time and was told my time would come. McDowall on the other hand would always play him even when he was injured. It was around this time he really did a big favour for my confidence. He was trying to shake off a muscle strain and the manager was anxious for him to play in the game on the Saturday. I used to go to the Ping Yong Chinese restaurant in Manchester once a week after training, with Bert, Ken Barnes and a couple of other players. Bert told me he was fed up being forced to play and was going to teach McDowall a lesson. Every Friday I used to look at the first team pinned up on the board and then shrug and walk away. That particular Friday I couldn't believe that my name was in. Bert had stuck to his guns and I had got the benefit.' At the turn of the year, it became apparent Manchester City were in relegation trouble and by the end of April they were one match away from losing their First Division place. On 29 April 1959, 50,000, the largest crowd for months, turned up at Maine Road to watch the last game of the season against Leicester City. Manchester had to win by 4–0 to avoid the drop while Aston Villa, playing at West Bromwich, needed to win 1–0 to stay up.

Leicester scored within the first 10 minutes before City, urged on by the huge crowd, scored three. Trautmann had kept his team in the game with a number of marvellous saves but even he could do nothing about the score from the Hawthorns.

'The Villa game started at 7.15pm and ours at 7.30pm. The noise from the crowd was deafening and then there was the most awful groan as the news came through that Villa were winning 1–0. We were pounding away at the Leicester lads but as the game went on we were becoming more and more fretful. The spectators behind my goal kept shouting to me news about the other match and I was finding it difficult to concentrate. About 15 minutes before the end of our game the most incredible roar went up from the crowd and people kept shouting 'Bert, West Brom have equalised'. I saw big Bill Leivers jump into the air with delight and we managed to hold on. At the end the crowd surged on to the pitch and carried us off to the tunnel. I think the noise and emotion of that night will be an abiding memory of how much a crowd can encourage a team and also how much the intense loyalty of the Manchester supporters meant.'

For the first time in six years the Manchester City players were not required to undertake a post-season football tour, and Trautmann took full benefit of his time off to be with Margaret and Stephen. He took them off to Anglesey for a long idyllic holiday. It was around this time he started to consider realistically the possibility of retiring and gave some thought to his future.

He had just completed one of his most exceptional seasons in football, and his contribution in keeping City in the First Division had been outstanding.

'I thought if I could keep my fitness I would have at least four more seasons left in me, but I had also to consider preparing for the future. I wasn't unduly worried, the City directors had told me time and time again there would be a job for me at Maine Road when I did retire and I had other irons in the fire. My idea was to stay on in football in some capacity but to try and develop some form of business also.'

In August 1959 Manchester City returned from a pre-season match in Berlin to face yet another season of poor results and discontent, and the signing of a young player who had an energizing effect on the team.

Trautmann started the season with a feeling of foreboding, the atmosphere at the club seemed muted and the organisation haphazard. McDowall was even more sombre and distant than usual and the team made jokes behind his back about him hatching more plans in his office. To be fair, the players were now heartily fed up of his plans. McDowall was desperate to recapture the flair and attitude of his previous team, but as Trautmann commented, 'The problem was we no longer had the talent at the club, it was simple, we just did not have players that were good enough.' Ken Barnes was also concerned about the playing strength at the club and he and Trautmann, as the senior players, constantly commented to the manager and coaching staff about the need for an injection of talent into the side. McDowall, on the advice of George Poyser, was merely buying players with good records in the lower divisions who could not do the business in the First. At the turn of the year it was apparent the team and supporters were in for another torrid time. In early January they faced Third Division Southampton in the third round of the FA Cup at Maine Road.

Colin Barlow, a young forward of exciting possibilities, gave City an early lead against Southampton and the supporters sat back and awaited an avalanche of goals. They watched as the avalanche started, in a calamitous game for the wretched City players, Southampton crashed five goals past Trautmann and Manchester City became the butt of football fan jokes across the country.

'What team is known as the Potters?'

'Stoke City?'

'No Manchester City, they've got ten mugs and a Jerry (chamber pot).'

The disastrous season continued with some awful displays by the team, and by March they looked certain to go down. Denis Law's arrival was like a breath of fresh air into the dressing room. Against all the odds, McDowall had persuaded him to sign for City in a deal worth £55,000 to Huddersfield, which shattered the British record transfer fee. The City manager and board were gambling everything on his mercurial talent.

Law's own observations on his arrival at Maine Road were less than complimentary, he had fully expected to join Arsenal or his old manager Bill Shankly at Liverpool. 'I moved to Maine Road in order to play First Division football,' Law recorded in his autobiography, 'but it didn't take me long to realise that City were going to have an uphill struggle to stay in the First Division. I had known that they were near the foot of the League table when I joined them, but I suppose I imagined they were going through a bad patch – only when I actually played for City did I appreciate the full extent of their problems – the Maine Road pitch is one of the best in the country and everything about the club and the ground was first class; everything except for the kit – at City the kit was in rags.' Law summed up exactly the state of things at Manchester City in the spring of 1960.

Trautmann too was appalled by the deteriorating standards on the field and behind the scenes at the stadium. His pride in appearance and his exact kit requirements were legend at the ground. When City had played in hooped socks Trautmann was exact to the centimetre in ensuring the right formation of sky blue and white hoops were lined up. In 1960 he was receiving socks with holes in them and moth-eaten shorts. The enormous acreage of Maine Road had the heavy pall of despondency and the atmosphere was muted and gloomy. Law further commented, 'Apart from Bert Trautmann only Ken Barnes and George Hannah could really play – it seemed to me the rest were either runners, or players past their best.'

Denis Law summed up succinctly the immense problems at Manchester City.

Trautmann observed Law's arrival with the hope McDowall and the board would make further money available for players of his ability.

'He was a brash and confident bugger, but my God he was a good footballer. Unfortunately, McDowall seemed to think just one young and gifted player would turn our fortunes around and make all the difference.'

Law's irrepressible humour and capacity for mickey-taking gave him an immediate admirer, Beaky Barnes, and they developed what would prove to be a life-long friendship. Revitalised by Law, carried by Barnes and Leivers and inspired by Bert Trautmann, Manchester City once again managed to avoid relegation to the Second Division.

The wind of change was now blowing through the professional football world: a number of footballers were becoming increasingly militant towards the maximum wage and contractual conditions the League clubs were enforcing on the players. Trautmann was the Professional Footballers' Union representative at Manchester City, and he was becoming concerned about the rewards and conditions of his profession towards the end of his magnificent, yet materially unrewarding, career. Jimmy Hill, who had taken over the chairmanship of the PFA from Jimmy Guthrie, was proving to be a forceful and articulate leader and it soon became inevitable a change to the wage structure and contracts of the players would bring them into conflict with the clubs. In the previous 20 years, stories of illegal payments and signing-on fees to players had become legend, and none more so than in the North East and at Sunderland in particular. Ken Barnes, playing in a match at Roker Park, had cheekily knocked a ball back to Trautmann who collected it calmly from the feet of the on-rushing forwards. Barnes remarked to one of the Sunderland players, 'I bet you couldn't do that to your fucking 'keeper.'

The stinging reply was, 'No, but is your goalkeeper getting paid as much as ours?'

Barnes did not remember Trautmann as a particularly militant man, but he was concerned as the rest about pay and conditions.

'I think we got Bert to be our representative when he broke his neck, perhaps when Don Revie left, but certainly to give the bugger something to do. One time he collected all our subscriptions, about 2/6d then, and some bastard broke into the dressing room and nicked the lot. He insisted on paying the loss out of his own pocket though. In terms of our wages and contracts, he reflected a lot of our attitudes and hopes.'

The biggest objection of footballers then was the binding contracts in favour of the clubs – the most often quoted description of them was slave contracts. The contracts were renewable once a year while the clubs had total control over transfer negotiations, regardless of whether he wanted to go to a particular club or not. Trautmann, like all the others, wanted the maximum wage deal scrapped and the freedom for a player to negotiate his own contract with his club.

The words spoken to Ken Barnes by the Sunderland player came back to haunt them when the news of illegal payments to the Roker Park staff suddenly broke in the newspapers and several reports of other clubs being involved with under-the-counter deals were openly mentioned. The PFA were brought in to defend the players before an FA commission and were treated lightly in terms of punishment. A while later, in the North-East, George Eastham was having a battle royal with Newcastle United to leave the club, who in turn were holding on to his registration for dear life without paying Eastham's wages.

In the last stages of his career, Trautmann watched the developments as the new decade in football began with the players threatening to go on strike if the Football League did not negotiate a new deal with the PFA. Trautmann's own funds had received a boost by being awarded a £750 benefit cheque for his 10-year loyalty to the club just in time to meet the needs of an enlarging family. On 28 August 1960, just as the season began, Margaret gave birth to another son and the couple named him Mark.

Manchester City opened the season with a run of six unbeaten games, with Denis Law in irresistible form, but by October the early-season promise faded into mediocrity. For Bert Trautmann, however, the month proved to be memorable. The Football League, for the first time, decided to include non-English players to represent the English League in representative matches, and not only was Trautmann selected but he was also made captain.

On 12 October 1960 Bert Trautmann led out the English Football League team against the Irish League at Bloomfield Road, Blackpool, with his young colleague from Manchester City, Denis Law, also in a side estimated to be worth £500,000 in transfer values.

When the League changed the rules about non-English players there had been an immediate lobby among the Press and players for Trautmann's inclusion, and people were delighted for the man when their clamour on his behalf was acknowledged.

'I really felt so proud when I led the team out, hundreds of supporters and friends travelled from Manchester to cheer me on. The Irish fought hard against us. I was the only player who was not an international, but we eventually overcame their resilience and won 5–2. I suppose I should have been a happy man, but I could not help thinking about what I had missed by not playing in international football.'

Also in October, Manchester City travelled to Tottenham Hotspur to play a side that had won their opening 11 games and who were walking away with the League Championship. Spurs turned on a wonderful exhibition of attacking football, matched only by the outstanding skills of Trautmann. Danny Blanchflower said to Ken Barnes, 'It's frightening, he seems to be getting even better as he gets older.' The game finished 1–1 and City became the first team to take a point off Spurs. Bert Trautmann left the field to a standing ovation after a breathtaking display, which at times left the home crowd in awe.

The autumn had not been without incident at Marsham Road either. Margaret was becoming preoccupied with the two children and had become overbearingly protective towards them, to the exclusion of Bert who felt increasingly cut off from his wife. Steve Fleet noticed Bert's attitude becoming more volatile around this time: 'I suppose Bert's Achilles' heel was always his short temper. We always put it down to his Continental temperament and allowed for it, because he really was such a gentle giant and caring man most of the time. We guessed things at home were a little difficult, we always used to joke with players if they were having a bad patch and suggest he had been rowing with his wife. Bert never opened up about his problems, we had heard rumours that he was unhappy but the subject was never broached, probably our macho attitudes in those days made the subject of problems at home taboo.'

Things were not helped by publicity given to a summons by the local council claiming Trautmann had not paid his rates bill of £44, which in turn started rumours he was in financial trouble. Trautmann was angry at the stories.

'It simply was a case of refusing to pay on two counts, I was unhappy with the rating assessment and unhappy with some of the council services at the time.'

In early 1961 the PFA party won their battle with the Football League and for the first time restrictions on maximum wages were lifted. The news Fulham were to pay Johnny Haynes £100 per week staggered the football world, making many players saliva at their own expectations. Many, like Bert Trautmann, were to be bitterly disappointed with the remuneration offered by their clubs.

In the midst of the PFA negotiations, Manchester City played in a remarkable Cup tie at Luton. On an absolute bog of a pitch and playing in torrential rain, Trautmann picked two shots from the back of his net within 17 minutes then spent the remainder of the game watching with the drenched spectators as his side scored six goals, or rather Denis Law scored them. The referee promptly decided to abandon the match with City having a 6–2 lead. The following Wednesday they travelled to Luton again to replay the game and of course managed to lose 3–1.

With yet another early exit from the Cup, they now had to concentrate, yet again, on avoiding relegation. Trautmann became involved in a number of unsavoury incidents as his frustrations grew with now what was becoming an annual struggle to avoid relegation, while Denis Law was also revealing the fiery side of his nature.

At Cardiff, on 6 February, Law was involved in an incident in which Steve Gammon broke a leg. A pushing and shoving mêlée started and Trautmann was seen to kick at a Cardiff player causing a full-scale punch-up. At the end of it he found himself fortunate to receive only a finger waved under his nose by the referee, who gave him a verbal warning.

Towards the end of the season, in a game against Wolverhampton Wanderers, Trautmann dived desperately to save a shot from the Wolves forward Ted Farmer. The ball squirmed away from him and into the net. Farmer stood over Trautmann and applauded him cynically before Trautmann's right hand smashed into his face. A brawl developed, with the officials trying to separate fighting players, and once again Trautmann was lucky to escape with a warning. Sadly the game had been recorded by news cameras and the incident was broadcast to the country. The term 'clogging' had just entered usage in the football world and the day after the match the Sunday newspapers branded Trautmann and Manchester City as a team of 'cloggers'.

'I was deeply offended by the remarks,' he said later, 'Farmer had breached the terms of sportsmanship for me and, though I was not proud of what I did, I did not regret it. His action was synonymous of the way the game was developing then and the whole attitude of players was changing rapidly.' Trautmann was right, a new breed of player was entering the game, and with wage restrictions being removed the development of the mercenary attitude was beginning where loyalty and commitment to one club would become a thing of the past. Denis Law and Bert Trautmann saved Manchester City from relegation in 1961, within weeks of the season ending; however, Law was gone when, after a short tour of Austria, Torino signed him to play in Italy with a cheque of £110,000 for Manchester City.

Trautmann entered into negotiations on his new contract with club secretary Walter Griffiths, fully expecting to reap the rewards of his ability and commitment to Manchester City. Les McDowall had gone through his ideas with Griffiths before retreating to his office. The club secretary put the offer before Trautmann; it was £30 a week on a one-year contract. He listened in disbelief as Griffiths told him that Bert's age and limited time left at Maine Road could not induce the club to offer him more.

# 1961–1964 – RETIREMENT

*Stranger, pause and ask thyself the question. Canst thou do likewise? If not, with a blush retire.*

CHARLES DICKENS

BERT TRAUTMANN was devastated by City's offer, he was certainly expecting at least £50 a week and he was all the more angry to find out Peter Dobing, who had been bought to replace Denis Law, was reputed to be on a £70-a-week contract.

The change in the playing staff at Maine Road was also affecting his thinking. The younger breed of player was different in attitude and approach, very few of them thought of the game of football with the deep commitment and positive thinking Trautmann's generation had. He began to feel more isolated as the age gap became obvious and Trautmann reflected on that time with bitterness.

'City, before the maximum wage restraints were lifted, always said they would have liked to pay me more if they could and then that derisory offer of £30 a week. I thought from 1958 on I was having my best seasons but they obviously didn't. The directors, who had promised me so much, were behind the wage offer, Dobing's high wages kept mine down! I found out later the board felt that I was playing on my reputation and when they put the offer on the table I argued with Walter Griffiths he should be paying me on my ability. OK I was slowing down and my reactions were slower but my positional play was developing to cancel out any problems that could have developed. I was very angry indeed at the start of the 1961–62 season.'

Bert Trautmann decided that this would be his last for Manchester City.

Les McDowall was now pinning his hopes for the First Division Championship on a mixture of seasoned professionals and, at last, some of the younger players who were being given a chance. They opened in some style, winning the first four matches, with Trautmann determined to show there was still life in the old dog yet. All his skill and guile were needed over the next few months as the team fell into their usual relegation position, and by the turn of the year they were bottom of the table. In the FA Cup they scraped through to the fourth round after a 1–0 win at Notts County before being dumped out by Everton at Goodison Park.

Manchester City put up a remarkable revival over the last few weeks of the season and finished in 12th position, and after the last match at the end of April speculation began immediately about Trautmann's future. He spent part of the summer in Anglesey to contemplate the future with his two boisterous sons and an increasingly hostile Margaret. She was turning life into the worst possible nightmare for Trautmann. After all the racial taunts and bigotry he had put up with, his wife was now beginning to make remarks about his nationality. Margaret Trautmann had started to goose-step around the house and shout 'Sieg Heil' at him, embarrassing friends and visitors with her behaviour, yet publicly she was giving interviews that intimated that all was well with them and she was a supportive and interested partner.

In an interview with Bob Gray of the mass circulation *Weekly News* in March 1962, she was asked if Bert received any hate mail. 'He still gets some occasionally. Always they refer to the fact that he is German. If possible I never let him see them. I throw them on the fire. A few weeks ago, somebody 'phoned to say they were coming to shoot Bert. I think they are cranks.'

When Gray asked her about the snags of being the wife of a man continually in the public eye she replied, 'You must keep up a pretty high standard of living. People always expect you to dress well and be in the latest fashion. We have little time to ourselves. Fans call at the house all the time. It is virtually impossible for us to be alone together, even when we go out. Bert spends all his time signing autographs.'

In reality, Margaret had never come to terms with Trautmann's fame, her jealousy of it had caused continual problems in the marriage and now she was isolating him from the two boys in an orchestrated campaign of petty and unnecessary remarks against him. Trautmann, with his quick temper, rose to the bait every time.

Matters had not been helped by a series of anonymous letters to Margaret, bearing a Manchester postmark, which had made accusations against Trautmann concerning extra-marital affairs. The couple returned from Wales at the end of the summer with a rapidly deteriorating relationship, and with Trautmann still unsure of what to do regarding his future.

He had formed some vague plans of going into business, primarily acting as a consultant for Anglo-German businesses, possibly on the public relations side. Stan Wilson thought he would be snapped up by one of the British car manufacturers.

'He was mad keen on Rover cars, I used to make fun of him when he bought one, I called them the poor mans Jaguar, but I knew Rover did not have a great share of the market in Germany and Bert would have been a great asset to them in breaking into the market.'

Trautmann also wanted to keep in football in some capacity, and with the thought of the promises by successive directors at Maine Road wanting him to stay on after his retirement he did not feel any sense of urgency about the future.

Les McDowall asked him to sign another contract for 1962–63 with an improved offer of £35 a week and Trautmann signed, but without much hope or enthusiasm for the season. The atmosphere at Maine Road was grim, when normally at the start of the season there were high hopes and expectancy for the new campaign.

Dave Ewing had left the club during the close season, leaving just Trautmann, Bill Leivers and Joe Hayes as the survivors of the mid-50s side. McDowall, in an effort to bolster his playing strength, bought Alex Harley and Matt Gray from Third Lanark and tried a number of formations from 3–4–3 to 2–5–3, causing one player to complain to a journalist, 'plans, plans, plans, I'm fucking sick of plans'.

Trautmann was now regarded as second-choice goalkeeper. Harry Dowd had been introduced into the team, making Trautmann unhappy on two counts: he thought he still deserved to retain his own place, and if he was to be denied that place Steve Fleet should be in the first team. Unfortunately, Fleet had cooked his own goose as far as McDowall was concerned. He had proved argumentative with the manager and was out of favour – soon he was to be out of the club. Alex Harley proved to be a revelation, his goalscoring ability was prodigious and his bustling style quickly established him as the League's leading scorer. Matt Gray also fitted into the team well. An industrious worker in midfield, he combined well with Harley and provided him with most of the goalscoring opportunities. The season, however, had started off disastrously for City and on the opening day of the season, on a scorching hot day, Wolves had hammered City 8–1. Trautmann's own performance was as abysmal as the rest of the team, and he and the rest of the players were not a happy group when they reported for training the following Monday.

Mike Doyle, who was just starting his splendid career at Manchester City, was allocated boot-cleaning duties when the first team arrived. Referring to the Wolves result, Doyle asked Trautmann how his back was feeling after bending to pick the ball out of the net so many times.

Trautmann's answer was an enormous whack around the back of Doyle's head. 'Your job is to clean the bluddy boots and that's all.' Trautmann was a little sorry afterwards but did not regret his action. 'I was obviously feeling a little peeved but I thought Doyle was a cocky little bugger and needed taking down a peg. Also, as the senior professional, I thought I deserved a little more respect.'

Trautmann's inner frustrations with his career and private life were now building up inside him, his temperament became increasingly tetchy and finally exploded on the field of play in a match against West Ham United at Maine Road. The team again performed with inefficient skill and were soon 4–1 down. Trautmann found himself flapping at nothing as the goals fired past him, he was in a foul mood as Malcolm Musgrove shot a fifth goal past him. Trautmann rushed out at the referee, Ken Stokes, to dispute the goal, claiming Musgrove was offside, but Stokes waved his protests aside and trotted off to the centre-circle.

'I just seemed to lose control completely, I was so angry with Stokes and I rushed back for the ball and kicked it as hard as I could towards him.'

The football hit Stokes in the back with the force of a cannon. He turned slowly and marched back towards the goalkeeper. The crowd were in uproar as the rest of the City players crowded around and they were bewildered to see Trautmann tear off his goalkeeper's jersey, throw it to the ground and walk off the pitch. Many people thought Trautmann had simply walked off in protest, it was only later established that Stokes had sent him off the field. Stokes needed a police escort from the ground as an angry crowd gathered after the match was finished, while inside McDowall concluded that Bert's days as the first-team goalkeeper were at an end.

Trautmann was fined £10 by the FA, given a seven-day suspension and lost £35 in pay. McDowall and Trautmann talked about the future, the manager still felt Bert had a lot to offer the club and Trautmann did not want to finish his career in the reserve team. He decided to play out the season and then make a decision.

Bert Trautmann played only 15 games in the First Division, his lowest number since joining the club, even less than the season he was recovering from his broken neck. Excluding that particular year, he had missed only 19 games through injury or illness in 11 years, a remarkable record, by now, however, it became obvious he had reached the end of his career.

Les McDowall was also coming to the end of his time as the manager of Manchester City. His communication with the players was virtually non-existent and his countenance became more dour as relegation loomed.

In one Final desperate effort to inspire his team, he called in a psychiatrist friend to try and instil some confidence into the players. Trautmann listened, fascinated, as he applied techniques in a pre-match talk.

'I sat there in the dressing room and listened in disbelief as he started to ask us to analyse our faults and to bring out any criticisms. He started to ask our younger players like Colin Barlow and David Wagstaffe what they thought of me as a goalkeeper and they just sat in embarrassed silence. It was a ludicrous situation and we all felt we had been made to look stupid. If anything it had an adverse effect on the team and I bloody well told McDowall what I thought about it.'

McDowall, the great ideas man, had now run out of them and his team, without effective leadership and skill, tumbled out of the division. The supporters were now baying for his blood and the directors, despite their impressive loyalty to him, also decided it was time for a change.

Les McDowall's final acts as the manager of Manchester City were to place Steve Fleet on the transfer list, allow Ken Barnes to join Wrexham as manager and persuade Bert Trautmann to sign a contract for one more year. On 29 May 1963 he resigned as manager after 13 years.

George Poyser was a portly, pipe-smoking man who was totally uninspiring, with the charisma of an outside lavatory. The directors decided to appoint him as McDowall's successor on 12 June.

Trautmann had every reason to feel disappointed by the board's decision. 'The directors wanted continuity at the club; I think they saw Poyser as an interim measure until Jimmy Meadows was groomed to take over. George was not a man who had the confidence of the players and he alienated me straight away by telling me he had never really rated me as a goalkeeper. I announced my retirement soon after.'

Steve Fleet had good reason to remember Poyser, and he was also unimpressed by him. 'He always tried to give the impression he was a worldly and sagacious man but he was really very dull and limited in his knowledge of football. The first thing he did as manager was to sell me to Ken Barnes at Wrexham. I had played only five first-team games at Maine Road in 10 years. I was more pleased to get away from the awful stench from George's pipe than anything else.'

Poyser had proved himself as a hard working and intrepid scout. In that capacity he had introduced some good young players to Manchester City and he decided to introduce more of them to the first team. He signed the former England player Derek Kevan and another former international, Jimmy Murray, to play alongside the youngsters, which worked for a while and the team had an encouraging start in the Second Division. In Trautmann's last season at Maine Road he played only three first-team games and eight for the reserves. It was a poor end to his glorious career and one that saddened him deeply.

Trautmann played his last first-team game at Maine Road on Good Friday, 27 March 1964, when over 27,000 spectators watched Manchester City defeat Norwich City 5–0. The following day he made his last appearance in the Football League in a 2–0 defeat at Preston North End.

Manchester City finished in sixth position, with Derek Kevan scoring 30 goals, but the team, the famous old stadium and the supporters had only one thing to honour at the end of the season, Bert Trautmann's testimonial game on 15 April 1964. Together with Eric Todd, Eric Thornton and the secretary of the Manchester City Supporters Club, Trautmann's last few weeks of the season were spent preparing for his final game.

Thornton wrote later, 'We met several times in a room underneath the main stand, gradually hammering out details. Finally it was decided to field a joint City-United team against an all-international line-up. The interest was quickly obvious. Once the match date was announced there were almost immediate applications for tickets from all parts of Britain, before we had even started inviting players, dozens of stars with clubs in all parts of the country were asking if they could play. What's more, none asked for payment. Often established topliners state their terms and hotels and everything has to be arranged to their satisfaction. In this instance, we merely wrote to the players we wanted in the opposition and, in the majority of cases, got replies by return of post.'

Bert Trautmann's Testimonial match attracted one of the largest attendances assembled for such a game. The official attendance was a doctored 47,951, the more realistic figure of 60,000 was revealed in later years.

The build-up and publicity for the match was incredible, the sportswriters pulled every possible cliché out of the hat in praise of his career, and Trautmann was the subject of countless interviews in England and Germany.

A truly magnificent collection of football talent lined up at 7.30pm that Wednesday evening. In the Manchester XI were Trautmann, Law, Charlton and Kevan, in opposition the team included Matthews, Finney and Armfield.

The atmosphere of the game was charged with emotion, and the noise from the crowd when Trautmann led out the two teams was ear shattering, he could feel pinpricks at the back of his eyes as the wall of noise welcomed him on to the field.

In a match of no consequence other than to honour one man, the players exhibited all their tricks and skills to entertain the spectators, but as the end of the game approached, with the Manchester team leading 5–4, the intense sentiment of the crowd started to interrupt the game. It started with a few small boys running on to the pitch to hug Trautmann, they were followed by larger boys and finally a torrent of humanity flowed from the terraces to engulf the man of the moment. The Manchester police cleared a path to the safety of the main stand where Trautmann, choking back tears, said his farewell.

'I have had some great moments in my life, I have had the honour of playing with some great players. I have had the honour of living among some of the best people in the world. Tonight, I am very grateful and very humble, not only for myself but on behalf of my family and the German people. I hope in some small way I have contributed something to make the world a nicer place to live in, God bless you all.' Trautmann withdrew to the dressing rooms to be toasted in a champagne-drenched, boisterous farewell from the players.

After the match a reception and party was held at the Cromford Club, the main nightclub, which the north-west sportsmen and sportswriters frequented. He was joined by Margaret and the Friar family.

Barbara had attended the match with her husband Ken. 'I stood behind the scoreboard end goal, which was packed with City and United supporters. I could not believe the sadness of the evening, even more the fact that, really, bitter enemies were standing side by side to watch Bert's last game. At the end, when the supporters poured on to the pitch, my own set of friends started to pull up the goal posts and destroy them. They reasoned no other Manchester City goalkeeper would ever stand between that particular set ever again.

Margaret was in a particularly effusive mood, she fussed around Bert as if all their problems were now over, he had now relinquished his role as a prominent figure in the football world and perhaps she could now have him to herself.'

When Trautmann left the Cromford Club in the early hours of Thursday morning, the reassuring words of the Manchester City directors came back to him: 'You will always have a job at Maine Road.'

The following morning he read with immense pride some of the letters he had received over the last few days:

*'I am still not quite sure whether I shall wake up one day to discover it has all been a dream. I will never forget your wonderful gesture that led to my once-in-a-lifetime experience.'*

Trautmann had paid the fare for this particular fan to attend his testimonial match.

*'It was always with mixed feeling we welcomed Manchester City to White Hart Lane. Naturally, as Spurs supporters we wanted our team to win – and by as big a margin as possible. At the same time, however, we knew we could bank on you to keep the score down to a reasonable number. I'm sure a lot of Spurs fans have never forgiven you for saving that Cliff Jones penalty in Spurs' vital League game at Easter, 1960, and again later the same year when, but for your brilliant form, Tottenham's 100 per cent record would have been further extended. We certainly look back on those games with very mixed feelings and the visits of City will never be the same again.'*

George Robb was never mentioned.

*'Thank God you've retired, I doubt if United forwards would ever have scored many against you in derby games and we couldn't have that could we?'*
**A Manchester United supporter**

*'My sister thinks you are 'FAB', what more can you ask from a Beatles fan.'*

*'When you joined Manchester City 15 years ago, I was one of the people who wrote to the club saying that I would never watch them play while you were on the books. My anger at the time was based on you being a member of a people who had deprived me of seven years of League Football – I do have the greatest admiration for a player who remains with one club for the whole of his career and who had the reputation for sportsmanship among players, spectators and writers. Will you please therefore accept my apologies for what I wrote nearly 15 years ago.'*

*'I am aged 13 and a United fan, despite this you top the list of my top ten goalkeepers.'*

Trautmann spent several days reading through his letters and sorting out the various bills from his testimonial match before banking a cheque for £9,000, the net result from the generous donations of the supporters and local businesses. He now looked forward to a relaxing summer, a time for reconciliation with his wife and the hopes of a new job in football at Manchester City.

# GO, GO, GO, COUNTY

*Dear Bert,*
  *The Chairman has asked me to write to thank you for your letter of the fifth of*
*May and to say it will be discussed at the next board meeting on Wednesday 27 May.*
                                                                    *Yours sincerely*
                                                          WALTER GRIFFITHS


W HEN Walter Griffiths asked Trautmann to write to Manchester City for
       a job he had assumed it was a mere formality. He was not particularly
       happy to make such a formal application for a job with a club he had
served with unswerving loyalty for 15 years, he felt a little insulted.

'The constant promises over the years from the directors had given me a false
sense of importance to the club I suppose, but I had not taken the promises lightly.
When I took the family to Anglesey for the summer I fully expected to be back at
Maine Road in some capacity in August.'

Bert Trautmann never did find out what was discussed at the board meeting on
27 May. He had no further communication from Griffiths or the board regarding
employment, as far as Manchester City Football Club seemed to be concerned he
was just another former player. In terms of unswerving loyalty, some board
members had possibly cast their minds back to 1952 and 1953 when that loyalty
had been brought into question by the Shalke 04 plots.

It was also known that the severe differences between Trautmann and George
Poyser would not allow for a constructive working climate between them, and the
possibility of Poyser himself asking the board not to employ Trautmann has been
suggested by a number of people. Whatever the reasons, he was now an ex-
professional footballer, out of the limelight and out of a job. For a short period after
his retirement he had continued his column in the *Manchester Evening News*. More
than once, Trautmann made known his ambitions to work either in football in some
capacity and to also develop Anglo-German business links. The response was
underwhelming. It is the unhappy consequence for anyone under the intense glare of
publicity and adulation of the public to suddenly find that source of esteem and glory
severed by the conclusion of a career, for professional footballers, who in Trautmann's

era represented so much to the huge numbers of people who watched them, all suffered particularly from the depressing syndrome of forgotten heroes. Few had made any money from the game they had graced so well, while the clubs had little interest in their welfare after retirement. Many went on to humdrum jobs, living off memories and anecdotes in their local pub. Trautmann's old friend Roy Paul was then driving a lorry around Wales with little to show from his career in football, and often many ex-professionals were reliving their feats of long gone Saturday afternoons through an alcoholic haze. Trautmann, at least, had the cushion of his unparalleled testimonial cheque to safeguard his immediate term, not enough for his long-term financial future but more than most had in the bank. Two approaches had been made by League clubs. Scunthorpe United and Sunderland had both made offers for Trautmann to play on short-term contracts. Surprisingly, at the start of the 1964–65 season, he accepted an offer from Grenville Hair of the Southern League team Wellington Town. He was offered £50 a match to play for the Shropshire side in an effort to generate interest in the obscure club.

In his second game Trautmann was sent off for violent conduct and did not play for them again. The association was a complete disaster for both parties. He brooded at Marsham Road with a further blemish on his playing record, hardly helpful to his coaching or managerial ambitions.

The previous summer, when Trautmann was contemplating his retirement from football, Jack Friar had persuaded him, after a number of years of trying, to become a member of his Masonic Lodge. Bert was introduced and accepted by the Torkington Lodge in July 1963. Friar assured him the contacts within the brother–hood would be worthwhile.

The year 1963 was also a significant one for German football, the Germans had reorganised their league system and full-time professionalism had been introduced with the formation of the Bundesliga. This development provoked intriguing possibilities in Trautmann's mind of perhaps finally returning to Germany to contribute to the professional football industry there. He had two definite obstacles to his plans: he was not fully qualified as a coach or trainer in German football terms and Margaret's obstinate and total refusal to even consider living in Germany. Trautmann had attended a number of coaching courses over the years, organised by the Lancashire Football Association, including two by the England team manager Walter Winterbottom, but he had no recognised coaching qualification. This would not exclude him from any job in Germany but the exacting standards made any choice of club more difficult.

In the autumn of 1964 neither the Masons nor the football world seemed to have anything to offer Bert Trautmann, until suddenly one evening in October Margaret answered the telephone.

'It's someone from Stockport County for you.'

Victor Bernard was a small, unattractive man whose flair for business, and particularly show business, had made him a prominent figure in the North West. In his early years he had been a professional dance-band singer, later becoming the manager of the Ted Heath Band, Denis Lotis and other well-known singers.

Bernard also had a keen interest in sport, he presented a programme called *Sportscene* on television, and in 1964 he had joined the board of the run-down, poverty-stricken Fourth Division club Stockport County. He brought to the board some much needed dynamic energy to set about transforming the club.

Stockport, lying south of Manchester, half in Lancashire and half in Cheshire, was yet another grimy industrial town in the North. Trautmann's home in Bramhall was only a few kilometres away from the dilapidated little Edgeley Park stadium where the club were just about surviving with a small band of loyal supporters watching a team of limited ambition and ability.

The attractions of the two Manchester clubs were always going to draw the crowds, while the suburbs of the Cheshire elite were far more interested in the middle-class sporting pursuits of tennis, rugby and horse riding.

Stockport County had performed without any great distinction since their formation, occasionally finding the right form to linger around the promotion area for a while, but since 1959, when they had been relegated from the Third Division, a place in mid-table was regarded as something of an achievement.

Bernard invited Trautmann to Edgeley Park, outlined his plans for the club and offered Trautmann the job of general manager. Without second thoughts he accepted. The first task they had to tackle was to get rid of the air of neglect and decay that permeated the club and to create an image of success, a new go getting organisation arising from the ashes. If nothing else, Victor Bernard knew the value of good public relations and how to create image. Bert Trautmann's name and charisma was the first part of Bernard's plan to rejuvenate the football club. The glamorous 60s had started to swing with gathering momentum, and the image of football and the profiles of footballers was becoming a great part of the decade's prominence. George Best at Manchester United had become the focus of the media and teenage adoration and even humble clubs like Stockport County could benefit from the new glamour.

Trevor Porteous, the County team manager, represented more than most the epitome of the lower division manager's responsibilities and attitudes. He had joined the club in the 50s as a player from Hull City, progressed to player-manager and then to team manager. As the fierce economies of the Fourth Division took hold, with average attendances of 2,000 generating little in terms of revenue, he found himself acting as secretary, scout and general administrator with a workload to make a Japanese executive blanch.

Porteous's knowledge of the lower divisions and players had enabled the club to continue between the constant threat of re-election and the bailiffs. When Bernard joined the board, Porteous welcomed the promise of an injection of funds into the club and the ambitious plans Bernard outlined for Stockport County. The great problem for Porteous was that Bernard wanted to run the club almost on his own.

'I read about Trautmann's appointment as the general manager in the newspaper, Victor had not bothered to tell me. Initially I welcomed the news, it meant I personally would be relieved of a great deal of pressure and could concentrate on the team. Bert was such a bloody nice guy and I think to a certain extent he was unsure of himself when he first arrived. He seemed to be searching for himself, for something. I had the impression he was desperate to prove himself but did not have any real direction. He had been such a wonderful player and had great appeals wherever he went, but in terms of managing or coaching I wasn't sure he had the character to do it. Bernard had quite a hold on him in the beginning, I could deal with Victor well enough but I believe Bert was greatly influenced by Victor's sheer and powerful personality.'

Bernard's character was indeed forceful, but his energy and commitment carried the banner for Stockport County that generated hectares of newspaper and television coverage. The triumvirate of Bernard, Trautmann and Porteous brought Stockport County forcefully from a desperate, unappealing football club to the centre of attention in the North West.

They did not have the money to rebuild Edgeley Park, but they had the foresight to transform the ragged and frightful old football ground into a gracefully made up dowager. Paul Doherty, the journalist and television producer, wrote at the time, 'It doesn't cost a packet of money to slip eight neon bulbs over the Stockport County sign outside the ground, but it works wonders on a watching public. Technically it only illuminates a weathered club sign, but it also lights up the fans to know something is changing, things are definitely on the move at Edgeley Park.' Besides the use of neon bulbs, County ripped out parts of the dilapidated stands and rebuilt them with cheap but cosmetically appealing materials, litres of paint were used to spruce up the stands and the terrace barriers, while the traditional white team shirts were changed to blue.

Bernard and Trautmann decided to switch home games from Saturday afternoons to Friday evenings, a masterstroke of initiative. The motive behind the idea was to attract the thousands of Manchester City and United fans in the area to come to Edgeley Park without any conflict of interest and as a result gained them a huge number of bi-partisan supporters. To do this they adopted that great marketing slogan, the sign of the times, 'Go, Go, Go, County'. The words appeared on car stickers, match posters and programmes. The Northern Press caught the mood of the club and the careful manipulation of the media by Victor Bernard, who thrust both himself and Trautmann forward as the messiahs of the regeneration of Stockport County, caught the imaginations of the local public.

Bert Trautmann spent his first season learning to manage on a shoestring budget. Despite all of Bernard's promises of money being pumped into the club, most of it went on entertaining and publicity. The Go, Go, Go, County image had raised attendances to an average of 6,000 during the season, but Trevor Porteous could not instill the message into the players. Stockport finished bottom of the Fourth Division and had to apply for re-election. At the start of the following season, just after his testimonial game, Porteous resigned and moved on to Crewe Alexandra.

'Many people thought Bert was responsible for me leaving, but it was not true. I got on well with him and we had a good working relationship. It was Victor Bernard who made my position difficult. He was good for County in what he was doing but he interfered in everything. We called him Little Caesar, he was a bad tempered man if he did not get his own way and his drinking played havoc with his temperament. Bert, at the time, was trying to please everyone, he was probably too easy going and Bernard was walking all over him. Trautmann was also having problems at home as well, I used to go around there for a meal occasionally and Margaret was so bloody rude to him, giving him Nazi salutes all the time and calling him a Kraut. She embarrassed everyone and less and less of their friends were calling around.'

With Porteous's departure, Trautmann took on the responsibility of the team and saw this as his chance to put into practice some of his ideas. His immediate need was an infusion of new, experienced players to gain promotion. Victor Bernard had already told the Press that County would get promotion in 1965–66, which considering the previous year's performance was highly optimistic.

Trautmann thought long and hard about the playing problems and the need to have a definite style to be successful because the Fourth Division was an extremely difficult division to get out of. Any team playing attractive and flowing football were hammered physically, so there would be a need for a gritty team of experienced professionals with the odd touch of class.

Trautmann brought in Eddie Quigley from Blackburn Rovers to replace Porteous and persuaded his old Manchester City colleague Jimmy Meadows to join them as first-team trainer.

A small colony of former Manchester City players became established at Edgeley Park. On a visit to Wrexham, Trautmann coaxed Beaky Barnes into letting Steve Fleet join up with him again, and former City players Billy Haydock, David Shawcross and Bert Lister were already at County.

More adventurously, Trautmann had arranged for Stockport County to go on a pre-season tour of Germany playing against regional league clubs and invited German clubs to visit humble Edgeley Park. FSV Frankfurt had come to Stockport the previous April and the support at the club started to swell even more as a result of his decision to bring continental opposition to the town. Steve Fleet had no regrets at joining up with Trautmann.

'There really was a buzz about the club and Bert had built up the club's reputation for looking after players. I remember Johnny Price, a young lad from Burnley, joining us. The digs in Stockport were not the best, so Bert moved him in with the Friars who spoilt the lad rotten. Bert persuaded the board to pay us extra money based on attendances, we received a couple of pounds for every extra 1,000 fans over 7,000, we finished up with average gates of over 10,000. The only problem at Stockport County was Victor Bernard's ego and Bert was slowly but surely beginning to resent Victor's constant interference in team matters.'

Trautmann had indeed become more assertive in dealing with Bernard's egotistical meddling and the virulence of their disputes was becoming more pronounced.

During the 1965–66 season Stockport County had a run of injuries that broke the promising promotion challenge they were mounting; indeed, Trautmann had played in one match for the reserve team when the injury list had become so acute.

Bernard, ever mindful of his bragging prediction that County would achieve promotion, constantly pressurised Trautmann and Quigley, who realistically were doing wonders with the limited playing resources. Over the Easter period the club were so short of forwards that Norman Sykes, a burly defender, had been picked to play as a forward. Bernard telephoned Trautmann on hearing the news and disagreed with Sykes's selection.

'Eddie and I pick the team Mr Chairman, if you don't like it you can have my resignation.'

The honeymoon with Bernard was over, and irreconcilable differences were about to end the association.

Stockport County finished the season on the fringe of the promotion pack, a creditable performance in comparison to the previous season, and the hopes of the team and the supporters were high for the next campaign.

Early in the summer of 1966 Trautmann, Quigley and Meadows put their heads together to plan for the following year. In a masterstroke of collective guile, they persuaded two exceptionally experienced players to join the club. Matt Woods and Eddie Stuart were players of outstanding service with clubs in the higher divisions. Stuart had collected three First Division Championship medals with Wolverhampton Wanderers in the 50s, while Woods was a dominant and successful former First Division centre-half.

With the rest of the team restored to full fitness, the managerial team were convinced they now had the resources to gain promotion during 1966–67.

In 1966 the World Cup was held in England for the first time and Victor Bernard had one thing in common with Alf Ramsey, the England manager; both had made predictions. Bernard had predicted success for County, while Ramsey had predicted England would win the World Cup. With home advantage, England were made favourites to win the tournament, with West Germany and Brazil also keenly fancied to do well. The English Football Association had allocated an interpreter to each team, also acting as official attaché, who they assumed would be acceptable to the various competing nations, and in most cases the selection was favourable. In the case of West Germany it was not.

When Wilfried Gerhardt heard who had been chosen to be the attaché with the German World Cup party in Sheffield, where they were to play their opening matches, his immediate action was to disagree with the choice. For Dr Gerhardt only one man could meet the criteria of the Deutscher Fußball-Bund and that man was Bernd Trautmann. The German Football Association, through Wilfried Gerhardt, immediately contacted the Secretary of the English FA, Denis Follows, and requested that Trautmann was installed as their attaché in England. 'You do realise Dr Gerhardt that Mr Trautmann is in the employ of an English League club who pay his wages, we cannot allow any conflict of interest.'

Stockport County and the West German national team? Denis Follows secured the grudging agreement of Victor Bernard for Trautmann to act as the official attaché to the German team for the 1966 World Cup Tournament, but the sting was he could not receive any payment from the German FA or his club and he would have to act purely in a voluntary capacity.

Wilfried Gerhardt had been as clear as possible without being rude to Follows in his request for Trautmann.

'As such he (Denis Follows) was in the highest position of the World Cup organising committee, finally they granted our wish and we were very happy to have Bernd Trautmann because you see he was the one and only logical solution to the problems for us, he knew everything about English football, he knew all the details, everybody knew him, he was a man who could open doors for us if we needed someone to do this. I think his selection was a very happy one, we were very satisfied with Bernd's work and in terms of team spirit he was one of the team from the very start.'

Paradoxically for Trautmann, it was yet another conflict in his life that was to exaggerate the personal turmoil he was experiencing. Wilfried Gerhardt was right about Trautmann's ability to open doors for the German party, his knowledge of the area and his contacts within the football world of Press, clubs and players was immense, yet this was the same world that had rejected him when he retired, watched with detached interest as he struggled to make a success of working for an unknown, in world terms, Fourth Division football club, while suddenly he was thrust into the limelight in the greatest of all football competitions, with one of the best teams in that competition.

For Trautmann at last his country had given him the recognition he had so desperately longed for, and he represented them with pride and vigour.

The German national side arrived in England a week after Wilfried Gerhardt had set-up their headquarters at the Peveril of the Peak Hotel in Dovedale, Derbyshire.

Trautmann completed his plans for Stockport and then travelled to Dovedale to meet up with Gerhardt, who was supervising the equipment and Press facilities. They travelled to Manchester together to meet the team arriving at Ringway Airport amid the expected blaze of publicity, and Trautmann could feel his adrenalin and excitement building up as he became a part of big-time soccer again.

'I knew what I had been missing in 1962 when I played for the English Football League side, but to be a part of the German National side and to train with the players was a great high for me, the talent in the team was incredible and I knew they were going to have a good World Cup and possibly win it. At the same time I had my hopes for England to do well also, but in my heart during that wonderful experience for me I was German through and through.' The players showed a great deal of respect and regard for Trautmann, him and the squad goalkeepers forming a natural bond, and when they travelled to Sheffield for the opening match in their group at Hillsborough the team spirit was high.

At that time the stadium was the most modern in Britain and the first electronic scoreboard had been installed. During the final minutes of the game a message flashed up.

'Bernd Trautmann, be at the players entrance after the match.' An intrigued Trautmann waited outside afterwards wondering what was going on. He was approached by a tall, smart-suited man in his sixties who held out his hand and introduced himself.

Franz Schain ran a haulage and garage business in Aachen and was in England to support the German team.

He told Trautmann, 'I have been a great admirer of yours for years and I just want to thank you for all you are doing for the team. I read in the papers that your club or FA are not paying you for the work you are doing and I want you to accept this.' Schain handed Trautmann an envelope, inside was a month's wages. The two of them became firm friends and Schain was to come to Trautmann's aid again a few years later.

West Germany went on to lose the World Cup Final 4–2 against England and, despite the disappointment of losing, Trautmann was utterly exhilarated by his experience with his countrymen, more importantly he was sounded out by officials about returning home to work there. The prospect became more and more appealing.

When Trautmann attended the reception given for the teams and officials after the Final, he was approached by a beaming Joe Mercer, who, together with Malcolm Allison, was reviving the fortunes of Manchester City.

Mercer shook Trautmann's hand and said, 'Unlucky Bert, but I doubt if we would have won if you were at your best in the German goal.'

Trautmann felt a lump form in his throat at this genuine compliment from an honest man, but fate and circumstance had denied him the honour. He felt deflated by his return to Marsham Road and the reality facing him at Stockport County, which was to gain promotion. Margaret spent the summer in Anglesey, returning only the day before the school term began in September. Without the pressure of his home life causing him immediate problems, Trautmann's utterly professional approach, together with Eddie Quigley's organisation, saw Stockport up with the leaders, and in one home match at the end of September nearly 14,000 attended the game against Southport. County were on their way, but unfortunately so was Trautmann, shortly after this game.

Victor Bernard's interferences and his self-aggrandisement were making life unbearable for both Trautmann and Quigley.

The atmosphere they had created at Edgeley Park was first class, with a squad of players who were fired by the interest and enthusiasm Trautmann was generating. His concern for people was such that even the groundstaff were benefitting. The club was still being run on a shoestring, Trautmann's budget was particularly low for the groundsmen, who had worked for the club for years on peanut wages. Stockport were selling up to 10,000 match programmes a game, which was providing some extra revenue, and Trautmann diverted some of the money raised by the programme sales into the pay packets of the grateful groundsmen.

Steve Fleet thought Trautmann would become a great manager. 'His approach to everyone was good, he had the respect of the players, the human touch with the other staff and enormous appeal to the supporters. He really was laying the foundations for a good club, but Victor Bernard and he were having more and more clashes. Bernard's interference was breaking up the harmony in the team as well. He was a small man with a small man's inferiority complex, not helped by his drinking problem. I remember we were waiting at Luton station after a game, we were in a great mood after a 2–1 win and I was laughing at some crack or other. Bernard turned on me with his face bright red and accused me of laughing at him behind his back. Bert intervened and they had an enormous row on the platform, there was no doubt the resentment between them was building up. Victor had a show-business mentality and used to throw lavish parties at his home in Marple. He always referred to us as his team. I believe he was jealous of Bert's popularity, which towered above him in both size and character.'

Trautmann arranged for Hamburg to play against Stockport, whose team was bolstered by the temporary inclusion of First Division players. The great Uwe Seeler played in the match for Hamburg and it proved to be an outstanding success. At the Belgrade Hotel, which was owned by one of the County directors, Bernard had laid on a lavish reception in honour of the German visitors and he watched through drunken eyes as Trautmann became the centre of attention. As the evening wore on Bernard approached Trautmann, who was talking to Steve Fleet and his wife.

'Bert was in a great mood, the atmosphere was exceptionally friendly and he said to my wife, if I could dance I would dance with you'. Just then Victor arrived, spun Bert around and said if you dance with anyone, you'll dance with my wife. He put a damper on the whole evening. Bert just walked away in disgust.' Trautmann was now reaching the end of his patience with Bernard and the final break came quickly.

At the end of October, Trautmann and Quigley were choosing the team to play at Hartlepools United when the telephone rang in Trautmann's office, – it was Bernard asking what team had been chosen. The chairman disagreed with the selection. 'I said that's fine by me Victor, come over and pick the team yourself, I'm off. I just picked up my things, said goodbye to Eddie and walked out, I really had had enough.'

Trautmann returned to his home, took the telephone off the hook and told Margaret to tell any Press who called at the house that he had gone away. The *Manchester Evening News* reported the following day that Trautmann had gone into hiding. In other papers he was quoted as saying: 'It's no use looking for me, I'm not available.'

Bernard stated he was 'surprised by Trautmann's actions and could not understand his reasons for leaving'.

The team were shattered by the news, although not too surprised, but they received a further shock when Eddie Quigley also left the club and returned to Blackburn Rovers. Jimmy Meadows took over, brought Trevor Porteous back to the club and worked hard to boost the players' morale.

The groundwork done by Trautmann gave them the basis of the team that won the Fourth Division Championship at the end of that season. When Stockport County collected their Championship trophy at the end of April 1967, Bert Trautmann was entering into negotiations for a job in West German football.

# FAILURE, HEARTACHE
# AND A SAD DEPARTURE

*'I'm satisfied with having tumbled off my ass,' Corchuelo replied, 'and with having learned through experience a truth of which I was ignorant.'*

MIGUEL DE CERVANTES SAAVEDRA

AFTER walking out on Stockport, Trautmann had to think long and hard again about his future. Despite his success there, no offers came in from any other British clubs, in some minds he had gained a not unjustifiable reputation for being temperamental and difficult, but the experience with Bernard had made him single minded to run any future club his own way.

His thoughts of employment were now firmly on leaving England to work in Germany. He contacted Wilfried Gerhardt in Frankfurt and asked him to let him know if any clubs would be interested. 'Our clubs were keen to help him settle as a coach, we thought very highly of his calibre as a football personality and [that] it would be good for our football if he could pass on his vast knowledge to our teams.'

In 1967 Preußen Münster, a team in the German Regionalliga West, contacted Trautmann and asked him to become the trainer of the team and he accepted immediately. Margaret refused to go and live in Germany and in a statement to a newspaper reporter, who asked her why, she said revealingly, 'He is one German, the boys and I are three English people, I want them to remain so.'

Trautmann moved to Germany on his own in June 1967 to work in Münster, an industrial town some 100 kilometres north of Düsseldorf. His immediate priority was to take a coaching course organised by the German FA, which would qualify him as a trainer in German football. He attended the Duisburg Sports Centre for an extensive three-week course, emerging with his coaching Grade A licence to start work with his new team. Preußen Münster were not dissimilar from Stockport County in terms of success and playing standard, although the German club had far more advantages in terms of a good little stadium and training facilities.

The president of Preußen Münster, Herr Overmann, welcomed Trautmann to the club at a considerably well-attended press conference, and he told the journalists of his excitement and hopes for his football team now they had the famous Bernd

Trautmann as the trainer. The 'famous Bernd Trautmann' looked on apprehensively as he realised the great expectations from him.

Preußen Münster were a mixture of full-time, part-time and amateur players, some of whom had performed with more well-known clubs in the Bundesliga.

It was a struggle from the start for Trautmann. He needed time to assess the playing strength of the club, to establish himself within the German system and to also build up his contacts within their football world, particularly on the scouting side. He saw this opportunity to actually try what he wanted, blend that superb German technical ability with the commitment and tenacity of the English style.

He set about his job under the eagle eyes of Overmann; Bernd had found the German equivalent of Victor Bernard.

There is no doubt that Preußen Münster had an awful start to the season, a 5–0 hammering at home by Bayer Leverkusen followed by a 1–0 defeat at Essen. They won only one of their opening eight matches. Trautmann did not panic, slowly sorting out the dead wood in his squad, again working with little money for new signings and introducing new, younger players with experienced, part-time professionals alongside. In Trautmann's first season Preußen Münster finished 13th in the 18-team league, but he was not unduly worried, again he felt he had laid the foundations for a good side. He returned home for the summer in England optimistic for his team the following year, but apprehensive about meeting up with Margaret.

He had received little communication from her during his stay in Münster, while hearing virtually nothing from Mark and Stephen, despite his long, though irregular, letters home. Barbara Friar, now Pearson after her marriage to Ken, felt sad for him on his return. 'Margaret had started to hide letters from Bert, which he had written to the boys, she hid them unopened under the mattress or ripped them up, it was a very difficult time for the boys without their father and Margaret began to alienate them from him. When he came home he had a very bad time indeed.'

Margaret had become more haphazard in her home. She developed the disrupting habit of cleaning and general housework in the middle of the night and then sitting silently for days without doing a thing. Communication between Trautmann and his wife was virtually nil, the trauma of John's death still a major, malignant factor in the crumbling relationship. Margaret Trautmann, despite the presence of her other two sons, would never recover from that trauma. The tragedy had, in reality, triggered her already fragile mental health into its downward spiral. She also made it clear to her husband that she had also been involved in other relationships. Bert Trautmann returned to Münster at the end of the summer distressed about his apparent irreconcilable relationship with his wife. He tried to pre-occupy himself with the new season.

Overmann immediately started to impose his own views on how the team should be run, he made it plain he was unhappy with the style and intimated some of the players were also dissatisfied with the way their trainer was running things. The selection of the team once again became an issue.

Trautmann was defensive: 'I was not completely closed to the views of Overmann, I would always be open to any ideas that were constructive, if the president suggested a certain player I would listen and in some cases agree, but in the long run I chose the team, and I was responsible for the players. The fact that players were going behind my back to the president was alien to me but I suppose the concept of player-power was beginning in England then also, certainly in Germany it was rife.'

Trautmann's attitude to his players was, from the beginning, relaxed and easy going. He coaxed rather than barked and he wanted to be close to them. The aloofness of his own manager, Les McDowall, had convinced him of the need to be accessible to the players, to build up the camaraderie and to solve any of their problems. The attitude of the German players reflected their conviction Trautmann was a soft touch. He couldn't win.

In October 1968, after the start of his second season in Germany, Overmann came down to the training ground and asked Trautmann to look at a young player who was the son of a friend of his. He did so and was not impressed, but to Trautmann's alarm Overmann signed the player anyway.

Trautmann attended the board meeting to register his complete disgust at the way the player had been signed.

He was told by Overmann, 'In Germany we have the say, not you, you're not in England now.' Trautmann resigned his job as trainer, packed his bags and returned to England, out of work and wondering what to do next.

Chastened by his experience and unhappy at home, Trautmann had no offers of work for three months until a sudden call came from the president of Opel Rüsselsheim, Carl Rhodenheber.

Rüsselsheim, a few kilometres west of Frankfurt, is the home of the giant Opel car plant. Although the team bore the name, the car company had little to do with the football club in February 1969 when Trautmann joined them.

The team were struggling in the Regionalliga Sud, in grave danger of being relegated, a familiar story for the new trainer. They were surviving on gates averaging 3,000 with a team of amateur and ex-professionals now playing on a part-time basis.

Once again Trautmann rolled up his sleeves and got to work. In response to his efforts, the players staged a revival to their dismal season. A run of wins and draws carried them up the table, and it seemed that Trautmann had worked a minor miracle. He told Rhodenheber he would be looking for an unambitious mid-table position the following season. With the limited resources available to provide new players, he was building his hopes on establishing a good youth policy and, like his ploy at Stockport County, to pick up a couple of good, experienced professionals.

After the summer break Trautmann returned to Rüsselsheim for the 1969–70 season. He had picked up three or four new players to augment his squad, who included among their number two with Bundesliga experience, and he set about blending them into a cohesive and hardworking team.

Trautmann had a promising opening season in the Regionalliga Sud and Rüsselsheim picked up the points to set them on target for a respectable if unspectacular placing in the table. But as they approached the midwinter break around Christmas they had slipped into a bad patch and the two ex-Bundesliga players were exerting their influence on Rhodenheber for a change of trainer. Trautmann had no knowledge of this when he returned to Bramhall for the holiday. He arrived back unsure of his reception from Margaret and the two boys, he tried hard to make up for his absence with lavish gifts, as his own father had done all those years ago, and he tried to bring a sense of fun to the household. The atmosphere between Margaret and Trautmann was muted and strained. When Barbara Pearson called round to see them at the tail-end of an enormous row, she recalled, 'Bert had pulled the tablecloth off the table and the kitchen was a mess. Margaret sat in the debris and was saying to the boys not to worry because he would be back in Germany soon.'

Trautmann left Bramhall after his depressing short visit to face a long and lonely drive back to Rüsselsheim through the snowy West European countryside, and he arrived back at his flat in the early hours of the morning.

When he reported for work Rhodenheber told him the players were not happy with his methods, that the club had expected more from him in terms of success and would he like to offer his resignation. Trautmann did so, quickly returning to England.

The instant triumph expected by the German clubs from Trautmann had eluded all the parties involved, the plans and the hopes he held were shattered and now he was back to square one again. Professionally, he felt hurt and let down, he had been given so little time to achieve his ambitions by his German employers and the realisation of the harsh world of failure gave him little hope for the future.

In his personal life he had to face the prospect of a difficult relationship with his family, together with a future without the promise of any improvement.

'I have been involved with sport all my life, I could not contemplate a future without being involved in football in some way, but I had also to make up to Margaret and the boys somehow the neglect of a husband and father. When we finally got around to talking seriously about things, I agreed to move to Anglesey.'

Margaret had wanted to move there for years, the successive years of temporary residence had fuelled her ambition to live on the island all the year round.

Her mental health was now of grave concern to Trautmann and the Friars.

The psychological blow of John's accident had not really been adequately considered by her doctor, but at the same time if any of the family had suggested she ought to seek treatment they would have been treated to the full onslaught of her fury, by now her mind was impregnable to any suggestion of her own contribution to the accident, for her, any blame lay entirely with her husband.

Trautmann was also going through his own mental anguish, the failures in Germany were depressing him deeply, while six years after his retirement from football he had still not really come to terms with no longer being in the public eye. The exceptional success Joe Mercer and Malcolm Allison had brought to Manchester City, who in 1970 had three major trophies at Maine Road, including the European Cup-winners' Cup, brought home to him the unkind fate that had excluded him from those triumphs in terms of age. He felt further cut off from his former club when Allison brought in Bert Williams as a goalkeeping coach while commenting, 'I consider Bert Williams to be the finest source of goalkeeping knowledge and ability.'

A move from the Manchester area seemed to him the best alternative to start afresh with his family. The house in Marsham Road was sold and the Trautmanns moved into Bron Haul, Benllech. It was an enormous property needing a complete overhaul, but the new home held exciting prospects for Bert and Margaret as they set about the task of restoring the house with vigour.

They had the idea of making part of the house into bed and breakfast accommodation and turning some of the outbuildings into summer chalets for holidaymakers.

Trautmann used the profit from the Marsham Road sale, together with some of his savings, to turn Bron Haul into a beautiful and admired home. The project took all of his time and energy through most of 1971, with periodic newspaper articles and television reporting being his only source of income.

Initially, Margaret responded well to his hard work and the local environment for which she had so much feeling, mentally she recovered some of her old humour and mischief as her walks along the sand dunes had a therapeutic effect. The benefits were, unfortunately, only short term. The arguments and her goading of Trautmann became an unwelcome feature of their lives once more, and eventually the hostile atmosphere of Marsham Road was recreated at Benllech. Margaret's enthusiasm for the house waned, and she reverted to her old habits of spurts of housework in the middle of the night, then cutting herself off from everyone in the darkness of one of the rooms.

In December 1971 the Trautmanns' marriage broke down completely. At Christmas Bert had bought two wooden boats for Mark and Stephen, who put them in pride of place on the dinner table. Their behaviour was a little unruly so Trautmann admonished them with a threat to box their ears if they did not behave. Margaret called him a bloody Nazi and asked him not to use Gestapo tactics on the boys. She later appeared on the stairs with his Iron Cross around her neck while performing the Nazi salute.

Trautmann could stand no more, in a rage he smashed the two boats, packed a few things and drove off into the night. Two days later the newspapers and television reported Bert Trautmann was missing from his home in Anglesey. More dramatically, Interpol had been called in to investigate his disappearance.

Mavis Pleat, an attractive blonde dental receptionist, had known Trautmann for a number of years. They had met when he visited the dental surgery where she worked and formed a close friendship. Bert often visited Mavis at her semi-detached home in Chorlton-cum-Hardy, the suburb housing many of the football celebrities from Manchester. When he left Anglesey he drove straight to her home.

The newspapers were full of speculation concerning Trautmann's whereabouts. One suggested he was on the verge of a breakdown after the death of his mother, while another, that he was allegedly upset after his application for the manager's job with the Welsh club Bangor City had been turned down. In the first instance, he was distressed by the death of Frieda a few weeks earlier, in the second he was mystified about the reports connecting him with Bangor. The papers had identified the source of the reports as coming from a close friend. The story in the *Manchester Evening News* stated 'his Sunbeam Rapier JLG 252C had been spotted outside a house in Chorlton-cum-Hardy,' it also quoted a police spokesman as saying, 'he has been reported missing from home but it is not known by whom'.

Margaret had issued a terse statement, which did little to alleviate the speculation: 'My solicitors are dealing with the problem.' When Mavis brought the newspapers to show Trautmann he immediately telephoned the Manchester police informing them he was in the area.

'They told me anyone could 'phone and say they were Bert Trautmann, I would have to call in at the local police station to prove who I was, I did so and then drove over to Davenport in Stockport where Barbara lived.'

Barbara Pearson had just rushed home from the hairdressers where she had learned the news of her brother-in-law's disappearance from home. 'Just after I arrived back, Bert turned up in a stressful state and I knew straight away he was having problems with Margaret. We telephoned her in Anglesey but she was not happy about speaking to us. Bert decided to drive back to see her, he was also worried about the boys.'

Margaret would not speak to him. He stayed just long enough to pack his suitcases then drove back to Manchester, leaving his wife and sons for good.

After staying with both Mavis and Barbara for a few days he made up his mind to leave England once and for all. He left everything for Margaret, Mark and Stephen, borrowed £100 from Mavis and flew to Frankfurt. On his arrival in Germany he contacted Franz Schain, who immediately invited him to stay at his home in Aachen.

Trautmann was shown great kindness by Schain and his family. He used the opportunity to take stock of his life and to consider his future, whether that future lay in Germany remained to be seen. Certainly, in terms of managing or coaching jobs, he would have difficulty in obtaining employment. In his mind he had to consider his qualifications for any future and reflect on his tattered personal life. He had burned his bridges as far as his family were concerned, at the same time he had severed his sporting links with England, while in Germany his reputation was not revered, now the vultures were ready to pick the carcass.

Schain put no pressure on the penniless Trautmann, he allowed him to bide his time and to think carefully towards his next move. Trautmann himself had the seeds of an idea, which began to sprout positively. The German government and the

Deutscher Fußball-Bund were involved in a number of aid projects with Third World countries and part of the package was to provide sports development programmes and support to help overseas Football Associations. Trautmann had discovered this programme when he contacted Wilfried Gerhardt just after the German Press had broken the news that he was living in distressed circumstances.

Life in Aachen with the Schain family had been helpful for him to clear his thoughts, and he felt he owed something to Franz. He insisted on doing some work for him to repay his generosity and also for something to occupy his time.

In realistic terms, the only other skill Trautmann had developed was concerned with vehicles, driving and maintaining them, but even his attempts to utilise his knowledge in a business had brought him problems in the past. During his career at Manchester City he had been persuaded to invest in a garage and car rental business in South Manchester by two local businessmen. The venture had collapsed within a year leaving huge debts and Trautmann losing his investment.

He offered to help in one of Schain's garages, it was almost full circle for him as memories of Hanomag came flooding back, however, he enjoyed the workshop atmosphere and was accepted by the workforce as one of the boys, unfortunately one of the boys tipped off the Press.

The small town environment of Aachen quickly became a source of gossip and rumour, including one story of Trautmann's romantic involvement with one of Schain's daughters. As the cauldron of conjecture bubbled the Press came to Aachen.

Trautmann was working in one of the tyre bays, stacking a pile of discarded tyres, when a photographer arrived and took a few pictures of Trautmann's labours. The photographs appeared in the nationals the following day, one, accompanied by a headline story 'From a King to a Pauper', appeared all over Germany.

Hurt pride and a feeling of humiliation overcame the 'pauper', to him it was the final straw of the last few months of torment. Wilfried Gerhardt, a man of intense loyalty and commitment, listened to Bernd's request for help with deep sympathy. The stories in the German Press had been distressing for a number of people who knew Trautmann, and it was of particular regret to Dr Gerhardt to have to read them. He did not know the full extent of the problems, but he was ready when the call for help came through.

'I realised he was going through a crisis, he needed help, not in the material sense, but he was looking for someone he could trust and help him start a new professional and personal life, whatever my advice and help was worth, I gave it.'

The help and advice of Wilfried Gerhardt provided the lifeline Bernd Trautmann so desperately needed.

The basis of the German Football Association's football coaching courses had been worked out and developed from the ideas of Sepp Herberger in the early 1950s. In true Germanic style it had been developed with little influence from other football nations. The Germans had worked out their own system, which had been a proven success in world terms, and other countries, particularly in the Third

World, were realising they had something to offer. When aid packages were agreed, part of the deal included using the German expertise and technical coaching ability in developing national teams.

As far as Wilfried Gerhardt was concerned, Bernd Trautmann had the qualities and the character to be of use to the programme. 'The overseas appointments were funded by the government, using our expertise and advice, for the qualifications of the candidates, so we made suggestions, but the position as such coach, in wherever, was government controlled and funded by our Foreign Office.

We helped to recommend the candidates who were properly qualified and had been through our system and passed our examinations, reached our standards of football expertise. Bernd Trautmann was of course ideal.'

Gerhardt was not dissuaded in recommending Trautmann by any adverse criticisms of his work in the German Regionalligas, or his reputation. 'I think Bernd Trautmann was always showing his convictions in a very open and frank way, if he was convinced of a thing he did it, if someone asked him to do a thing he said 'I will do it my way or not at all.'

'He must have been slightly unlucky in his choice of clubs because, well, every–body expected instant success from him, he wanted to bring to bear his ideas and this would have taken him time, he needed two to four years, but nobody gave him those years, they wanted the famous Bernd Trautmann to do it straight away, be champions tomorrow, that was the idea and of course no coach in the world could grant the success they were looking for, and this may have been increased even more by the clash of personalities that must have happened.

His great strength, as far as I could see, was always determined hard work, but in the long term rather than the short term, he laid foundations.'

In February 1972 Trautmann found himself on board a plane overlooking the palmed landscape of Burma as the aircraft made its final approach into the airport of that country's capital, Rangoon.

# A NEW BEGINNING

*May he ever be cool as water and fragrant as a flower.*

BURMESE TRADITIONAL PRAYER

O
N THE long flight to Rangoon Bernd looked forward to his new challenge with relish, the depression of the last year had been cleared from his mind like the spring sun relieving the greyness of winter.

Before leaving Germany he had cleared up his affairs in England. A legal separation from Margaret had been obtained through his English solicitor, while formal settlement of terms was arranged for her and the future of the boys. He now looked forward to his own future and the beginning of a new life.

In Germany he had undergone a briefing from the German Foreign Office, which was both comprehensive and revealing about the Burmese and their culture. Burma, an isolationist country under a socialistic, military regime, was the beneficiary of a considerable German contribution to their interests. Trautmann was told of the economic and agricultural background of the country and the role the German Government adopted towards the regime. It was one of supportive and constructive aid and Bernd Trautmann's own role was to serve as the official coach, paid by the Germans, of the Burma Football Federation.

He was met at Rangoon by an official from his embassy and driven to the German diplomatic compound, which housed officials on postings, together with a number of German industrial representatives working for their companies in Burma. Trautmann unpacked his things in the white-painted bungalow he had been allocated and spent two days on a brief familiarisation tour before meeting up with the president of the Burma Football Federation, Colonel Kyaw Sein Tun. Sein Tun was a delightful man whose commitment to football over-rode his obligations to his Army background. Trautmann found him to be a man of charming character and he also became immediately aware of the wonderful disposition and gentleness of the people. The Buddhist religion touched all aspects of the population, and their peaceful nature touched him deeply. He became determined to pass on all his expertise in developing the structure of Burmese football.

Trautmann's immediate problem was the restriction placed on him in terms of being able to travel within the country. Despite Sein Tun's support, travel difficulties in Burma were caused by insurgents in the country areas who were in opposition to the government. Power lines and rail tracks suffered from numerous attacks by the rebels, while the problems on the Burmese borders with Laos and Thailand, relating to drug or political issues, caused further restrictions on internal travel.

Trautmann was also bound by the constraints of his brief from the West German government, which confined his contacts to Sein Tun's sphere of influence.

Bernd spent the first weeks in his new job assessing the potential of the national Burmese football team, looking at any local and national political influences before devising his plans within the German Football Association's coaching guidelines.

Trautmann's initial observation was that the Burmese had no influences at all on their style. It was developed from a natural ability within the limitations of their characteristic size and build, but that natural ability was, however, exceptional. He needed only their commitment to his organisation to build up an impressive, teachable group of players and, more importantly, to establish a positive and equable group of Burmese coaches to pass on the benefits.

The travel restrictions meant all of his coaching and working environment had to be conducted around the Rangoon area, with his main base at the National Aung San Memorial Stadium. Trautmann recognised instantly the lack of egotistical selfishness in the players compared to their European counterparts. The Burmese were eager to learn, while the pressures of interference from club chairmen or presidents did not exist. Trautmann now had the time and the facilities to do what he wanted.

The isolation of Burma had deprived the country of any serious international opposition for many years and the new coach recognised that. Regardless of the enormous enthusiasm of his team, plus the supportive attitude of the Burmese Football Federation, international competition was a much-needed stage for him to fully assess the potential of his charges. He had no problems in persuading Sein Tun to bring Burma out of the self-imposed wilderness or in gaining the approval of the government for the team to re-enter South-East Asian international football. The immediate priority was for Burma to do well in the Asian Zone Olympic Qualifying Tournament. The Burmese squad became immediately responsive to Trautmann's ideas, and with intense hard work, coupled with new training techniques, they won the qualifying group. In September 1972 the Burmese won the Fair Play Trophy in the Olympic Games football tournament. Trautmann chalked up his first, albeit non-winners, honour for Burma.

The experience of international competition enabled him to hone the talents and commitment of his team to face their next task after the Olympics, when they travelled to Seoul in South Korea to compete for the President's Cup, organised specifically for South-East Asian nations.

In October 1972 Trautmann and his squad returned to Rangoon with the President's Cup and against all the odds they had won the trophy. The response of his players and the Burmese Football Federation heartened him immensely. He felt perfectly at peace in this unique country and the graceful simplicity of the Buddhist attitudes in turn helped him to look within himself at his own attitudes. Within the first year of living in Burma he was as relaxed as a cat in a linen cupboard, while his recent, turbulent past stored itself away in his mind without too many emotional scars.

He missed Mark and Stephen. His letters to them in England were not swiftly answered and the rare replies he did receive were brief and hurried.

Colonel Kyaw Sein Tun became a close friend of Trautmann's, the Burmese football president entertained him regularly, and through him Bernd was able to meet a number of prominent families. He adapted to the lifestyle with ease and, as his confidence returned, he found himself an able diplomat.

Through Sein Tun, Trautmann was able to escape the confines of Rangoon on a more regular and protected basis than others, and he used the opportunity to do so as often as possible, travelling eventually to many parts of Burma out of bounds for most foreigners. As a result, his experience and knowledge of the people and the country grew, providing him with a further insight in to the attitude and minds of his players.

After the success in Seoul, the Burmese, at the instigation of their coach, entered the Djakarta Anniversary Football Tournament in Indonesia. Trautmann was keen to keep the momentum of the recent triumphs going, and his players were also anxious to prove themselves further in international competition. In early June Trautmann travelled with the team to Djakarta with their reputation as an emerging football nation in Asia preceding them.

The main claim to football fame of the Asian nations was the exceptional victory of the North Koreans against Italy in the 1966 World Cup. The Koreans had become the major force in Asian soccer and had dominated the area in competitions. Their success had rejuvenated interest within that part of the world, and by 1973 football was achieving great popularity among the South-East Asian countries.

Trautmann notched up further distinction for the Burmese Football Federation when the team won the Indonesian competition.

Within the Burmese domestic system, he also worked hard with the Football Federation. With their assistance he set up a number of coaching clinics for division and state coaches. He became the catalyst for the Burmese First Division coaching manuals and taught a number of seminars for the development of junior football within the country.

Trautmann had at last found the environment to give him the time to develop his ideas and the response had been positive and also tangibly rewarding. His own reputation was unequalled within the sports community as his loyalty and convictions towards his responsibilities became proven by the elevation of Burmese football into a force in Asia.

In his personal life Trautmann was also experiencing a romantic development, which had started shortly after his arrival in Rangoon. Ursula Van der Heyde came from a prosperous family of lawyers in Rüdeshiem, one of the Rheingau wine-producing towns and villages nestling along the banks of the Rhine between Weisbaden and Koblenz. Ursula had spurned the family tradition of her father, mother and brother, for she had not gone into law but into industry and was working for the industrial company Fritz Werner, which was based in the town neighbouring her own, at Gesenheim.

She had been sent to Burma to represent her company's interests just a few months before Trautmann's arrival, and when they met there was an instant attraction. Just as Bernd's work bore the fruits of his efforts, his relationship with Ursula, or Ushi as she was generally known, blossomed.

Ushi's employers had set up a number of projects in Burma, ranging from chemical plants to printing works. She had established a good working relationship with the Burmese Government and had also succumbed to the charm of the people and the relaxed way of life.

Shortly after Trautmann took the Burmese team to win the gold medal in the South-East Asian Games in Singapore, his commitment to the relationship with Ushi became more binding as he received news from England that his divorce from Margaret had come through. A few weeks after his 50th birthday a decree nisi had been granted at Caernarfon Divorce Court in Wales to Margaret Trautmann on the grounds the couple had lived apart for more than two years.

In a national newspaper report it merely stated the divorce had been granted and 'Trautmann's last known address was a PO Box number in Rangoon, Burma.'

Trautmann celebrated the news after picking up the documents from the PO Box by asking Ushi to marry him. Bernd and Ursula Trautmann moved into their new home in the German diplomatic compound shortly afterwards.

The Burma football team responded by retaining the President's Cup in the competition in Seoul.

During 1974 the Trautmanns had to face the prospect of leaving Burma. His term as the national coach was due to be completed at the end of August and the German Foreign Office now had to consider moving Trautmann on. His last duty as the official coach to the Burma Football Federation was to accompany the team to take part, once again, in the Indonesian Anniversary Football Tournament. His team arrived back in Rangoon with the Trophy. At the height of his triumphs in Burma, Trautmann also had the unexpected opportunity to appear at Maine Road to wear the goalkeeping jersey of Manchester City.

Johnny Hart, who was the last of the 1950s side to have remained at City for his entire football career, had been a player, trainer and, for a brief period, the manager before ill health had forced him to quit. Manchester City granted him a testimonial and one of Hart's great wishes was for Trautmann to appear.

Flying via Bangkok, the Middle East and Paris, Trautmann arrived at Maine Road a few hours before the game and rested for a short time before turning up at the stadium.

He looked fit and lean and, as usual, tanned when he entered the dressing room. Some of the players from his day looked in amazement, time had not been kind to the majority of them and pot bellies were much in evidence as they donned their playing strip, while Trautmann looked 10 years younger.

It was agreed that Joe Corrigan, the current Manchester City and England goalkeeper, would play one half for the City past and present team, and the jet-lagged Trautmann would play in the second. He came out on to the pitch to a welcome of old, a roar and thunderous applause.

Trautmann was back in the City goal and older supporters wanted to savour every minute. It was significant that Corrigan came out in the second half, squatted with the photographers behind Trautmann's goal and studied every move.

A brief appearance at Hart's reception party following the game allowed Bert to catch up with a few old friends before he had to dash to Ringway and make the long return leg of the journey back to Burma. Back in Rangoon, Bernd and Ushi packed their bags and said a fond farewell to all their friends, returning to Germany in order to prepare for the next posting by the German Government. He left the Burmese Football Federation with its most accomplished and successful team ever.

## Tanzania

Trautmann's sense of achievement from his work in Burma gave him an immense feeling of satisfaction. He was hoping to find a year's extension to his contract had been considered by his Government, but in Bonn they had other plans for him. His reputation within the department was sky-high, while a number of countries had been in touch with the sports-aid programme administrators trying to obtain Trautmann as their football coach.

Bernd and Ushi stayed at her parent's home in Rüdesheim while awaiting the new posting, and Trautmann, as part of a Government department, had to complete his own reports on the programme in Burma. Part of his task was to brief his replacement on the set-up before he, in turn, was briefed on his next programme – it was to be in Tanzania, East Africa.

The Trautmanns arrived in the capital, Dar Es Salaam, in the spring of 1975 and settled in to their home overlooking the Indian Ocean. Tanzania as a country was constituted from the old British Colonial countries of Tanganyika and Zanzibar. Since they had gained independence from Britain, the leaders adopted a socialist philosophy and political system but were struggling to maintain the basis of their economy as the Europeans had left in droves when the government nationalised businesses and implemented state agricultural policies. The Tanzanians were grateful for any overseas aid they could get.

Dar Es Salaam, once a prosperous and bustling trading port with links to the Arabian and Indian trade routes, was a little down at heel when Trautmann looked at his new challenge.

His parameters were different to those he had in Burma, for he was to advise the Tanzanian FA rather than be in full control as the national coach. Within the guidelines of the German coaching manuals and applying his own techniques, he set up coaching clinics and seminars for the players and officials while developing an education programme, which led to full coaching status for the participants. Bernd Trautmann, in effect, became a teacher.

He missed Burma from the start of his new job. In a way he felt his first posting had spoiled him, more so when he heard the problems other coaches on the programme were experiencing elsewhere. He was, however, to have his own share in the fullness of time. The application and commitment of the Africans was in direct contrast to the disciplined and organised approach of the Burmese, and Trautmann had to assimilate and acclimatise for the first few weeks. The slower pace of life and the laid-back attitude of his students meant it would take them longer to respond to his inductions, but Trautmann's ability to adapt to a new domicile soon brought results. His education programme was not confined to soccer, the Tanzanians were eager to learn about life in Europe, and he was often sidetracked into discussing the social and cultural differences between the two continents.

'They had a fixation about all white people being rich and no real idea about the pressures of living in a large European city. I tried to explain to them a house, a car, material benefits were not that necessary for a fulfilling life. This was something I had come to accept while in Burma. I explained the advantages they had over us, a beautiful climate, land where you could grow anything and no great social commitment or convention to weigh them down. They had a richness to their lives which we do not have in Europe. I couldn't go on too much into their political situation, they certainly had problems but even so they were untainted then by material greed and I loved their simple lives. They were happy people.'

The happy people responded to Bernd's unpretentious approach. Under a scholarship scheme a number of coaches were sent to the Duisburg Sports Centre in Germany and returned to Tanzania to set up their own schemes within the country. As the time came for Trautmann to move on again he had laid the foundations for a comprehensive football coaching system and the basis for a good national team to compete against other African nations. Bernd and Ushi once again returned to Rüdesheim for a break. Trautmann completed his reports, then learned he had been put forward to take the highest coaching qualification in Germany, the *Fußball-Lehrer* at Cologne University. A somewhat more mature student than most, Bernd Trautmann started his course in November 1977, at the end of March 1978 he emerged from his intensive studies with the *Fußball-Lehrer* Diploma.

## Liberia

A few weeks after his university course, Bernd and Ushi found themselves back in Africa, this time in Monrovia, the capital of Liberia. In contrast to Tanzania, the population of this dusty and poverty-stricken country on the west coast of the continent was weary and deprived. The country's main claim to fame was shipping, Monrovia was a port of convenience for shipping companies to register their vessels and the national flag was probably one of the best known in the world. People knew very little else, or cared, about Liberia. The main economy was based on its commercial maritime activities, while the Americans had provided aid packages to the government and a number of US companies were based there. The result was a direct American influence on the local population, old American cars acted as taxis, the shops were full of expensive American commodities, but the majority of Liberians lived in extreme poverty under the government of President William Tolbert.

The Liberian Football Association were struggling to maintain its national team as an identity and were dependant on the hard work of a handful of dedicated coaches, who struggled along with little money and few resources. Trautmann joined them as national coach. Nearly all the teams were based around Monrovia, the US influence of baseball and American football had pervaded into shanty towns and villages. That influence had more significance to the people than Western European cultural activities.

Trautmann had to revert to basics, set up basic coaching clinics and decided on a national squad from his limited pool of talent to compete in the immediate goal, the African Olympic qualifying group.

Trautmann and his assistants slowly built up the confidence and the technical ability of the Liberian players and they began to perform capably in friendly matches. The first big test was an Olympic Qualifier to be played in Monrovia against Ghana, the African champions and a nation they had not beaten in 25 years. Against all the odds, Liberia defeated the Ghanaians 1–0. The return match to be held in Accra in November 1979 would be of great importance in deciding the West African qualifiers; it would be a great test of character for the Liberian team.

As Trautmann and his squad prepared for the match in Accra, he heard the first rumblings of political instability and revolution through the diplomatic staff at the German Embassy. The population as such were not holding mass demonstrations or rallies, the discontent stemmed from the armed forces and the threat of a coup was in the air, not unusual for African states, but one that could not be taken lightly. Nevertheless, after consideration and advice from the diplomats, Trautmann decided to continue with the trip to Ghana. The Minister for Transport had laid on the presidential Boeing 707 for the team and Trautmann persuaded him and another minister to accompany the team to Accra. As they lifted from the runway at Monrovia airport and headed east to Ghana, events in the city exploded.

Master-Sergeant Samuel Doe organised and completed a murderous coup with his Army unit. President Tolbert and 13 of his ministers were ruthlessly executed and the country was in a state of emergency with rigid curfews being enforced. The two government ministers with the Liberian party tried desperately to find out what was happening, but no contact could be made with Monrovia and any news was coming through the embassies there.

Bernd Trautmann managed to contact the German Embassy and was relieved to find out Ushi was under diplomatic protection and unharmed. He now had to sort out his own predicament in Accra, with a large party of players and officials stuck in a hotel without any funds or any idea of their future. Following discussions with the Ghanaian Government and the Ghana FA, it was agreed the match should continue, at least it would give the players something to occupy their minds until the situation at home could be analysed. The Liberians offered a spirited performance, considering their pre-occupation with events at home, losing 2–1 before a large crowd at the Accra National Stadium.

In the hotel afterwards, Trautmann made frantic efforts through the German attaché to organise some funds, and he eventually raised 6,000 marks through his own bank to provide what he could for the party of 27 people. A shortage of commodities in Accra made things all the more difficult, even a box of matches cost as much as US $2, while the markets had few foodstuffs for sale.

Trautmann and the Liberians were in Accra for seven days, subsisting as best they could until news came through that the airport in Monrovia was open again. The Liberian officials, together with the crew, arranged for the 707 to take them home, while their protector and organiser, on advice from Bonn, was asked to return to Germany.

When Trautmann arrived back home he had to spend an anxious few days appraising the German intelligence services of the difficulties he had experienced, then returning as quickly as possible to Monrovia to be reunited with his wife.

Any real signs of the coup were not that apparent as he was driven from the airport; the tanks and military vehicles dotted along the roads gave only a minimal indication of anything untoward. The violence had been limited to the uncompromising eradication of the previous political establishment.

Trautmann and Ushi remained in Monrovia for just a few more weeks, winding down their affairs, and then returned to Germany to decide their future. The tour of duty in Liberia had been concluded rather more quickly than was anticipated and no new assignment was immediately available. Bernd and Ushi stayed with the Van der Heyde family in Rüdesheim, Trautmann made a brief coaching trip to Burma for a month until, in the late summer of 1980, they moved on again.

### Pakistan

From his home in the diplomatic compound in Islamabad, Trautmann quickly realised that his attachment to the Pakistan Football Association would prove to be a difficult challenge and one which would require a great deal of diplomacy, together with some brutal frankness. His work in Pakistan also required him to travel extensively within the huge areas of the country which, in turn, meant Ushi would have to be left on her own for lengthy periods. Ushi had no immediate problems, she was used to the diplomatic social structures and she was also intrepid enough to plan her own life while Bernd was away. Above all Islamabad offered her the facilities to partake in one of her great passions, horse riding. While Trautmann set up his coaching structure, Ushi set up her circle of social friends and her equestrian diversions.

Bernd's problems as coach to the national team were compounded by the fact the Pakistanis had not played international football for 10 years, by now not an unfamiliar situation for him.

Trautmann's initial dilemma was to confront the regional associations, who were influenced by political or religious differences, or where nepotism and petty briberies were endemic among team selections and national competitions. The new broom had to sweep clean from the start.

On a plus side, the Pakistan Football Federation gave him a free hand to sort out their problems. He appointed two unbiased assistants to help him to communicate his ideas and he persuaded the Pakistani FA to consider seriously the prospect of international competition again. Trautmann sought and was rewarded with entries to the ASEAN games and also the King's Cup Tournament in Bangkok.

The new national coach and his staff travelled the length and breadth of the country to assess the players, which the regional associations had put forward for consideration as candidates for the new international team. In addition, they also had to look at the local coaching set-ups. Trautmann was appalled by the standards of players, who in many cases were related to local officials and were as adept at football as Richard Nixon was to cover-ups. The new broom swept out 75 per cent of the players who had been under consideration for the international team and started again. He was plagued by regional dislikes and differences; the people in Karachi disliked the people in Islamabad, Lahore or Peshawar, while the citizens of Multan and Hyderabad were unhappy about working with anyone.

Because of the local differences and attitudes, the one most important factor was missing. In Trautmann's words, 'No player seemed to feel any love or passion in playing for Pakistan. There was no pride or fire or feeling for the football team that was found in their cricket or hockey teams.'

He adopted a patient and pragmatic approach to his job. He had the advantage of being in complete control of events without any interference from others and he appointed new coaches and officials in the various regions to replace the indifferent standards set by the incumbents.

He instructed that all candidates for new coaching courses met one important criterion – they had to have had playing experience and were not just related to local officials. Organisation was difficult at first and Trautmann based the national team trials in Peshawar, which seemed the less effected of the local associations to any furtive influences. Within a few months he had established the exact standards he wanted for his coaching classes, while at the same time patiently building up a committed and reasonably talented squad of Pakistani footballers.

After a long gap the Pakistan Football Association re-emerged into international football, at the King's Cup competition in Thailand. The tournament at that time included Western European nations like Norway and one or two East European First Division sides from Poland, Hungary or East Germany, which greatly varied the competition and the style of play. Pakistan finished in fifth position overall, in a competition of 16 teams.

Trautmann and his coaches had established an excellent start for the new team, and above all else the Pakistani players gained a pride in their football. Trautmann's chameleon-like ability to adapt to his surroundings played a huge part in the response he gained from the football establishment and more implicitly from the Pakistan national and local Government officials. They realised his ability to motivate and organise had given a great impetus to their football, they saw positive signs for the long term and Trautmann was sounded out by some of them about remaining in the country after his official term was completed.

The years of empty promises, which had begun at Manchester City, made Trautmann wary of any commitment. He showed only a polite interest in the initial offers but unfortunately he had other problems that he had to deal with.

While Trautmann's wholehearted commitment to the fortunes of the Pakistani football cause had brought both himself and the team great credit, the enforced separation of Bernd and Ushi while he was establishing his career credentials did little to enhance their personal relationship.

They had grown considerably apart as their own separate interests developed, and Ushi started an affair with a career diplomat on the German Embassy staff, which was to end their marriage. In 1982 Bernd and Ushi returned to Germany, he with promises of a job for life in Pakistan if he so wanted but which did not materialise, Ushi with a decision to make about the relationship. She chose to go on her separate way and the Trautmanns parted.

Trautmann told the Foreign Office in Bonn of his personal problems and with understanding they allowed him a period of compassionate leave in order to sort out his personal life. Strangely enough, the only place he now regarded as home in Germany was Rüdesheim, and while Ushi made plans with the man who had replaced Bernd in her life, Trautmann stayed with her parents.

The actuality of the marriage disintegration was less traumatic than his first to Margaret, although obviously harrowing. His own mind and maturity accepted the reasons more readily than the awful circumstances of Margaret and his children. Trautmann fulfilled some short-term coaching assignments while he went through his divorce from Ushi, and he returned to his beloved Burma and also to East Africa over a four-month period.

During 1983, while he was still a guest of the Van der Heydes, Trautmann was invited to one of the summer houses, non-residential chalets high up on the banks of the Rhine. These tracts of land had been purchased over the years by Rüdesheimer families to enjoy the view of the river and the sloping vista of the twiggy Rheingau vineyards. They provide a summer retreat for the local community, away from the throngs of tourists who pour into the town and allow the professional and business people who own them a welcome retreat from the crowded little town.

Socially, the summer plots are the main meeting point for the local people, away from the crowded Drosselsgasse and the Weingartens of the narrow streets below.

## Rüdesheim-am-Rhein 1983

Marlis Winau was born into and was a part of the Rüdesheim social structure all her life. As a young girl she had seen the Allied forces inflict untold damage on the historic town, and after the occupation by the Americans she had sold them ice from her grandfather's business and home in Bleichstrasse near the town centre. When her marriage ended, she moved into the beautiful, but somewhat neglected, house with her two children, Angelica and Reiner, struggling to rebuild the home and to establish her printing business. On one of her few free evenings she was invited to one of the summer chalets for an evening with the Van der Heydes, where she was introduced to Bernd Trautmann. Trautmann, at 60 years of age, was fast approaching his retirement, but he was still a fit man and felt he had a lot to offer as far as his career was concerned. When he met Marlis she became a serious consideration in his plans.

## North Yemen

When Bernd Trautmann was offered the post of advisory coach based in San'ā' in North Yemen, the job presented him with one of his most daunting challenges and it proved to be one of the most unsatisfactory episodes in his coaching career.

The Yemenis had, in truth, little interest in football. When Trautmann arrived he had a budget of just 25,000 marks for the year, most of which was used to buy transport for his Yemeni assistant, to pay the man's expenses and to buy equipment. It was a totally inadequate sum but, in the view of the German Government, a realistic figure. As far as they were concerned the North Yemen administration were only interested in one thing, obtaining as much as possible in terms of hard currency from whatever source. They had little interest in the peripheral aid programme foreign governments were offering, in football terms, the development of the sport was of as much interest to them as an anti-cocaine poster in Colombia.

Trautmann soon realised the lack of interest but tried hard to instil some enthusiasm. He used his contacts at Adidas to scrounge further equipment outside the scope of his budget, but to no avail, the North Yemenis did not respond. They did not co-operate with any of his plans, showed little enthusiasm for his coaching clinics and, in real terms, the whole project was a waste of time.

The Germans wanted to get their feet in the door to develop trade interests in North Yemen, but the Arab nation were unwilling to open it too far.

Marlis joined Bernd for a short time in San'ā' and they used the opportunity to tour the country, a privilege denied to many other people. But after Trautmann had been there for just a year he was brought back to Germany with both his time and effort wasted, no progress having been achieved in North Yemen Football standards.

Bernd Trautmann's last posting for the German Government was in Malta, where he did much to develop the island's football interests. He worked patiently and with skill at teaching the Maltese coaches, setting up a comprehensive series of clinics and seminars. He was helped considerably by having Marlis with him to enjoy the Mediterranean sunshine. They married on 4 July 1987.

Trautmann retired from his job with the German Government in October 1988.

# TRAUTMANN THE PLAYER

*It is not simply a question of showing off. It is merely that goalkeeping seems to call for more calculated drama than centre-forwarding or inside-forwarding.*

*Goalkeepers assume more picturesque positions and shapes than any of the other players – and there is no doubt in my mind that every goalkeeper had the idea that he would be Ulanova of the Bolshoi Ballet, if only he had the time.*

*It seems to be simpler to take on this 'star' quality between the goalkeepers than in any other position.*

JOHN MACADAM

WHEN John MacAdam wrote his view on goalkeepers in the late 1950s, he had the benefit of knowing and watching a group of truly charismatic and superb goalkeepers in an era popularly known as the 'Golden Age'. In Britain, George Younger, Gil Merrick, Bert Williams and Jack Kelsey were outstanding players, while in the rest of the world, Yashin, Grosics, Beara, Gilmar and Dominguez were all world-famous goalkeeping talents. They all had one thing in common, each of them played in international football and were recognised through the national teams.

The honour of playing for his country was denied to Bert Trautmann, to his lasting regret and to the disappointment of many others. It is all the more remarkable, therefore, that his ability and reputation as a goalkeeper was established worldwide without the benefit of international games while playing for most of his career with a struggling English League side.

The title of the 'World's Best Goalkeeper' and the 'Best British Goalkeeper Ever' have been applied to him, not just from supporters but also from renowned international players.

*'There have only been two world-class goalkeepers, one was Lev Yashin, the other the German boy who played in Manchester – Trautmann.'*

Lev Yashin

In analysing Trautmann's skill, it was perhaps his natural athletic ability and superb physique that made him stand out above all the others, together with his charismatic character and genuine humility. His technique was certainly unparalleled in the British game, while his reflexes and anticipation made him exciting and daring. Together with his immense bravery, he was a formidable opponent. These qualities were evident in his early days at St Helens.

*'I once saw Trautmann pull off two saves in almost one continuous movement, a feat I still believe physically impossible for any other goalkeeper except for him. Someone unleashed a thunderous volley from outside the area, Trautmann leapt across from one side of his goal and somehow palmed the ball back out to the edge of the area, where another forward fired back an equally powerful shot to the opposite corner. To our amazement he picked himself up off the ground from the first save and hurtled through the air to catch and hold the second shot at the far post. We could not believe the speed of his acrobatics.'*

Bill Twist

When Trautmann moved into professional football his application and concentration were second to none. Considering his original introduction to the Football League being fraught with difficulties, his mental preparation for each game was remarkable. He managed to become so singular that he cut out everything else from his mind and developed an acute ability to 'psyche out' opposing forwards. His confidence was such that he left gaps for forwards to aim their shots at and then would dive the way he had forced them to shoot. This ability was particularly disconcerting for forwards, while his physique always seemed much greater than his appearance would suggest, his superb positioning skill always made the goals seem that little bit smaller.

*'Bert Trautmann became, without a doubt, one of the greatest goal-keepers in the Football League. One of the things that I remember about him was that he was a huge man who had very large hands. He filled the goal and made it difficult to beat him. He had great anticipation and agility and his courage was second to none.*

*I remember him well because after I was transferred from Fulham to West Bromwich Albion in 1956 for £25,000, my first game at The Hawthorns was against Manchester City. West Brom, having invested that amount of money in me, were looking for a convincing win – but we lost 4–0. Bert just filled the goal. We never looked like getting the ball past him. Furthermore, I stood on the Wembley terrace in 1956 with a 3s 6d ticket and watched him give a memorable, brave, efficient and technical performance. In the match Bert broke his neck and never left the pitch – one doesn't have to say anymore.'*

Bobby Robson

Trautmann's powers of concentration and ability were also noted by another unique footballer.

*'He was a tall, powerful 'keeper, using tremendous powers of concentration and technique. There is no doubt that he was one of the world's great goalkeepers.'*

Sir Stanley Matthews

The anticipation that Bobby Robson thought so much of really was outstanding. Trautmann developed an almost uncanny knack of knowing where the ball was going to be. If he displayed any vulnerability it was on rare occasions in dealing with shots at his near post, most prominently when Bobby Mitchell scored against him in the 1955 FA Cup Final. For a big man, however, his ability to get down quickly to low shots was all the more remarkable.

*'I remember when I was due to play in an international against Northern Ireland at Maine Road in the 1950s, Walter Winterbottom, the England manager, arranged for us to do some light training. I met Bert at Maine Road and he agreed to help me with some shooting practice. I hit them high, low, with power and precision. Bert's said to me: 'Come on, Nat, you can do better than that'. I was giving them everything I had. We are talking of an era when there were some great guys playing – Gil Merrick, Bert Williams, Ted Ditchburn, Sam Bartram to name but a few. I would put Bert at the very top of the list.'*

Nat Lofthouse

His Manchester City colleagues in the successful Cup years were unanimous that his ability outshone any other goalkeeper.

*'When our new style was brought into action at Maine Road we had a goalkeeper who was possibly the finest thrower of a ball the game has ever seen, and I thought he was the world's greatest goalkeeper. Until the 1954–55 season Bert Trautmann had stood between City and heavy defeat more times than I care to remember. Those fantastic leaps would do credit to a circus acrobat, that wonderful anticipation, which enabled him to catch balls quite coolly when lesser men would be glad to fingertip the ball to safety. No doubts – Trautmann was the best.'*

Don Revie

*'People have asked me who was the best goalkeeper and only two come into the reckoning, both from Manchester City, Frank Swift and Bert Trautmann. Swifty had a knack of winning over a crowd by his antics. Trauty had to win their approval by his daring and courage in the face of adverse criticism about his nationality. I have no doubt in my mind that Trautmann was the greatest goalkeeper I have seen. There is only a cigarette papers width between him and Swift in skill – but Bert would be my first choice.'*

Roy Paul

'Beaky' Barnes was less erudite, but none the less positive about his own opinion: 'If there was a better goalkeeper on his day than Trauty, I'd like to have seen him. That's all I have to say on that subject.' The influence on his fellow goalkeepers and of the next generation that followed was quite profound. Bob Wilson modelled his own style of play on Trautmann, while Steve Fleet, who had more chance than most to study his style, maintained there would never be another like him. Says Fleet, 'one of his most notable accomplishments was his unerring knack of catching a ball. He caught more shots than any other goalkeeper. And then there was that amazing throwing ability which gave City an extra dimension to play.'

The throwing talent undoubtedly impressed others.

> *'Tom Whittaker, our manager at the time, always emphasised to watch out carefully when Trautmann cleared his goal area with a throw because Bert never used the usual over-arm throw mainly used by English goalkeepers. His throw always came straight-arm, always with great distance, accuracy and speed. The throw, in fact, was so quick and accurate that many opposing defenders were taken by surprise and many goals were added to City's tally as a result of Bert's attacking throw outs.*
>
> *It was my pleasure to be a player at the same period. He will always be remembered by British fans as a goalkeeper who graced the football grounds in Britain with great ability and, furthermore, great dignity. Bert will always be ranked in Britain with the greatest.'*

Jack Kelsey

One young goalkeeper, who was just emerging into prominence towards the end of Trautmann's career, was also impressed.

> *'Bert, for me, was a very great goalkeeper because he made things look so easy. He never panicked at all under pressure and he was the first goalkeeper I ever saw start an attack by throwing a ball deep. I'd seen others throw, but he always looked for someone nearer the half-way line and bypassed the others.*
>
> *The big thing also for me was he was such a sportsman and played as if he owed us something because he was a German and had been a prisoner-of-war. If anything we should owe him a debt of gratitude for staying here and showing us what a great goalkeeper he was. I certainly learned a lot from him.'*

Gordon Banks

Across the city from Maine Road, one other man had studied Trautmann's play.

> *'Bert Trautmann occupies a special place in my mind, because I knew every time I played at Maine Road I'd learn something – there were many occasions on which his goalkeeping skill excited my admiration.*
>
> *I'll go along with most people who say one man doesn't make a team; but I do believe that there are times when one man can save a team. Bert Trautmann was such a man.'*

Harry Gregg

One major feature of Trautmann's play was his immense courage. He always faced oncoming forwards directly and went into a dive at their feet head first without shirking his responsibility. The greatest testament to that courage was when, after suffering his neck injury against Birmingham City, he twice more went down at the feet of forwards at a time of great pain and distress.

*'His handling was absolutely sound, his reflexes razor-sharp, but also he communicated an air of calmness and security alongside his brilliance. There is little need for me to emphasise his bravery because without that talent other skills are useless to a goalkeeper. But history records that Bert was a lion in that department.'*

Jimmy Hill

Trautmann had many things to prove when he came to prominence in English football. One of the first was to help restore respect and civility back to the minds of the English towards his country. Many men could have hidden behind a curtain of apologetic excuses about Germany's past, Trautmann was proud of his nationality and never flinched publicly when the wrath of the anti-German feeling descended on him, despite the fact that inside it hurt him and his family deeply. He was determined to prove that as an individual and a sportsman his ability and his qualities as a human being would transcend the prejudice and hate. He chose to face his problems head on and with single-minded conviction to represent his country with pride. His contribution outside the football world was memorable in the way he contributed to the lives of the Manchester people and particularly the positive, deep feeling towards the Jewish community, who, above all, had directed the worst cynicism towards him. The way in which he healed the deep wounds is a testament to his commitment.

*'The respect that he commanded for himself and, as a result, the German nation, was perhaps the beginning of the healing of the wounds caused by the war. He was in fact more than a brilliant goalkeeper.'*

Jimmy Hill

Many great footballers have said many things about Bert Trautmann. The following three perhaps sum up the great respect and feelings he commanded.

*'Bert Trautmann was a goalkeeper who earned everyone's admiration for his bravery, outstanding ability and agility. His handling and positional play was faultless and he would have played for England had he been able to do so.*

*He was a likeable fellow, with a great sense of humour, and I had great respect for him as a fellow professional. He served the game with distinction and has a special place in the memory of English soccer players. I have no hesitation in naming Bert as one of the greatest goalkeepers.'*

Tom Finney

*'Whenever we played against Manchester City in the 1950s we were always going to be involved in a great game of football but, regardless of how we planned our tactics, we knew we would have Bert*

*Trautmann to contend with. He was simply the best. I was one of the few forwards to score regularly against him but at the same time, for every one I did score he saved what I thought were one or two certainties. He had the quickest reflexes I have ever experienced and he was a bloody nice bloke as well.'*

Jackie Milburn

*'I played against Bert Trautmann many times for Preston North End and his games for Manchester City were always quite fantastic. He was the worry of our lives. I also saw him many times against other clubs, his consistent form, skill and ability won the hearts of all sports people after the terrible war. He had everything you look for in a world-class goalkeeper. I still get asked today, who was the best goalkeeper I have ever seen. It's about opinions, but I think he might just be the best ever.'*

Tommy Docherty

The final words on Trautmann are left to two men who had diverse paths in the world of football.

*'He was a unique player and the best-ever distributor of a ball, with no equal, then or now. Jimmy Murphy used to tell us not to look up when we hit shots, almost as if Trautmann could read your mind because his anticipation was so uncanny. At Maine Road once, a ball was headed out to me around the 18-yard area and I caught it on the volley with full power. The area was packed with players and my shot was going straight into the top corner. For me and the other United forwards it was a goal all the way, when suddenly, Bert pulled off quite the most outstanding and the best save I have ever seen. How he could have ever seen my shot through the mass of players I don't know, but he dived from one side of the goal to the other and tipped it over the bar. Bert Trautmann was the best goalkeeper around at the time.'*

Bobby Charlton

*'He may not have got the material rewards he desired, but he will always have the spiritual reward of the love and admiration of the people of England. Bert Trautmann will always belong to, and be a part of, the people of Manchester.'*

Steve Fleet

# THE TRAUTMANN FOUNDATION

In the summer of 2003 Mathias Paskowski, a journalist working for the football magazine 11 Freunde (11 Friends), telephoned Bernd Trautmann at his home in La Llosa, Spain. Mathias wanted an in depth interview and Bernd, knowing of the magazines more cerebral reputation for football writing, readily agreed.

During the interview, Bernd touched on his continuing hope to somehow further develop Anglo-German relations. As the years had passed since his retirement from active involvement in football, he had been in constant demand to attend sporting or trade functions, and also charity fundraising events in the UK, Manchester in particular of course, but also in Germany.

Shortly after the interview was published, Mathias contacted him again and explained that he and another group of anglophiles, who had either completed their education or were regular visitors to the UK, thought they had an ideal way for him to leave a lasting legacy. They were particularly concerned with the negative stereotypes that still existed, nearly 60 years after the end of World War Two, among a generation of young people in Britain who seemed to have a widespread ignorance of modern Germany. This concern was also felt by the British Embassy in Berlin. The feeling was not being helped by perhaps an over emphasis in the British school history curriculum on the Nazi period.

In addition, regular physical attacks on German school children visiting the UK were causing a spate of negative press articles in Germany, while the British Embassy were encountering an overwhelming number of complaints. They had become increasingly worried that their work in developing and strengthening UK/German economic and social links was being undermined.

Trautmann had forged many contacts in the sports world; he had sponsored and accompanied German junior football teams on tours to the UK and also encouraged reciprocal arrangements in Germany. This was exactly the area the British Embassy staff was looking at, their reasoning being that although most German young people had good English language skills and a large number had visited Britain, there was a significant imbalance in the opposite direction. At the same time, there was a steady decline in the number of British pupils electing to study German.

Mathias Paskowski, together with Ingmar Leue and Ronald Kaduk, approached the British Embassy with Bernd's approval and outlined their ideas. They wanted to concentrate on fostering and improving relationships through football-based activities. With the British onside, and promise of active support from the German government, they set up the Trautmann Foundation.

At the Kaiser Cup in Hamburg in June 2004, the Foundation was formally launched. Trautmann attended the event, supported by Uwe Seeler and other leading sports people; more importantly the British Ambassador, Sir Peter Torry, agreed to become a patron. Bernd, together with Paskowski, Leue and Kaduk, explained the main aims of the foundation.

The Trautmann Foundation would be embarking on a number of ambitious projects, the main focus of which would be establishing football camps for youth organisations in Britain and Germany, a learning through football week of social and developmental activities, all culminating in a mini-tournament. The 'Kick and Think' academies would bring youngsters together, not only for sporting activity but to look at future perspective in social and cultural development. They also outlined plans for young people to be given three-month placements at football clubs, associations or football-related companies, financed by the foundation and its sponsors.

They would be setting up a Trautmann Award to be presented to a person or institution from Germany or Britain for their contributions to football and sportsmanship. After the launch, the German Government showed their commitment by appointing Otto Schily, the German Minister for the Interior, as a patron.

Bernd Trautmann returned to Spain with his lasting legacy firmly in place.

Bernd Trautmann Foundation Förderverein
Postfach 120815
10598 Berlin
Germany
Kontakt@trautmann-foundation.org


In late October 2004 Bernhard Trautmann arose early, his limbs aching as usual. He brewed coffee and made his way to the terrace. The warmth of the sun and the effects of the caffeine brought life to his body and mind.

The post arrived with the usual volume of mail, autograph requests and letters from fans around the world. He was intrigued by an official letter with an impress from the British Embassy in Berlin. He opened it expecting some update on the Embassy's involvement with the foundation. Marlis, his wife, came into the lounge to find him sitting quietly, his eyes welling with tears. He handed her the letter, and she feared the worst that it was bad news. She read the letter and broke into a huge smile of pride.

He had been awarded the Order of the British Empire – the OBE – in recognition of his ongoing work to improve British-German relations. He was to travel to Berlin to receive the honour, which would coincide with the Queen Elizabeth II state visit.

He arrived in Berlin on 1 November 2004, nearly 70 years after his very first visit, to attend a reception at the British Embassy hosted by Sir Peter Torry. In a private ceremony he was awarded his medal by the Ambassador together with a notation signed by the Queen and Prince Philip.

After the ceremony he and Sir Peter faced the Press. Trautmann gave an emotional speech of thanks.

On 3 November he had been invited to the Berlin Sinfonia to attend a concert and be formally presented to the Queen. He waited nervously in line, and when the monarch arrived she moved along the group briskly until she reached Trautmann. They shook hands. As Prince Philip looked on with an acknowledged smile of recognition, the Queen said, 'Ah! Herr Trautmann, you are the one who received my OBE'. After an unprecedented three-minute chat, the royal couple moved on. A proud and honoured man followed them into the concert hall.

He returned to La Llosa the following day. As he stood on the veranda at this home, nestling between the orange groves and the Mediterranean, he could look towards the shimmering sea, at last a man with a life fulfilled.

# BERT TRAUTMANN'S CAREER STATISTICS

## St Helens Town FC Appearances

|         | Liverpool Co.Comb | Lancs Comb | FA Cup | G.Mahon Cup | Total |
|---------|-------------------|------------|--------|-------------|-------|
| 1948–49 | 34                | 0          | 1      | 6           | 41    |
| 1949–50 | 0                 | 9          | 1      | 0           | 10    |
| Total   | 34                | 9          | 2      | 6           | 51    |

*Honours:* George Mahon Cup-winners' medal **1949**

## Manchester City FC Appearances

|         | League | FA Cup | FL Cup | Central | Lancs Cup | Manch Cup | Friend's | Tours/ Others | Total |
|---------|--------|--------|--------|---------|-----------|-----------|----------|---------------|-------|
| 1949–50 | 26     | 0      | 0      | 5       | 0         | 0         | 2        | 0             | 33    |
| 1950–51 | 42     | 1      | 0      | 0       | 0         | 0         | 3        | 0             | 46    |
| 1951–52 | 41     | 2      | 0      | 0       | 0         | 0         | 4        | 0             | 47    |
| 1952–53 | 42     | 3      | 0      | 0       | 1         | 0         | 0        | 0             | 46    |
| 1953–54 | 42     | 2      | 0      | 0       | 1         | 0         | 13       | 0             | 58    |
| 1954–55 | 40     | 6      | 0      | 0       | 0         | 0         | 8        | 0             | 54    |
| 1955–56 | 40     | 7      | 0      | 0       | 0         | 0         | 2        | 0             | 49    |
| 1956–57 | 21     | 2      | 0      | 2       | 0         | 0         | 3        | 0             | 28    |
| 1957–58 | 34     | 1      | 0      | 0       | 0         | 0         | 5        | 1             | 41    |
| 1958–59 | 41     | 2      | 0      | 0       | 0         | 1         | 0        | 0             | 44    |
| 1959–60 | 41     | 1      | 0      | 0       | 0         | 0         | 6        | 0             | 48    |
| 1960–61 | 40     | 4      | 2      | 1       | 0         | 0         | 4        | 0             | 51    |
| 1961–62 | 40     | 2      | 1      | 0       | 0         | 1         | 2        | 0             | 46    |
| 1962–63 | 15     | 0      | 1      | 20      | 0         | 0         | 0        | 0             | 36    |
| 1963–64 | 3      | 0      | 0      | 8       | 1         | 0         | 0        | 0             | 12    |
| Total   | 508    | 33     | 4      | 36      | 3         | 2         | 52       | 1             | 639   |

*Honours:* Football League Division Two runners'-up medal 1950–51; FA Cup runners'-up medal 1955; FA Cup-winners' medal 1956; Manchester Player of the Year 1956; English Footballer of the Year 1956.

### Representative Honours
English Football League v Irish League, 12 October 1960 (captain); English Football League v Italian League, 1 November 1960 (substitute).

### Wellington Town
Southern League, 1964–65 (2 appearances).

### Stockport County FC
General manager, October 1964–October 1966. Cheshire County League, 1965–66 (1 appearance)

### FC Preußen Münster
Trasner, 1967–68

### FC Opel Rüsseisheim
Trainer, 1968–69

### Qualifications
German Football Association – Grade 'A' Trainer's Licence, July 1967; *Fussball-Lehrer* Diploma, Cologne University, 1978.

### Coaching Assignments
Burma national coach, 1972–74 Team Honours: Asian Zone (2) Olympic Qualifying contest winners, 1972; Olympic Fair Play Trophy, 1972; President's Cup winners, 1972; Jakarta Anniversary Cup winners, 1973; ASEAN Games Gold Medalists, 1973; President's Cup winners, 1973; Jakarta Anniversary Cup winners, 1974.
Tanzanian Football Association advisory coach, 1975–77.
Liberian Football Association national coach, 1978–80.
Pakistan Football Association national coach, 1980–83.
Yemen Football Association advisory coach 1984. Maltese Football Association advisory coach, 1985–87.

# BIBLIOGRAPHY

*Manchester City – My Team*, Mike Doyle (Souvenir Press, 1977).
*Determined to Win*, George Eastham (Stanley Paul, 1964).
*Soccer in the Fifties*, Geoffrey Green (Ian Allan, 1974).
*Denis Law – An Autobiography* (Futura Publications, 1980).
*A Red Dragon of Wales*, Roy Paul (Robert Hale, 1956).
*Soccer's Happy Wanderer*, Don Revie (Museum Press, 1955).
*The Rise and Fall of the Third Reich*, William Shirer (Secker & Warburg Ltd, 1960).
*Go Go Going Up*, Stockport County FC (Macclesfield Press, 1967).
*Football from the Goalmouth*, Frank Swift (Sporting Handbooks, 1948).
*Adolf Hitler*, John Toland (Doubleday & Company Inc 1976).
*Manchester City – Meredith to Mercer*, Eric Thornton (Robert Hale, 1969).
*Steppes to Wembley*, Bert Trautmann (Robert Hale, 1956).
*The Manchester City Story*, Andrew Ward (Breedon Books, 1984).
*The Manchester City Story*, David Williams (Newservice Ltd, 1947).

# ARCHIVE SOURCES

Axel Springer Group
BBC Television
British Movietone News
German Football Association
Central Library, Manchester (Newspaper Archives)
*Manchester Evening News*
*Pathe News*
*Picture Post*
Public Records Office, Kew, London
*St Helens Reporter*

# TAPED SOURCES

Ken Barnes, Jim Barrett, Roy Clarke, Steve Fleet, Dr Wilfried Gerhardt, David Leach, Freda Leach, Barbara Pearson, Beryl Paul, Roy Paul, St Helens Town FC, Bill Twist, Audrey Wilson, Stan Wilson.

# STATISTICAL INFORMATION

Jim Barrett of St Helens Town FC
Dr Wilfried Gerhardt, General Secretary of Deutscher Fußball-Bund
Richard Harnwell of Stockport County FC
John Maddocks

6576944R00142

Printed in Great Britain
by Amazon.co.uk, Ltd.,
Marston Gate.